The Myth Of Post-Racial America

Searching for Equality in the Age of Materialism

H. Roy Kaplan

ROWMAN & LITTLEFIELD EDUCATION

A division of

ROWMAN & LITTLEFIELD PUBLISHERS, INC.
Lanham • New York • Toronto • Plymouth, UK

Published by Rowman & Littlefield Education
A division of Rowman & Littlefield Publishers, Inc.
A wholly owned subsidary of The Rowman & Littlefield Publishing Group, Inc.
4501 Forbes Boulevard, Suite 200, Lanham, Maryland 20706
http://www.rowmaneducation.com

Estover Road, Plymouth PL6 7PY, United Kingdom

British Library Cataloguing in Publication Information Available

Library of Congress Cataloging-in-Publication Data

Kaplan, H. Roy.
The myth of post-racial America : searching for equality in the age of materialism / H. Roy Kaplan.
    p. cm.
    Includes bibliographical references and index.
    ISBN 978-1-61048-005-5 (cloth : alk. paper) -- ISBN 978-1-61048-006-2 (pbk. : alk. paper) -- ISBN 978-1-61048-007-9 (electronic)
    1. United States--Race relations. 2. United States--Race relations--History. 3. Racism--United States. 4. Racism--United States--History. 5. Post-racialism--United States. I. Title.
    E185.615.K276 2010
    305.800973--dc22   2010034109

∞ ™ The paper used in this publication meets the minimum requirements of American National Standard for Information Sciences—Permanence of Paper for Printed Library Materials, ANSI/NISO Z39.48-1992.

Printed in the United States of America

I want to thank my teachers for the impact they made on me: Joseph Roucek, Glenn Vernon, Bhopinder Bolaria, Charles Page, Gene Piedmont, Curt Tausky, and William Julius Wilson. (They're not responsible for the final product.)

Contents

Acknowledgements vii

Preface ix

Chapter 1 Facing the Challenge of Diversity 1

Chapter 2 The Origin of Our Species 7

Chapter 3 The Rise of Racism 17

Chapter 4 Darwin's Descendants:
Contemporary Scientific Racism 47

Chapter 5 Justifying the Indefensible:
Rationalizing Domination and Exploitation 59

Chapter 6 Why People Hate 73

Chapter 7 Surviving White Culture 81

Chapter 8 You Have to be Carefully Taught:
Learning about Race and Racism 93

Chapter 9 Thinking about Race 105

Chapter 10 Teaching about Inclusivity in Schools 117

Chapter 11 Corporate Diversity and the Cost of Color 129

Chapter 12 Social Inequality from the World of Work to Society 141

Chapter 13 Racial Disparities in Health and Wellness 149

Chapter 14   Crime and Punishment   159

Chapter 15   How the Military Shaped Blacks' Progress   173

Chapter 16   The Myth of the Meritocracy   189

Chapter 17   More than Talk: Why Dialogue is Not Enough   199

Postscript   215

References   221

Index   233

About the Author   239

Acknowledgements

Many of the ideas contained in this book were generated over the years in my classes on the subject of racism. Education is an interactive endeavor, and I have learned much from my students as we wrestled with the issues presented in the following pages. I hope that this project will inspire them to engage in constructive social action to resolve the inequalities which prevent our nation from fulfilling the promise of "liberty and justice for all."

My colleagues, Lionel Lewis and Edward Kissi, made thoughtful comments on a draft of this manuscript. I am grateful for this and even more so for their friendship. I would also like to thank Jennifer Strouf for identifing sources about racial disparities in legal settlement.

Working in the Department of Africana Studies at the University of South Florida under the Chairmanship of the late Dr. Trevor Purcell and currently Dr. Debra Plant, has deepened my perspective about race and racism. I would like to thank Drs. Eric Duke and Cheryl Rodriguez for sharing insight and sources that strengthened this work.

I would be remiss if I didn't mention the influence that my previous stint with the National Conference of Christians and Jews had on my life and work. To my former colleagues and staff, thanks for all your good fellowship and inspiration. I am forever grateful for being enriched through working with you.

Tammy Jaycox Kaplan did an exceptional job of reviewing the manuscript, correcting grammatical errors, and arranging the index and reference sections. She's a talented copy editor and a great daughter-in-law.

I could not have completed this work without the encouragement and understanding of my wife, Mary, who graciously let me bounce ideas off her and shared our over-used computer. My sons, Eric and Ian, and daughter-in-law Toni, demonstrate the power that love and understanding have in creating families of respect and understanding. Lastly, it is my expectation that my granddaughters, Zoey, Keeley, and Nia, will help make the promise of America a reality. We all need to leave this world better than the way we found it.

Preface

Not a day goes by in the United States without a racial incident. From the savage beatings and murders of people of color, to job and housing discrimination and the myriad of petty insults that mock the founding principles of our society—all Americans are faced with the consequences of racism. With the election of Barack Obama, some people assumed that the United States was entering a post-racial era. A black man in the White House signified that we had finally matured as a nation, embraced diversity, and were forging a future of equality. That idyllic view obscures the reality that color still permeates life in a society born from an economic system based on human bondage. A system bolstered by social and theological rationalizations for the treatment of human beings as insensate animals.[1]

Incidents of blatant racism surface regularly in the United States. Some of the most memorable include the legal system of Louisiana which revealed the disparate treatment of six teenage African-American boys; the portrayal of the first African-American President of the United States as a goggle-eyed Sambo selling waffles, as a caricature of the Joker from Batman, and as primitive medicine man with a bone through his nose; numerous public gaffes ranging from the racist *macaca* remark of former Virginia Senator George Allen to the arrest of Professor Henry Louis Gates for breaking into his own home; the banishment of African-American children from a country club pool in Pennsylvania; the politically insensitive remark of Senate Majority Leader Harry Reid about then-candidate Obama's skin color and speech, and his use of the word *Negro* to describe him; the ill-tempered outburst by Congressman Joe Wilson during President Obama's Congressional health care speech; and the astonishing, callous, and insensitive comments of televangelist Pat Robertson following the devastating earthquake in Haiti, and conservative talk show host Rush Limbaugh's warning to listeners not to contribute to the Haitian relief effort.

These are but a few reminders that race and racism are still deeply woven into the fabric of our society. This book is about racism and why it's important to identify and eliminate it. What we mean by racism is the domination, exploitation, degradation, and disparagement of dark-skinned people by whites. Of course people of color can be racist, but in a society founded on and run *of, by,* and *for* white people, in most situations, dark-skinned people lack the power to control large numbers of whites. Nor can they establish and enforce policies that perpetuate unequal treatment of whites, or view them from a social, biological, and historical frame of reference that depicts them as intellectually, morally, and biologically inferior. But such is the way many whites, whether they admit or recognize it, view dark-skinned people.

The FBI's annual report on the incidence of hate crimes in the United States shows that the vast majority (72.6 percent) of the hate crimes committed in 2008 in this country were offenses by whites against blacks, compared to 17.3 percent committed against whites.[2] Often, people of color perpetrate crimes against whites as a reaction to being discriminated against. As we will see, it was whites who exploited the world in search of natural and human resources, and it was they who slaughtered and enslaved people of color. Although color consciousness has been documented for thousands of years, racism as we know it is a modern white invention used to dominate and exploit people of color physically, politically, economically, and emotionally.

In a real sense, racism connotes not only negative prejudicial thoughts about dark-skinned people. It is more than an emotive, visceral repulsion, and repugnance of them. It has an action component. It is a transitive verb that implies the implementation of these negative beliefs into discriminatory behavior to the detriment of the victims. As we will see, the legacy of racist beliefs and behaviors still influence relationships between dominant whites and dark-skinned people, even the way the victims of racist thoughts and actions feel about themselves, and these beliefs have a devastating impact on children of color in and outside of the classroom.

This book will trace the development and manifestation of racist ideologies that were used to justify the dominant position of whites because it helps us understand the origin of myths and stereotypes, as well as some of the behavior that stigmatize and devalue people of color today. Gaining an understanding of the reasons why people are prejudiced and how our economic system perpetuates discriminatory behavior will, ideally, serve to improve understanding among whites about the impact of their actions on people of color.

Perhaps there is no more crucial institution that affects the future of our society than education. Educators have the power to shape our nation's future and the future of our youth. It is my hope that this book will help clarify issues about race and racism that affect the way they view students of color and their relationships to them. If we, as educators, can dispel the myths and stereotypes that have crept into our culture and intrude into classrooms and campuses, we can create egalitarian learning environments that ignite and sustain the creative energies of all students. Classrooms which are culturally aware and sensitive can be the way we can close the achievement gap. Such classrooms become inclusive enterprises that pique the curiosity and imagination of all students. They become places of respect where enthusiasm is nourished and the prospect of brighter futures becomes reality and not just shibboleth.

This book is not meant to be a diatribe against whites. It is intended to illuminate how racism helps to perpetuate social inequality in the classroom and society. At bottom, racism is a struggle for power and privilege. It is the domination of one group in our society, whites, over another—people of color. One way of looking at this situation is to consider who runs things. Another is to ponder the question, "Who can do what to whom and how often?"

While there have been dramatic changes in the social, political, and economic status of people of color from the time of the Civil Rights Movement in the 1960s, any impartial observer can easily discern that whites still control this society. Despite growing affluence and visibility of people of color—African-Americans, Latinos, Asians, Native Americans, bi-racial individuals—most of the day-to-day decisions that affect peoples' lives are made by white males from the classroom to the boardroom. Because African-Americans and Latinos are the most disadvantaged and numerous ethnic groups in the United States, they will be the focus of this book.

WHY WRITE A BOOK ABOUT RACISM?

There are two reasons for addressing social problems. First is the humanitarian perspective—to seek justice because it is the right thing to do. Centuries of domination and exploitation must yield to freedom, as the Rev. Dr. Martin Luther King, Jr. noted: "The arc of the moral universe is long but it bends toward justice." As conscientious citizens in a country with great promise, it is incumbent upon us to take an active role in the elimination of racism and inequality from our society. As the Jewish philosopher Hillel noted in the first century C.E., "If I am not for myself who will be? If I am only for myself, what am I? If not now, when?"

The second reason for understanding the dynamics of race and racism in the United States is because demographic changes are occurring which threaten to tear our society apart. Already a third of the 307 million residents of the United States are people of color, and within 30 years minorities will be in the majority. Whites will still have a numerical edge, because many Latinos, (the largest ethnic group in the nation), are white; but many consider themselves members of a Latino ethnic group. Asians are one of the fastest growing ethnic groups, and they, too, are frequently discriminated against, but overall, their income and education levels exceed those of whites.

If, as a nation, we do not proactively approach the issue of racism, we will become accomplices in our own undoing, heirs to an inherently unequal and unjust social system that distorts human relationships and deprives millions of people of the opportunity to participate fully in society. Not acting now and denying the issue of racism is tantamount to depriving the nation of the productive contributions of a third of its populace. Acting later is a recipe for communal suicide.

The pragmatic rationale for ending racism will be reflected in the future nature of our society—mature, egalitarian, and compassionate; or frenetic, exploitative, and competitive. We are entering a period fraught with vast social, political, and economic upheavals that will challenge our commitment and ability to create and sustain our social system. From global warming and environmental degradation to heightened competition from emerging super-powers China, India, and Brazil; commodities we have taken for granted will become increasingly precious, expensive, and scarce.

The way we choose to face these challenges will be a measure of our commitment to the values this country was predicated upon. These values have rung hollow for millions of people of color in the past as dominant white capitalists maintained hegemony over the distribution of goods and services that affected the health and very lives of these people. The time has come when we must decide what kind of nation we will be. Will we act to create equity and dignity for all people, or will we perpetuate the struggle to preserve the entrenched status quo and perquisites that have flowed unremittingly to the few who have monopolized them? Our choice is simple. The former brings hope and the promise of survival in a collaborative inclusive endeavor. The latter portends extinction.

THE PLAN OF THE BOOK

This book is designed to provide the reader with historical, theoretical, and empirical information about the causes and consequences of racism. We begin our discussion by establishing the origins of mankind. The rationale for this strategy is to demonstrate that all humans are descended from common ancestors who lived in Africa 60,000 to 70,000 years ago. This fact serves as a point of departure for our exploration of the reason and rationalization for the construction of the concepts of race and racism.

It is the thesis of this book that competition and materialism led to the emergence of status distinctions among groups of people and later mercantilism, imperialism, colonialism, and capitalism. From these movements racism evolved to rationalize the existing social order established in white European nations. Pseudo-scientific methods were utilized to justify the domination and exploitation of indigenous peoples and the trans-Atlantic slave trade. White Europeans utilized racist categories of people to stereotype and denigrate non-whites. From Colonial times in the New World to the present—wealthy, dominant white males have managed to perpetuate their power and influence by preventing women and people of color from sharing in their power and privilege, and their perspectives and influence reach inside our classrooms to this day. They are manifested in the Eurocentric curricula and the glorification of competitive individualism which is expressed in our system of tracking and grading students to the diminution and often exclusion of cooperative, collaborative, and humanistic approaches which could create educational communities focused on making better citizens and people.

Following a discussion of how these trends affect our views and treatment of immigrants, our focus turns to analyzing why people are prejudiced and why they discriminate against one another. It is our contention that competition for increasingly scarce goods is driving a wedge between light and dark-skinned people. Relying on myths and stereotypes about purported biological and motivational incapacities of dark-skinned people provides whites with a method for justifying the present structure of society which adversely impacts people of color. Combined with rapid social change from demographic and technological trends, the fear of strangers and the unknown are potent allies in the perpetuation of discrimination and racism.

Racism takes social, psychological, and physiological tolls on its victims. It robs children of self-esteem and deprives adults of opportunities for upward mobility in society both socially and economically. We learn that corporate power resides almost exclusively in the hands of white males and, despite pressure to open up corporations to women and minorities, little change has occurred at the highest rungs of the corporate structure in more than three decades.

We next turn to an analysis of disparities between whites and non-whites in wealth and income and the impact this has on political and economic power in the United States. From there we focus on the role racism plays in creating and perpetuating disparities in education, health, criminal justice, and housing, looking at how government and the military prevented people of color from participating in policies and programs that materially improved the social and economic status of whites.

We also discuss the concept of merit and the cherished "American Dream" of success through individual initiative and industriousness, and find that the playing field is not level, but slanted to help whites maintain their privileges and rewards.

In the final chapter, we explore the importance of inter-racial dialogue as a means for preventing and resolving conflict and conclude that, while dialogue is necessary, it is in itself an insufficient activity for resolving the deep-seated emotional and behavioral distances among ethnic groups in society. We propose engaging people in dialogue and community service projects where they can work towards the common good and in the process breakdown myths and stereotypes about each other.

Finally, in a brief postscript, suggestions are made for improving the quality of life of all Americans by creating meaningful dialogues on critical social issues in conjunction with community service initiatives. This approach will provide communal benefits and positive individual interactions. We conclude that it is incumbent on everyone to collaborate and cooperate to avert communal disaster and ensure bright prospects for the future of our society.

A NOTE ON TERMS USED IN THIS BOOK

Just as technology thrusts new devices on us, challenging the way we ordinarily live, work, and play; so, too, does our culture change through time. Ideas, words, and expressions take on new meanings, become obsolete or part of the lexicon that didn't exist a few years ago. Any discussion of race and racism must employ terms commonly used so readers can understand and identify the concepts. Therein lies a problem because our terminology, just like our technology, is ever-changing, leaving some people, like Senate Majority Leader Harry Reid of Nevada, in a time-warp.

While I will not be using the term *Negro*, several interchangeable terms will be used throughout this volume. At times the term "people of color" may be used; however, this term is unacceptable to some Hispanics because they consider themselves white. In fact, the Hispanic population of the United States is over 45 million, over 15 percent of our population, but the majority of them, 29 million, are white. Many Hispanics prefer to be called Latinos over the demographic term Hispanic. Spanish is the principal language in over 40 countries, but Latinos have a wide variety of cultures with different holidays, customs, religions, music, art, dance, food, heroes, politics, and dress. While lumping them together under any category is risky—they disproportionately share the bond of poverty, deficient health status, low educational attainment, and discrimination in the United States.

Blacks are also a diverse mix of people comprising nearly 13 percent of our population (38 million), including Africans, West Indians, and some Latinos. They have a rich variety of cultures and traditions spanning the globe. While it would be wrong to lump all blacks in the United States under the category of African-American, the vast majority of blacks in this country are, and their historical and contemporary experiences in race relations differ to some extent from foreign-born blacks. Indeed, competition for scarce resources (i.e., jobs, housing, education, health care) and the disparate treatment afforded foreign-born blacks is a source of tension between them and African-Americans. Nevertheless, information will be presented throughout using the terms African-American and black because of their preponderance and circumstances which, along with Latinos, has left them behind in their quest for equal opportunities in this country.

We must also consider the sizeable proportion of Asians (over 13 million), bi-racial people (7 million), Native Americans and Alaskans (800,000), and Native Hawaiians and Pacific Islanders (over 400,000). Together these groups comprise nearly 13 percent of our population. Our focus will, however, be on blacks and Latinos, but to bridge the gap in our discussion of racism and discrimination with such a diverse group of people, I will often refer to them as darker-skinned versus the lighter-skinned or whites. I do not use the term Caucasian because of its racist derivation explained later in the text. Sometimes whites in the United States are referred to as Euro-Americans, a term that most whites think is a misnomer because they consider themselves "just American."

As we will see, the term race is itself a socially-constructed concept. Although people look different, scientists have established that humans are closely genetically linked, sharing nearly 100 percent of their DNA. Observed physiological differences among groups of people are the result of genetic inbreeding and interbreeding, migration, and evolutionary adaptations to the environment. Skin color, hair texture, the shape of one's nose, lips, or ears have nothing to do with athleticism or intelligence.

When a group lives in isolation from others or forms cohesive bonds in a larger community or society, it may develop a common culture with unique beliefs, values, and behavior; what social scientists refer to as an ethnic group. Since genetic variation among different groups is so miniscule, a more appropriate term than race would be ethnicity—a term I prefer and sometimes use, but which has not been widely accepted as a substitute for race in a society preoccupied with classification of physical types.

The continuum of variations in abilities within a group is as large as differences between and among groups. Unfortunately, for reasons we will enumerate, light-skinned people have, for more than 500 years, stigmatized and denigrated dark-skinned people. Racism is having the power and privilege to control access to opportunities, upward mobility, and resources in our society while depriving dark-skinned people of these advantages. Racism also carries with it social, psychological, ideological, and theological rationalizations for treating dark-skinned people differently, and sometimes not as people at all.

Another word that is used occasionally is minorities. This is a misnomer when applied to people of color because in a larger sense, whites are minorities on this planet and within a few decades, they will be so in the United States. The term minority may have negative connotations because it can mean less than and unequal to, and many people of color resent being put into such categories. I am aware of the stigma associated with that term and hope readers will understand that no pejorative intentions were implied when it was used as a descriptor of groups of people who have been systemically denied equal opportunities in our society.

Many of the comparisons made and arguments derived from our discussion about prejudice and discrimination are equally valid for a discussion of the implications of social class, or for that matter, the other "*isms*" that plague our society, (e.g., sexism, ableism, anti-Semitism, and homophobia). Some authors even conflate racism with classism. They maintain that the contemporary liberal preoccupation with the culture of poverty and associated values often found among the struggling underclass has assumed the same attributes that were used to stigmatize supposedly different racial and ethnic groups from the seventeenth through the middle of the twentieth century when it became unfashionable to invoke racial classifications following the Holocaust.[3] While I do not accept the logic of this argument in view of the information contained herein, it is indicative of the similarities in treatment accorded minorities and marginalized people in our society. I could have written about any of these groups, but chose race because it is one of the most vexing and perplexing phenomena that has influenced relationships around the world for over 500 years. The following discussion will serve to elucidate the causes and consequences of racism in our society and to promote better understanding and cooperation among our increasingly diverse population. We all deserve better treatment than we have received.

NOTES

1. For a discussion of the implications of the election of Barack Obama for American society see: Eduardo Bonilla-Silva, *Racism Without Racists*. Third edition Lanham, MD: Rowman & Littlefield, 2010, chapter 9; and Adia Harvey Wingfield

and Joe R. Feagin, *Yes We Can?* N.Y. Routledge, 2010; Tim Wise, *Between Barack and a Hard Place,* San Francisco: City Lights Publishers, 2009. These writers dispute the assumption that the election of Barack Obama ushered in a post-racial society.

2. "Hate Crime Statistics, 2008," FBI, U.S. Department of Justice, November 23, 2009.

3. E.g., see Kenan Malik, *The Meaning of Race: Race, History, and Culture in Western Society.* N.Y.: New York University Press, 1996.

Chapter 1

Facing the Challenge of Diversity

...how can the people who have been the object of effective and productive domination by themselves create the conditions of freedom?

—Herbert Marcuse, *One-Dimensional Man*

Humans like to think they are different and superior to all other animals that inhabit this planet. Yet, people are imperfect, and depending on one's belief system, made so through innate spiritual deficiencies or the weight of societal pressures which promote negative, harmful tendencies that produce conflict and strife.

The struggle for survival increases competition and conflict among people over goods and resources. These are also used as indices of success, despite religious admonitions against the accumulation of worldly goods and ostentatious display of materialism.[1] Our attempts to create status distinctions among different racial and ethnic groups based on purported biological differences is even more preposterous given our professed spiritual values that embrace universal brotherhood and equality.

If the universe is under the dominion of a supernatural force that guides our lives, and this supernatural force resembles man and subscribes to a value system that embraces equality, brotherhood, truth, justice, and fairness, then how and why are so many humans deprived of dignity and social justice? What explains the misery and degradation that afflict millions of people in the United States and billions around the world? This book will expose the myths that have created and sustained schisms among us. It is imperative that we understand the role that race plays in the lives of people in the United States and around the world if we are to survive the demographic changes that are occurring and their social implications.

1

THE CULTURAL CLASH

Of specific import is the increasing diversity of the world's population and its mobility. Over ten percent (900 million) of the planet's population annually travels outside their country's boundaries. Large numbers of people cross national borders in search of jobs, freedom, and a better life. Whether for business or pleasure, escape or safety, people are being exposed to a diverse mix of cultures that are magnified by mass communications represented by the internet, telephonic technologies, radio, television, print media, and movies.

This unparalleled mixing of people is wreaking havoc on established societies as the different values, spirituality, dress, foods, living arrangements, customs, and traditions of the new interact and often clash with the old. From Russia to the Balkans, Great Britain to Europe, across Asia the Middle East and Africa, and throughout the Americas—migration, tourism, and mass communications are exposing indigenous populations to ideas, values, and behaviors that challenge established institutions causing stress, anxiety, and conflict.

The effects of this mobility of people and ideas on host/established populations has important ramifications. Along with the rise in hate crimes and the resurgence of old jingoistic antagonisms at the individual level, there has been an increase in nationalistic movements designed to socialize, indoctrinate, and assimilate newcomers. On the one hand are attempts to recast minorities into more socially acceptable versions of the dominant culture, such as French legislation primarily oriented toward Muslims outlawing the wearing of religious ornaments and apparel like headscarves (*hijab*). On the other are the demonstrative attempts to eradicate groups through "ethnic cleansing" as in the former Yugoslavia where Serbs, Croats, and Muslims sought to obliterate all vestiges of ethnic and religious opponents[2] through state-supported violence and the intentional destruction of cultural artifacts. The mass murder of 800,000 Tutsies by rival Hutus during the genocide of 1994 in Rwanda, and the ongoing violence against indigenous people in the Darfur region of Sudan, as well as Han Chinese assaults on minority Uighurs represent failures or the unwillingness of majorities to acknowledge and accept different lifestyles, values, and behavior.

Genocide, the physical and cultural destruction of a group of people by a dominant majority, has occurred throughout history. What differentiates more recent instances of this phenomenon is the frequency of cases, the application of modern technology as in the Jewish Holocaust in Europe between 1933 and 1945, and the prospects for new and more frequent clashes between ethnic groups because of the ephemeral nature of national and communal boundaries. In short, humans are faced with learning to deal with the challenges wrought by diversity—competition for jobs, education, mates, and "the good life" defined by an obsession with materialism— or they risk becoming extinct.

OUR CHANGING SOCIETY

Race relations in the United States are at a crossroads. While some African-Americans and Latinos have made enormous progress in education, employment, and improving their condition in our society, the social status of a significant proportion of people in these groups remains unchanged over the decades since the Civil Rights Era of the 1960s. This underclass, which may account for as much as 12 percent of households in the United States, is growing among African-Americans and the Latino population, which includes many of the 12 million illegal immigrants in this country. It is a persistent reminder that the American Dream remains beyond the reach of millions of ethnic minorities today.[3]

At present rates of growth our current population of 307 million people will reach 439 million by 2050. Over half of our population will be ethnic minorities. Non-Hispanic single-race whites will number 203.3 million or 46 percent of the total population, 20 percent lower than it was in 2008. Nearly one in every three people will be Latino (132.8 million) and 15 percent (65.7 million) will be black. The Asian population will rise to 40.6 million or 9.2 percent of the population. More than three-fifths (62 percent) of the nation's children will be minorities.[4]

The face of America is also changing with each passing day. We are experiencing a loss of a sense of permanence—a dissolution of groundedness that threatens established white majority ways of life. Many pressures are forcing people to confront the prospect of change, which creates fear and trepidation. Scarcity of resources and the threat to comfort are powerful forces that can tear society apart if we do not learn how to adjust and adapt to them.

In the 1950s whites were the clear majority. Even in places with sizable numbers of people of color (then referred to as colored people), whites were far more visible than blacks. Wherever you went, you knew who was in control, who had the power to make things happen, who you should befriend and emulate, who you should or could ignore, and who you should steer clear of.

John Wayne was everybody's hero, and television stars like Steve Allen, Jack Parr, Perry Como, Walt Disney, and Lloyd Bridges filled the airwaves. But there were no people of color in starring roles, only maids and butlers like

Rochester on the *Jack Benny Show*, and *Amos 'n Andy* pushing stereotypes about blacks to amuse whites. At one time there were TV shows starring a sea mammal (Flipper), a bear (Gentle Ben), a horse (Mr. Ed), a mouse (Mickey), and a dog (Lassie), but none featuring a person of color.

How times have changed! Now a third of our population is minorities, and half the students in public schools are children of color. Blacks and Latinos have their own television networks. The mayors of most of the largest cities in the United States are African-American or Latino. Ten percent of the House of Representatives are African-Americans, and an African-American man is the 44th president of our country.

Despite these advances, and the optimistic assumptions of some people that racism is dead in this country, there remains a gulf between the white majority and minorities on a host of critical social indices of power, privilege, and human decency. It is not the book's intent to delineate all the myriad ways that people of color are unequal to whites in this society. Nor do we wish to place blame or guilt on whites for benefiting from and perpetuating this system of privilege. Rather, we choose to write about how we got to where we are as a nation, and the ways we can, as individuals, work to create a more inclusive and responsible society based on mutual respect, collaboration, and cooperation.

Our country does not need to be colorblind, but cognizant and respectful of the differences that have made us who we are. Therefore, this book will demonstrate some of the effects of racism on people of color, especially African-Americans and Latinos because many whites do not recognize these and their implications for society. Focusing on disparities in the quality of life between people of color and whites provides prima facie evidence of discrimination.

It was difficult to limit the discussion of disparities between whites and people of color because of the voluminous research in each of the fields selected for analysis. Rather than engage in an extended discussion of these issues, we focused on some of the major findings to lay the foundation for the subsequent discussion that explores why such disparities exist, persist and, in some instances, such as in health care, have been increasing.

In reviewing the research it was abundantly clear that, as the Kerner Commission concluded forty years ago, we are indeed two nations, one black, one white, separate and unequal.[5] And while ethnic groups other than African-Americans and Latinos have grown since that report was released following tumultuous upheavals in this country, it is still a fact that darker-skinned people are treated differently than lighter-skinned people in the United States and in other white-dominated societies.

In recent years social scientists have debated whether social class has a more significant effect on social status than race. William Julius Wilson, past president of the American Sociological Association, helped to fuel this debate in his important work *The Declining Significance of Race*,[6] and most recently, *More Than Just Race*[7] where he argued that a combination of structural factors—for example, government policies which influenced the availability of mortgages to African Americans, and labor market changes that led to the loss of jobs in the inner city, as well as black culture and racism—contribute to the adverse situation of inner city blacks. For Wilson, and other adherents to his theoretical position, social class antagonisms derived from economic competition are the principal reasons for discrimination and the inferior position of African Americans in our society

This book is not designed to fuel the debate over the relative importance of class or race as the principal aggravating cause of prejudice and discrimination in American society. We do not intend to engage in a chicken-or-egg discourse about the relative importance of one over the other. In a sense, that debate is linked to the nature versus nurture (heredity versus environment) controversy that has embroiled and baffled social scientists for decades. We will not endeavor to create a misery or opportunity index predicated on the relative importance of color and class. They share in the definition and exclusion of people. There is no doubt that economics is an important component in the social status of people. On the other hand, the very fact that economic status is in part defined by barriers to full participation in our society based on color testifies to the importance of racism as a determining factor in the overall equation of discrimination. While the focus of this book is on color, it is not intended to diminish the important role of class in affecting the attainment of human potentialities, but it is designed to illuminate the role of color as a factor that has historically influenced human opportunities in and outside of the classroom.

On the surface, race and racism may be diminishing in their influence on educational attainment in the United States. Recent research[8] indicates that greater educational achievement is obtained for all groups of students when they are economically rather than racially integrated. However, America's inner cities have become storage bins where children of color are warehoused receiving substandard instruction from incompetent, inexperienced teachers in abysmal surroundings.[9] This twenty-first century residential and educational apartheid is based on economic segregation that was the result of government and private sector policies that legalized discrimination against non-whites. Though outlawed, the lingering effects of these policies and new variations of them perpetuate the disadvantaged status of people of color while advantaging whites.

For some observers the argument over whether race or class is paramount may seem little more than a chicken-and-egg discourse engaged in by academics with too much time on their hands. But establishing the relative importance of the duality of forces that perpetuate discrimination in our society, forces which impede the social and economic progress of what will soon be half our population, hardly seems irrelevant. Historical evidence indicates that racism, the domination and exploitation of people of color by whites with accompanying social and psychological justifications for doing so, is difficult to eradicate. It endures even in the best of times and flourishes in the worst.

This work is intended to help people understand the causes and effects of racism on a significant proportion of our population so that we may begin the dialogue advocated by Presidents Clinton and Obama, and clear the air of myths and stereotypes that have separated and divided our society for 400 years.

NOTES

1. See the classic on this by Max Weber, Talcott Parsons, (trans.), *The Protestant Ethic and the Spirit of Capitalism,* Mineola, N.Y.: Dover Publications, 2003.

2. See Michael Sells, *The Bridge Betrayed: Religion and Ethnic Genocide in Bosnia*, Berkeley, Cal.: 1996, for an account of the extremes ethnic cleansing can go, and Fergal Keane, *Seasons of Blood: A Rwandan Journey*, London: Penguin Books, 1997 for a perspective on the Rwandan tragedy. Michael Mann's *The Dark Side of Democracy: Explaining Ethnic Cleansing*, London: Cambridge University Press, 2004, is a comprehensive sociological analysis of ethnic cleansing.

3. For an elaboration of this thesis see: William Julius Wilson, *The Truly Disadvantaged: The Inner City, the Underclass, and Public Policy*, Chicago: University of Chicago Press, 1987, and Douglas Massey and Nancy Denton, *American Apartheid: Segregation and the Making of the Underclass*, Cambridge, Mass.: Harvard University Press, 1998.

4. "An Older and More Diverse Nation by Midcentury," U.S. Census Bureau News, U.S. Department of Commerce, Washington, D.C., August 14, 2008.

5. National Advisory Commission on Civil Disorders, Washington, D.C.: United States Government Printing Office, 1968.

6. Chicago: University of Chicago Press, 1978.

7. New York: W.W. Norton, 2009.

8. Gary Orfield and Susan Eaton, *Dismantling Segregation*, N.Y.: The New Press, 1997; Richard Kahlenberg, *All Together Now*, Washington, D.C., Brookings Institution Press, 2001; Emily Bazelon, "The New Kind of Integration," *New York Times Magazine*, July 20, 2008: 38-43.

9. See Jonathan Kozol, *Savage Inequalities*, N.Y.: Crown Publishers, Inc., 1991 and *The Shame of the Nation*, N.Y.: Crown Publishers, Inc., 2005, and H. Roy Kaplan, *Failing Grades*, Second edition, Lanham, Md.: Rowman & Littlefield Education, 2007.

Chapter 2

The Origin of Our Species

It has often and confidently been asserted, that man's origin can never be known: but ignorance more frequently begets confidence than knowledge: it is those who know little, and not those who know much, who so positively assert that this or that problem will never be solved by science.

—Charles Darwin, *The Descent of Man*

IN THE BEGINNING

The story of human evolution provides the foundation from which discussions about race and racism must begin. It is perhaps the greatest story ever told and has been referred to as "The Greatest Journey Ever Told."[1] If we can understand and acknowledge our common origins, we may be able to exorcise the demons in our heads that breed hatred and violence toward strangers and relegate millions of children of color to subordinate roles in our educational institutions.

The story of human evolution begins in the motherland—Africa, over 200,000 years ago. That is when our human ancestors began to resemble modern men and women. Prior to that time ancient "archaic" species of humans existed in Africa, Asia, and Europe, most notably the Neanderthals, but their smaller brains and inability to adapt to climatological changes in their environment brought on by ice age temperatures led to their demise.

New evidence reveals that Neanderthals shared habitats with our ancient Homo sapien (thinking man) relatives, but became extinct, leaving our ancestors to dominate the planet. It is thought that the last vestige of the ill-fated

7

Neanderthals occupied coastal caves on the island of Gibraltar 28,000 years ago, before modern humans predominated.[2]

Although archaeologists and paleontologists are continually discovering new information about our early ancestors, a considerable body of evidence indicates that humans descended from ape-like hominids six million years ago on the African continent. Modern humans began appearing in sub-Saharan Africa approximately 130,000 years ago, and then migrated around the world, travelling first to the Middle East, then on to Asia, moving into Australia about 65,000 years ago, Europe approximately 30,000 to 40,000 years in the past, and the Americas just 15,000 years ago.

The path they took is marked by their very essence—deoxyribonucleic acid (DNA), the building block of life. Along the way they left this indelible mark—a calling card of the ages, their biological imprint. Two of the most important elements of our ancestors' biological composition that are embedded in their DNA are mitochondria, which are found in the cytoplasm of cells and are passed on by mothers to their offspring, and the Y chromosome which fathers pass on to their sons from generation to generation. Changes in the Y chromosome become imprinted in the DNA of male heirs and reflect the identical DNA structure in all male relatives.

These two biological markers have enabled scientists to study and map the evolution and travel of our ancestors from pre-history to contemporary time. They help to explain why a group of black South Africans known as the Lemba, are indeed, as they contend, of Jewish descent; how Thomas Jefferson's liaison with one of his slaves, Sally Hemings, produced mulatto heirs; and why some Scandinavians carry the sickle-cell gene more commonly found in Africans and descendants of Africans in the United States.[3]

Our ancestors were distinguished from ancients by their larger brains which enabled them to better adapt to their environment. Their superior intellectual ability helped them to create tools that facilitated gathering food and hunting. These developments not only enhanced their survivability, but led to farming, the domestication of animals, creation of a surplus, and migration around the globe.

One of the most significant scientific findings of modern science is the fact that all humans are descended from one female (Mitochondrial Eve) who lived in Africa 200,000 years ago. This fact has been established through a combination of paleoanthropological research of human remains and artifacts on the African continent *and* the examination of DNA.

Only within the last few decades have scientists been able to understand, analyze, and apply knowledge about the sequencing of DNA to the origin and evolution of our species, Homo sapiens. The story of our evolution is filled with the richness of human of diversity and similarities, and refutes malicious stereotypes about people who, superficially, appear different from the majority.

Contemporary scientific research about the origin of our species based on analyses of DNA, has led scientists to conclude that all humans are related. Furthermore, analyses of Y chromosomes, passed on from fathers to their sons, corroborates this and indicates that all men are descended from a male (Mitochondrial Adam) who lived in Africa around the same time as Mitochondrial Eve (but he probably did not know her).

Because all humans have the same set of chromosomes (23 pairs), and share mitochondrial DNA, we are all biologically linked to our ancient ancestors.[4] Through the analysis of mitochondrial DNA scientists have concluded that all humans are 99.98 percent genetically identical. Only *0.2 percent* difference in genetic material exists between any two randomly selected people on the planet. The fascinating fact is that over 85 percent of those minute differences can be accounted for *within* a person's local group. The so-called concept of race accounts for just *0.012 percent* of the differences in genes between groups.[5] A person might have more similarities with someone on another continent than a neighbor because we are descended from common ancestors. This fact helps explain why the sickle-cell trait, most commonly found in West and Central Africa and people of African descent because it was an evolutionary marker that provided protection against malaria, turns up in people around the world who, on the surface, look different from Africans, such as Swedes.

The sickle-cell trait was a human evolutionary mutation that gave some measure of protection to indigenous Africans against malaria. Today it is found among millions of people in Africa, the Mediterranean, East Indians and people of Spanish ancestry. When both parents carry the trait their offspring may develop a debilitating, deadly disease known as sickle-cell anemia—a condition found among 1 in 500 African-Americans and 1 in 1,200 Latinos in the United States. Two million Americans, including 10 percent of African-Americans, carry the sickle-cell trait. The widespread occurrence of the sickle-cell trait testifies to the common origins of humans.[6]

THE REASON FOR HUMAN VARIATION

The question arises, if we are all related, why do we look different from one another? Hair, skin, lips, noses, ears and eyes as well as our physiques appear in many variations. The incalculable physiological differences that seem to defy generalizations about common origins and genetic heritage are actually evolutionary adaptations to our environment. As our ancestors began the long journey out of Africa in search of new habitats either in quest of adventure or for food, their external physiognomy underwent changes.

The English biologist Charles Darwin was one of the first scientists to publish observations about how species adapted to their environment through the process of natural selection. Darwin observed flora and fauna in the Galapagos Islands, an isolated chain off the coast of Ecuador, and attributed natural selection to the process of evolution that assured the survival of the strongest most adaptable members of a species. It was nature's way of ensuring the survival of the fittest.

The answer to why our external features vary then lies in the sequencing of the DNA which structures genes in myriad ways. Through the passage of time a number of processes occurred that influenced the structure of our DNA, causing changes in our physiology. Genes have many forms, or alleles, which are influenced by processes like genetic drift, where a population can become isolated and pass on biological characteristics with a minimum introduction of new genetic material from outside groups. Throughout human history, when different groups of people came into contact with one another, two social processes occurred: they mated and they fought. The flow of genes from one group to another through interbreeding leads to some genetic differences among humans.

In fact, geographic distance and migration account for most of the observable differences among groups today, but earlier in our history natural selection made important contributions to our genetic heritage. As Darwin perceived, plants and animals adapt to their environment in a never-ending attempt to accommodate to changes wrought by nature with the "weaker" or less flexible members of the species becoming extinct.[7] From time to time mutations occur in the DNA sequences or nucleotides, those vast strands of protein that determine our biological, and to some extent, psychological nature. Mutations may have positive or negative effects on the survivability of the species, such as the sickle-cell trait, or the epicanthic fold prevalent in Asians that helped their ancestors adapt to the sandstorms and climate on the Steppes of Central Asia by narrowing their eyes.

When combinations of genes through natural selection and mutation are inherited they form a haplotype indicating a common genetic origin. A haplogroup represents a cluster of related haplotypes and may create distinguishing biological differences among group members, especially when they have been separated by time and distance.

Some mutations can also be neutral like hair or eye color. It was recently discovered that some Neanderthals were red-headed. Red hair among us is the result of a mutation that impedes melanin in hair follicles and does not appear to serve any function.[8] However, red hair is an indication of pale skin which is found among humans who migrated out of Africa into parts of the planet with less sunshine. Having lighter skin is a mutation that assisted some of our ancestors by helping their bodies absorb ultraviolet light through their skin. This enabled them to receive vitamin D, which prevents rickets and scurvy and, significantly, depression.

Unlike their cousins, who live near the equator where the sun shines brightly year round, and have darker skin produced by more melanin to protect them from the harmful effects of sunlight (skin cancer), northern peoples suffer from higher rates of suicide, alcoholism, and drug addiction associated with depression-related vitamin D insufficiency. Skin color is a function of natural selection and does not determine behavior. Higher rates of such deviant behavior in northern climes are not biologically determined but social and psychological adaptations to environmental effects.

Although humans may have different physical appearances, everyone on the planet is related to his or her ancestors who lived in eastern Africa. As award-winning science writer Steve Olson notes, "Everyone on earth today is equally distant from the early modern humans of eastern Africa. In that respect, no one group ... is more closely related to our ancestors than any other. The same number of generations separates Australians, Canadians, and Ethiopians from early modern humans."[9]

TRACING Y CHROMOSOMES

Two recent illustrations of historical genetic links established by tracing the Y chromosome are the Lemba, a group of black Africans living in South Africa, and the purported heirs of Thomas Jefferson, the third president of the United States.

The Lemba people, numbering around 50,000, live for the most part in the Limpopo Province in the northern part of South Africa and in southwest rural Zimbabwe. Not much attention was paid to them until Tudor Parfitt, a Professor of Modern Jewish Studies at the University of London's School of Oriental and African Studies, fortuitously encountered them at a lecture he gave in South Africa in the mid-nineties.

Noticing that the Lemba men wore Yarmulkes (skull caps), he engaged them in a conversation and was surprised to learn that they claimed to be Jewish, supposedly descended from a group of Jews who migrated there from the Middle East over 3,000 years ago. Parfitt did not know of any scientific research to corroborate their claims but accepted their invitation to visit their village in the region of Venda in South Africa. There he observed the Lemba in their daily rituals which overtly corresponded with Jewish traditions, such as ritual slaughter of animals and the following of Kosher dietary laws such as adhering to the biblical injunction against mixing milk and meat in the same meal, and the circumcision of males, which Jews do when the baby is eight days old, but the Lemba practice at the age of eight years.

Still, no conclusive proof existed to support their claim until a research team of biologists headed by Professor Karl Skorecki on the Faculty of Medicine at Technion University in Israel established through Y chromosome analysis that a limited number of markers created a Y Common Modal Haplotype among Jewish male priests or *Cohanim*.[10] According to the Old Testament, Moses anointed his brother Aaron as the high priest or *Cohen* of the Israelites, and all of his male heirs are by lineage, priests or *Cohanim*. Since the Cohen Modal Haplotype is found almost exclusively among *Cohanim* in the Jewish male population, researchers reasoned that it would be a way of demonstrating whether the Lemba were indeed descendants of Jews.

A research team headed by Mark Thomas, including Tudor Parfitt, took DNA samples of Lemba men in the late 1990s and found evidence of their Semitic genetic link, with two-thirds of one prominent clan of Lemba men, the Buba, having Middle Eastern origins.[11] Although researchers at the time believed the Lemba men and other Jewish males with the Cohen Modal Haplotype were descended from a single Jewish priest (Aaron) approximately 3,000 years ago, subsequent refinements in DNA analysis by geneticist Michael Hammer at the University of Arizona along with Karl Skorecki and others, indicate that the Cohen Modal Haplotype is linked to multiple and unique lineages of Jewish priests who existed at that time, not one heir.[12]

The Lemba claim to be Jewish by birth. Samuel Moweti, a Lemba, and former member of the South African Parliament, noted in an interview with Leslie Stahl on the CBS show *60 Minutes* "Jewishness in us is inborn." Actually, most humans alive today have alleles in common with Jews from centuries of interbreeding. Although Jews' preponderance for endogamous marriages helped to establish and perpetuate different or unique haplogroups from other populations, the fact remains that all humans share the vast amount of their genetic material making his statement illogical and false. Jews are not a racial group. They do not differ in any structural biological way from non-Jews. They are an ethnic group of people found predominantly in two populations—the central and eastern European Ashkenazim and the Sephardim who inhabited the Mediterranean. Both lived in the Middle East until their lands were conquered and they were dispersed in what is known as the Diaspora under Roman occupation 2,000 years ago.

Jewishness is not biological but cultural. And while the Lemba seek recognition and acceptance by Jews around the world, South African Jews have asked them to convert before they are accepted into the religion. This is not a racist statement but recognition of the social and psychological foundation of Judaism, not a biological separateness that has been used to stigmatize, stereotype, and persecute Jews for 2,000 years. We will see that the same kind of warped thinking has led to the development and implementation of racist ideologies and behavior resulting in the torment of generations of people around the world.

THE SIGNIFICANCE OF BIOLOGICAL MARKERS

The Y chromosome and mitochondrial DNA are invaluable tools for tracing human existence. Together they have established incontrovertible evidence of the oneness of humanity—the fact that humans have more similarities than differences—we breathe air, eat food, create and work with tools, laugh and cry, congregate in groups, and feel pain when we are discriminated against. Because we are so genetically linked, we can exchange blood, tissues, organs, and bones. Organ transplants are most successful with living-related donors, but through immunosuppressive drugs, transplants between strangers are highly successful today. It makes little difference whether the donor and recipient are the same color, sex, or religion as long as their blood types match.

Six years ago my wife, who was teaching at the University of South Florida, began having difficulty with her balance and experienced head and neck pain. After being examined by several neurologists she decided to undergo an operation to replace two cervical discs in her neck. Knowing the operation would take approximately three hours, I was shocked to see her surgeon in the waiting room an hour and a half into the operation. "Is everything all right?" I asked nervously. "Oh, she's doing fine. I finished my part and the rest of the team is working on her now. I removed the two degenerated discs and they're putting in two plates, some screws, and bone grafts. It'll take about a year for the grafts to start growing, but she'll be fine."

"Where did you get the bone from for the grafts?" I asked.

"Cadaver," he replied. We never asked about the color of the donor.

I know my wife and most people undergoing similar operations, just like my father-in-law, a retired cardiac surgeon who had three cornea transplants to restore his vision, were ecstatic about receiving organs that could substitute for their own non-functioning ones. They didn't ask about the color, sex, height, or religion of the donor. What was important was that someone bequeathed these body parts to help improve the life of another human being—a living person who could use the donated material because we share common biology.

This means that the shape of our nose, lips, ears, eyes, and the texture of our hair is no indication of an atavistic throwback to primitive ancestors, nor are they related to how fast we can run, how high we can jump, and how well we can think and reason. Although humans look different, the essential fact is that we have far more similarities than differences. Flared nostrils and flat noses help people living in warm humid climates breath easier when they exert themselves, just as having curly hair (facetiously referred to as nappy, kinky, or bad hair) is another form of natural selection that helps cool individuals by facilitating evaporation through the scalp.

THE FALLACY OF BIOLOGICAL STEREOTYPES

Just as these characteristics found among dark-skinned people do not aid their athletic achievement or hinder their intellectual accomplishments, so, too, the epicanthic cleft that narrows the eyes of Asians has nothing to do with their academic success in math and science. Yet, common stereotypes about these groups permeate our culture, affecting our views of one another and poisoning relationships through misinformation and malicious rumors.

The single most pernicious assumption associated with contemporary racism is that skin color determines one's athletic and intellectual ability. There is no scientific evidence to support these beliefs yet our culture is permeated with messages that perpetuate this misinformation, just as a majority of Americans reject Darwin's long established theory of evolution.[13]

The term race has lost significance as a heuristic concept among social scientists.[14] They contend that it is more useful to focus on ethnicity, which is defined as the social and cultural characteristics that differentiate one group from another. Despite persistent public beliefs to the contrary, scientists know that physiological differences among people are insignificant and do not account for systematic variations in human behavior, but they do affect the way people are treated, such as racism and discrimination and their effects on health, income, employment, the dispensation of criminal justice, and educational attainment.

The paradox of race is that biologically insignificant differences in genetic structure have, nevertheless, led to the formation of enormous differences in the way people are perceived and the nature of our interactions. While it may be fashionable to dismiss race as inaccurate and superfluous, it is facile to assume it lacks importance in our society as a source of tension and harbinger of the social and economic status of large segments of our society.

Human behavioral variation is the result of social and psychological processes related to adaptations to the environment, custom, and tradition.

Though race exists as a social construct—in our minds—there are observable differences among us, and these have enormous power that have contributed to violence, wars, the demise of nations and peoples, and the perpetuation of human misery. Race only has the power we attribute to it. It is a shallow, hollow concept that evolved to justify and perpetuate the status of privileged light-skinned people. If we are able to identify the core elements that have been used to create racist ideologies of supremacy, perhaps we can deconstruct the concept and limit its power.

NOTES

1. James Shreeve, "The Greatest Journey Ever Told: The Trail of Our DNA," *National Geographic*, Sunday, March 12, 2006: 61–73.

2. Kate Wong, "Twilight of the Neanderthals," *Scientific American*, 301, (2), August, 2009, pp. 32–37. See also chapter 4, "The Fate of the Neanderthals," in John H. Relethford, *Reflections of Our Past: How History is Revealed in Our Genes,* Cambridge: Mass.: Westview Press, 2003, pp. 75–99.

3. For a discussion of the biological origins of modern humans see: Steve Olson, *Mapping Human History: Genes Race and Our Common Origin*, Boston: Mariner Books, 2002 and Relethford, loc. cit. The work of Luca Cavalli-Sforza and his colleagues are landmark studies in the quest of human origins. See: Luca L. Cavalli-Sforza, Paolo Menozzi, and Alberto Piazza, *The History and Geography of Human Genes,* Princeton: Princeton University Press, 1994.

4. National Geographic is conducting a world-wide genealogical survey to establish human origins and relatedness. The goal is to analyze DNA samples from 100,000 people to determine genetic commonalities. Their website *www.genographic. com* contains contemporary scientific and historical information about the origin of our species as well as opportunities to participate in the project and trace more recent family members. Another useful website about human origins is available through NOVA which also produced a fascinating three part series on evolution "Becoming Human." See: *http://www .pbs.org/wgbh/nova/beta/evolution.*

5. Paul Hoffman, "The Science of Race," *Discover*, November 1994: 55.

6. "About Sickle Cell Disease," U.S. News and World Report, August 28, 2008 at: *http://health.usnews.com/articles/health/blood-disorders/2008/08/about-sickle-cell-disease.*

7. Charles Darwin, *On the Origin of Species by Means of Natural Selection, or the Preservation of Favoured Races in the Struggle for Life.* London: Murray, 1859.

8. Brian Handywerk, "Some Neanderthals Were Pale Redheads, DNA Suggests," *National Geographic News,* October 25, 2007.

9. Olson, op. cit., p. 29.

10. Karl Skorecki, et. al. "Chromosomes of Jewish Priests," *Nature*, 385, January 2, 1997: 32.

11. Mark G. Thomas, et. al., "Y Chromosomes Traveling South: The Cohen Haplotype and the Origins of the Lemba—the 'Black Jews of Southern Africa,'" *American Journal of Human* Genetics, 66 (2), February, 2000: 674–686.

12. Michael F. Hammer, et. al., "Extended Y Chromosome Haplotypes Resolve Multiple and Unique Lineages of the Jewish Priesthood," *Human Genetics*, July 2009 at: *http://www.springerlink.com/content /357176p177623m41/fulltext/pdf.* See also: David Goldstein, *Jacob's Legacy: A Genetic View of Jewish History,* New Haven: Yale University Press, 2008. Another fascinating Y chromosome investigation has been the attempt to prove that Thomas Jefferson fathered children with his slave mistress, Sally Hemings, who was the half-sister of Jefferson's deceased wife, Martha. Some members of the Jefferson family acknowledge this relationship and embrace their bi-racial relatives while others do not. See the discussion of the genetic evidence of this debate in Relethford, op. cit. 219–223, and the definitive historical evidence in Annette Gordon-Reed, *The Hemingses of Monticello*, N.Y.: W.W. Norton, 2008.

13. On the occasion of Darwin's 200th birthday, a Gallup poll of people in the United States found that only 39 percent believed in his theory of evolution and only 55 percent of those polled could even associate him with the concept of evolution. *http://www.gallup.com/poll/114544/darwin-birthday-believe-evolution.aspx?version=print.* February 11, 2009. Retrieved: 10/14/09.

14. See the web site of the American Association of Anthropology for discussions of DNA, race and the social and cultural implications associated with that term at: *http://www.understandingrace.org/home.html.*

Chapter 3

The Rise of Racism

That no doubt can any longer remain but that we are with great probability right in referring all and singular as many varieties of man as are at present known to one and the same species.

—*The Anthropological Treatises of Johann Friedrich Blumenbach, 1795*

Racism and discrimination against dark-skinned people is nothing new. Historian Thomas Gossett discerned a preference for light skin over 5,000 years ago in India and ancient Egypt and China.[1] Since Africa is the source of the human species and all humans are nearly identical genetically, how did whiteness and white physiology become "normal" and superior, and dark skin aberrant and inferior? To understand this paradox we must examine the historical, philosophical, and "scientific" thought that created the foundation for racist ideologies.

HOW RACISM BEGAN

Racism emerged in the United States as an attempt to rationalize white European domination and exploitation of Africans and indigenous peoples in North, Central, and South America. Relying on theological, philosophical, social, and pseudo-scientific explanations of the natural superiority of whites over people of color, Europeans and their descendants in the New World endeavored to justify their theft of land and mistreatment of people of color.

Bolstered by the Bible, writings of intellectuals such as Englishman Thomas Hobbes and German philosopher Immanuel Kant, and scientists like Darwin,

17

Lamarck, Linnaeus, and Blumenbach, whites constructed an ideology to legitimize their hegemony over the lands and peoples which they desired. This ideology was composed of several layers, based on a foundation of religious and moral superiority of the white race over all others, especially dark-skinned peoples. Throughout history and even today, despite the fact that whites account for less than 10 percent of the world's population, they have managed to infuse their beliefs about white supremacy throughout the world and, through ideological, cultural, political and military excursions, promulgate their hegemonic perspective in an attempt to justify their position of domination and exploitation.

While money and avarice were in the final analysis the root of the evil of racism, theories of the natural superiority of whites over dark-skinned people were invented to rationalize and conceal their true intent. What higher authority could one cite than sacred texts which depicted dark-skinned people as the cursed descendants of Noah's recalcitrant son, Ham?[2] God had ordained white people to be leaders and explorers, to bring His word to the heathen, soulless savages whose primitive naturalistic lifestyles reeked from their profligate debaucheries.

In *Leviathan*, Hobbes referred to the savages and barbarians living in America. The land of the vanquished belongs to the conqueror, and though slavery is never justified, subordination of indigenous populations for economic interests is acceptable.[3] A hundred years later, Thomas Carlyle, Scottish writer and historian, contended that blacks inhabiting Britain's colonies in the West Indies were incapable of developing the natural resources of their lands and should be compelled to toil under the God-given natural order of white masters and black servants: "You are not 'slaves' now; nor do I wish it can be avoided, to see you slaves again; but decidedly you will have to be servants to those that are born wiser than you, that are born lords of you—servants to the whites, if they are (as what mortal can doubt they are?) born wiser than you. That, you may depend upon it, my obscure black friends, is and was always the law of the world, for you and all men; to be servants, the more foolish of us to the more wise; only sorrow, futility, and disappointment will betide both, till both, in some approximate degree, get to conform to the same."[4]

In their zeal to conquer the New World in search of fame and fortune and to spread the word of God, Portuguese, Dutch, Spanish, French, and English explorers ran roughshod over indigenous peoples, disparaging their cultures, slaughtering, pillaging, and enslaving for King, Country, and religion/Christianity. The two-fold justification of these actions were their belief in the natural superiority of whites over dark-skinned people, and their theological mindset which countenanced white dominion over people of color as part of God's natural order. These served as convenient subterfuge for obfuscating the mercantilist and nascent capitalist expansionist enterprises of nation states competing in a global struggle for power, privilege, and resources.

White European civilization not only carried new technology to far away lands, its emissaries harbored infectious diseases such as smallpox, bubonic plague, and other infectious and communicable illnesses that indigenous people had little or no resistance to. If thousands of indigenous people were slaughtered by rapacious encroaching conquistadors, millions of natives succumbed to the germs that silently invaded their bodies. It is estimated that within 40 years of Columbus' landing in Hispaniola in 1492, nearly all of the 300,000 to 400,000 Arawak/Taino Indians who had inhabited the region were deceased.

Geographer Jared Diamond documents the effects of European encroachment on the mortality of indigenous populations, noting that "Throughout the Americas, diseases introduced with Europeans spread from tribe to tribe far in advance of the Europeans themselves, killing an estimated 95 percent of the pre-Columbian Native-American population."[5]

While most of the illnesses were spread unintentionally, there were instances, like that of Jeffrey Amherst, English hero of the French and Indian War, who knowingly distributed blankets infected with smallpox to Native Americans to "Extirpate this Execrable Race."[6]

EXPLORATION AND EXPLOITATION

Ironically, Europeans' stereotypical views of indigenous people were reinforced through their encounters with societies they deemed primitive. Scantily clothed, nomadic, hunter/gatherers, and subsistence agriculturalists fit the prevailing European view of such people as inferior who, with their property, were like so many low-hanging fruit to be plucked for King and country. Travel outside the European continent in the fourteenth to the sixteenth centuries was limited for most people. Excursions to the New World and distant lands prior to Columbus and the Age of Exploration facilitated by Portuguese Prince Henry the Navigator had occurred, but such voyages were rarely undertaken for other than commercial purposes.

It was the propitious if not serendipitous technological coincidence of navigational improvements, and an increase in the availability of printing brought about by Gutenberg's invention of metal movable type in 1455, that created increased incursions and glimpses of whites into indigenous lands. This not only led to the Renaissance but European exploration around the world. As ethnocentric travelers glimpsed strange new cultures they transferred their stereotypical images of primitive indigenous peoples through word of mouth and, increasingly, print. Descriptions of beings more ape-like than human known as "oran-ootan" were accompanied by sketches that reinforced European chauvinistic beliefs in their natural superiority and the seemingly wretched existence of "primitive" peoples in Africa and the New World.

A man and woman att the Cape of good Hope

Figure 3.1   Male and female hotentot. Source: Sir Thomas Herbert, Some Yeares Travels into Africa & Asia The Great. London: Jacob Blome & Richard Bishop, 1638, p. 18.

It was no coincidence that racist theories in the form of human phylogenetic classifications began to surface in the seventeenth century. The colonization of the New World and excursions into the interior of Africa and Asia was spurred by the search for new markets and wealth to nourish the coffers of European nation-states. This travel brought Europeans into contact with diverse peoples who had been little known prior to the advent of new navigational aides.

Initial accounts of aboriginal indigenous people were sometimes based on sketchy recollections of travelers that bore little resemblance to reality. Some

Figure 3.2 "Oran-ootan" described by Beedkman (1718). Source: Captain Daniel Beeckman, A Voyage to & From the Island of Borneo. London: T. Warneretal, 1719.

groups in Southern Africa were likened to missing links between humans and apes, derisively referred to as *Hottentots*, and depicted as simian-like creatures. In 1708, naturalist Francois Leguat rendered the following comparison of an ape to a Hottentot: "[i]ts Face had no other Hair upon it than the Eye-brows, and in general it much resembled one of those *Grotesque* Faces which the Female *Hottentots* have at the Cape."[7]

In seventeenth century England, various groups of people on the African continent were likened to the devil and other ghoulish, nightmarish apparitions. The seventeenth century English traveler, Sir Thomas Herbert, traveled to Africa in 1627-1629 and likened Africans to monkeys.

"Comparing their imitations, speech and visages, I doubt many of them have no better Predecessors than Monkeys. Their language is rather apishly than articulately founded, with whom 'tis thought they have unnatural mixture. Having a voice 'twixt humane and beast, makes that supposition to be more of credit, that they have a beastly copulation or conjuncture. So as considering the resemblance they bear with Baboons, which I could observe kept frequent company with the Women, their speech ... rather agreeing with beasts than men ... these may be said to be the descendants of Satyrs, of any such ever were."[8]

One of the saddest and most sordid examples of Eurocentric racism surrounds the exploitation of a teenage African woman, Sarah Baartman. Born of Khoi Khoi descent in 1789 in South Africa, Sarah Baartman was "discovered" by a British ship's doctor, William Dunlop, while she was working as a slave in Cape Colony. She had unusually large breasts, buttocks and labia, a condition known as steatopygia not uncommon among people from her region of Africa, and thought to be an evolutionary adaptation that allows for the dispersion of bodily heat and storing of fat. Dunlop coaxed her into traveling with him to England where she spent four years exhibited for scientists and the public as an exotic specimen nicknamed the "*Hottentot Venus*." She then went on display in Paris. When the public lost interest in gawking at her naked body she turned to prostitution and died in 1815 at the age of 25 of "inflammatory and eruptive sickness." (Possibly syphilis.)

Sarah Baartman's travail did not end with her untimely death. French scientist Georges Cuvier made a plaster cast of her body, removed her skeleton, brain and genitals and preserved them in bottles that were displayed in French museums for 160 years. In 1974 they were removed from public view from the *Musee de l'Homme* in Paris. After eight years of public pleas and a request from Nelson Mandela, her remains were returned and laid to rest in her homeland in 1994.[9]

Her case was not unique. Professor Sadiah Qureshi points out that other exhibitions of people from colonized lands soon followed, including Laplanders and South Americans in 1822, "Bushmen" (San) in 1847, and Aztecs and Zulus in 1853. He notes that to this day there are still some 2,000 skeletons of Khosians in South African museums testifying to the racialization of indigenous Africans as inferior beings.[10]

HOW EXPLORATION LED TO CONQUEST

As competition between the mercantilist nation-states increased and colonization spread around the globe, propaganda demonizing adversaries was created to cast opponents in a negative light, although the behavior of these imperialist powers in occupied lands was universally reprehensible. In North America, conflict between the Spanish and English over colonization led to propaganda that demonized each other's behavior and intentions toward the Indians.

The English cited the writing of two Spaniards, Bartolomé de Las Casas, who was the first priest ordained in the New World and became Bishop of Chiapas in Guatemala, and Juan Gines de Sepulveda, an eminent theologian, as evidence of Spain's barbarous intentions toward indigenous people and the moral justification for English control over American colonies. The brutal treatment of Indians by Spanish conquistadors was observed first-hand by de Las Casas who helped subdue them in Cuba in 1502. Las Casas was given an estate (*encomienda)* by the Spanish government for his service, which also included the right to the treatment of Indians on the land as serfs and the free use of their labor.

Gradually Las Casas was repulsed by the exploitation of the Indians and renounced all his claims to them in 1514. Thereafter, he worked tirelessly for the rest of his life (he died in 1566 at the age of 92) for the recognition of Indian rights and humane treatment of indigenous peoples. He summarized his philosophy about the rights of Indians and his grievances against their mistreatment in his "A Brief Account on the Destruction of the Indies" (also known as "Tears of the Indians"), with the subtitle "Or a faithful Narrative of The Horrid and Unexampled Massacres, Butcheries, and all manner of Cruelties, that Hell and Malice could invent, committed by the Popish *Spanish* Party on the inhabitants of *West-India,* TOGETHER with the Devastations of several Kingdoms in America by Fire and Sword, for the space of Forty and Two Years, from the time of its first Discovery by them." Published in 1552 in Seville, the widely read report detailed the horrific treatment meted out against Indians by Spanish conquerors.

Describing the massacre of indigenous people, Las Casas wrote:

> ... of the Three Millions of Persons, which lived in Hispaniola itself, there is at present but the inconsiderable remnant of scarce Three Hundred.[11]

Further,

> ... the Spaniards by their barbarous and execrable Actions have absolutely depopulated Ten Kingdoms, of greater extent than all Spain, together with the Kingdoms of Arragon and Portugal....

> The decimation of the natives was all the more deplorable because ... the inhabitants of the islands were peaceful innocent Sheep, innocently simple, altogether void of and averse to all manner of Craft, Subtlety and Malice and most Obedient and Loyal Subjects to their Native Sovereigns; and behave themselves patiently, submissively and quietly towards the Spaniards, to whom they are subservient and subject; so that finally they live without the least thirst after revenge, laying aside all litigiousness, commotion and hatred.[12]

Las Casas was enraged that the Spaniards wreaked havoc on these non-threatening, peaceful natives in the most despicable and depraved ways, even taking pleasure from their torment and misery. The Spaniards

> ... spar'd no Age, or Sex, nay not so much as Women and Child, but ripping up their Bellies, tore them alive in pieces. They laid Wagers among themselves, who should with a Sword at one blow cut, or divide a Man in two; or which of them should decollate or behead a Man, with the greatest dexterity; nay farther, which should sheath his Sword in the Bowels of a Man with the quickest dispatch and expedition. They snatcht young Babes from the Mothers Breasts, and dasht out the brains of those innocents against Rocks; others they cast into Rivers scoffing and jeering them, and called upon their bodies when falling with derision, the true testimony of their cruelty, to come to them, and inhumanely exposing others to their Merciless Swords, together with the Mothers that gave them Life. They erected certain Gibbets, large, but low made, so that their feet almost reacht the ground, every one of which was so ordered as to bear Thirteen Persons in Honour and Reverance (as they said blasphemously) of our Reedemer and his Twelve Apostles, under which they made a Fire to burn Ashes whilst hanging on them....[13]

As controversy grew in Spain about the appropriate treatment of conquered indigenous people a law was passed in 1542 prohibiting Indian slavery and abolishing the system of *encomienda*. However, its weak enforcement led Las Casas to continue his crusade for Indian rights. This culminated in the creation of an historic *junta* convened by King Charles V in 1550 in Valladolid to hear arguments pro and con about the use of force with Indians in Spanish America.

De Las Casas and Sepulveda presented their case before a jury of learned scholars and jurists. Las Casas insisted on the natural rights and goodness of the Indians and Sepulveda on their barbarism, idolatry, lack of ability to place reason over their passions, and the justification for enslaving them when they refused to convert to Christianity.

Although neither of the scholars prevailed, the debate provided ammunition for adherents of both sides of the issue and the mistreatment of the Indians continued, despite the issuance of a papal bull, *Sublimus Dei,* by Pope Paul III, 13 years before, which proclaimed Indians were rational beings and had the ability to accept Christianity:

> The enemy of the human race, who opposes all good deeds in order to bring men to destruction, beholding and envying this, invented a means never before heard of, by which he might hinder the preaching of God's word of Salvation to the people: he inspired his satellites who, to please him, have not hesitated to publish abroad that the Indians of the West and the South, and other people of whom We have recent knowledge should be treated as dumb brutes created for our service, pretending that they are incapable of receiving the Catholic Faith.

> We, who, though unworthy, exercise on earth the power of our Lord and seek with all our might to bring those sheep of His flock who are outside into the fold committed to our charge, consider, however, that the Indians are truly men and that they are not only capable of understanding the Catholic Faith but, according to our information, they desire exceedingly to receive it. ... the said Indians and all other people who may later be discovered by Christians, are by no means to be deprived of their liberty or the possession of their property, even though they be outside the faith of Jesus Christ; and that they may and should, freely and legitimately, enjoy their liberty and the possession of their property; nor should they be in any way enslaved; should the contrary happen, it shall be null and have no effect.[14] —Pope Paul III

Perhaps it was some indigenous peoples' reluctance to convert which inflamed and encouraged their mistreatment by the invaders, but Spaniards were not alone in their maltreatment of residents in the New World. The Dutch, French, and English held similar negative views about First Nation people. While there were initial attempts to convert the Indians to Christianity and save them from eternal damnation, early explorers and settlers slipped into racist ideologies that denigrated and disparaged indigenous peoples' lifestyles and customs, rationalizing their domination, enslavement and annihilation. King Philip's War in 1675–1676 in New England marked the end of English missionary attempts to proselytize Indians. The abandonment of this philosophy led to the view that "the only good Indian is a dead Indian."

HOW RACIST IDEOLOGY AROSE

It is important to reiterate that the motivation to dominate indigenous people was two-pronged. Of paramount importance was the financial need to obtain wealth through gold and resources, including, as we will see, enslavement of native populations. The impetus for the acquisition of wealth and extension of markets under mercantilism and developing capitalism was bolstered by the formation of an ideology of racism that was peculiar to the West. According to historian Ivan Hannaford, this perspective was unknown in form and substance prior to its introduction at the time of European exploration and encounters with diverse populations around the world in the fifteenth century.[15]

Western (white) racist ideology was used to justify the domination and exploitation of indigenous people by linking it, or more properly using it, as a rationalization to explain the natural dominion of whites over indigenous people of color. They were frequently referred to as savages, barbarians, heathen, infidels, idolaters, wretched, promiscuous, primitive, hostile, cannibalistic, ape-like, docile, and sheep-like. It was the duty, even the God-given right and obligation, of white Europeans to spread the word of God to save these lost souls. Whites were destined, ordained by God, to conquer non-whites and in the process spread Christianity and their superior values to heathen lands.

According to Hannaford, numerous Bulls were issued by the Catholic Church from the eleventh century onward that stressed papal authority over heathen lands "'on the authority of the omnipotent God delegated to us through St. Peter and the Vicariate of Jesus Christ which we exercise on earth.'"[16]

THE RISE OF "SCIENTIFIC RACISM"

The imprimatur of theology was supported by the development of "scientific" theories of racial classifications. These helped complete the rationale for European domination and exploitation of indigenous populations by demonstrating that whites were biologically advanced, superior beings. Among the first so-called scientific attempts to classify racial differences was that of the German physician, Johann Friedrich Blumenbach (1752–1840), who is regarded as the "father of anthropology" or rather physical anthropology.

While other scientists were struggling to reconcile theological dicta about the nature of man and his preeminent unique position in the universe, scientists like Swede Carolus Linnaeus (1707–1778), the "Father of Taxonomy," whose work is still used today, and Frenchman Georges-Louis Leclerc, Comte de Buffon (1707–1788) endeavored to understand why and how differences among humans occurred.

Although their typologies sought to delineate different categories of humans, it was Blumenbach who proposed a systematic classification of people based on the geographical region they resided in. He believed that an organism's morphology or structure could be modified by its environment and resultant changes could be inherited.

Blumenbach's meticulous work, first published in 1775 as *On the Natural Variety of Mankind,* originally classified humans based on physical features created through interaction with their environment.

Initially, Blumenbach enumerated four regions and corresponding types of people found in them: Europe, Asia, Africa, and the part of America nearest to Europe, to which he added the southern world in a later edition. Although similar attempts at classifying humans had been done before, Blumenbach based his scheme primarily on cranial structure and he refused to designate different groups of people as superior or inferior. He believed that all humans were biologically linked to one another, and the varieties of mankind were not immutable.

His categories included:

Caucasian (White): Europe and the Lapps, part of West Asia, the Caspian Sea, Mount Taurus, the Ganges, North Africa, Greenland, and North American Esquimos.
Mongoloid (Yellow): The rest of Asia.
Ethiopian (Black): Africa
Red: The rest of North America
Maylay (Brown): The new Southern World of the Philippines, Molucca, Sunda, and the Pacific archipelago including New Zealand and other islands of that region.[17]

One of the most fascinating observations he made was his attempt to delineate physiological differences among these groups based on skin color, hair texture and cranial features. Another was his attribution of demeanor and psychological states to the people who inhabited these regions. For example, Caucasians were said to have a loftier mentality and generous spirit.

Mongoloids were crafty, and those in the north (China) were depraved and perfidious. People in the southern part of the world were said to be distrustful and ferocious.

This early attempt to construct personality types based on physical appearance and region led to a devastating trend in scientific circles that inevitably depicted darker-skinned people as less intelligent than lighter-skinned people. In the case of the Indians of the Americas, such labeling was part of the ideological framework that justified their exploitation by colonizers. Further evidence of their inferiority was their nomadic hunter-gatherer lifestyle which defied the logic of "civilized" God-fearing Europeans with their capitalistic exploitative perspective of dominating nature, expanding markets, and consumption. When indigenous people refused to grow crops for exportation by colonizing powers they were slaughtered, driven off their lands, and replaced by Africans.

In the third edition of his book, Blumenbach introduced the term Caucasian to describe white people living on the southern slopes of the Caucasus Mountains, in what is now Georgia. This term has remained a commonly used demographic category to the present time, despite its origins over two centuries ago as a quasi-racist term to denote what he considered to be the most beautiful and aesthetically pleasing people in the world. Though he did not rank order classes of humans, his terminology was later used to do just that. This was particularly evident in the development of the Teutonic, Aryan, and Anglo-Saxon myth which led to modern conceptualizations of racial superiority and inferiority based on skin color and geographical location.

RESISTANCE OF INDIGENOUS PEOPLE

In North, Central, and South America, Spanish, French, and English colonists were meeting with resistance from Native Americans in their attempt to dominate them and expropriate their property. Racial stereotypes in the New World were linked to the different types of people inhabiting these regions and the colonial policies of the occupying nations. Central and South American Indians encountered by the Spanish were often depicted as gentle, peaceful, and docile, being principally engaged in agricultural pursuits and farming.

In contrast, the English encountered nomadic hunters. In their attempt to enclose land for farming they denied a source of sustenance to the Indians. The French initially had an easier time interacting with the Indians because they were trappers and traders and did not seek to restrict Indians' access to traditional hunting territories. Nevertheless, the French also experienced conflict with them, and during the French and Indian War (1754–1763) the practice of scalping victims by the English, French, colonists, and Indians spread in what might be considered terroristic tactics that dehumanized Indians, casting them as bloodthirsty savages.

There is evidence that some Native Americans practiced scalping prior to the arrival of Europeans on the North American continent, but Europeans carried the practice to another level. Scalping, and the more common practice of beheading, had been done for centuries before in Europe, but now bounties were placed on scalps in the Northeastern colonies. The French offered 30 francs worth of goods to the Indians for English scalps. The practice backfired when the governor of Massachusetts offered 40 pounds for the scalp of an Indian male and 20 for a female, while the governor of Pennsylvania raised the ante to 130 pounds for Indian males and 50 pounds for females. What was initially a seldom used tactic spread through the colonies at the instigation of the French and English with the Indians being at once blamed, victimized and stereotyped for scalping.

AFRICAN SLAVERY

There were differences in the political and religious philosophies between the Catholic (French and Spanish) and Protestant (British) views of indigenous people. Catholics, as we have seen in the case of de Las Casas, were more accepting of the humanity of Indians, while the Protestants were more racially exclusive, taking the position of being superior (chosen) to Indians with the concomitant assumption that New World lands were destined for them to conquer and inhabit.

This theological and political ideology permeated the writing of travelers and influenced the treatment of indigenous people encountered by colonizers. When they failed to coerce sufficient numbers of Indians to do their bidding in the New World, and the supply of indentured Englishmen and Scotts dwindled as they succumbed to the rigors of hostile climate and terrain, the imperialist powers turned to Africa for a source of labor and resources. In a frenzied orgy of human trafficking that lasted from the early 1500s to the mid-1800s, approximately 12.5 million captive Africans were forcibly taken from their homelands across the Atlantic Ocean to the New World. About 10.8 million of them survived to become slaves in the Americas.[18]

From its inception, slavery was an attempt to provide a cheap supply of labor for the developing agricultural economy of the colonies in the New World. Having failed to domesticate large numbers of indigenous people, and faced with a dwindling supply of indentured servants from England, the institutionalization of slavery provided a pool of laborers who were more adapted to the rigors of plantation life and agricultural pursuits as well as the climate in the southern United States, Central and South America, and the Caribbean.

The trans-Atlantic slave trade spanned 300 years, from the sixteenth through the nineteenth centuries, and reached its height between 1700 and 1800 when 6.4 million people were shipped from Africa. Nearly a third of the captives were women and nearly a quarter were children. Portugal dominated the slave trade in its early years and after 1807, when the British outlawed the Atlantic slave trade. The British, however, were the principal marketers of slaves when the industry was at its height in the eighteenth century.

Nearly half of all transatlantic slave ship voyages were conducted by Portuguese and Brazilian ships, with the British accounting for 25 percent and the French 11 percent. The vast majority of Africans destined to be enslaved were transported to Brazil (40 percent), and the Caribbean (40 percent) with North America receiving approximately four percent. Sugar cane was the primary crop in which slaves were utilized in the Caribbean, followed by cotton, tobacco and rice in the United States.[19]

HOW EXPLORATION LED TO EXPLOITATION

Along with the growth of the slave trade arose religious and political ideologies that sanctioned, even justified, the institution of human bondage. The European presumption of racial superiority emanated from their conviction that they had been chosen by God to spread Christianity to heathens around the world. This mindset was linked to their belief that they were naturally superior to other racial groups by virtue of their possession of superior technology which enabled them to travel to distant lands and spread their religion by subjugating "inferior," "primitive" inhabitants.

Little did they know that their "superior" technology had been preceded by developments in Asia and Africa centuries before, or that their ability to produce a surplus was the result of fortuitous circumstances as geographer Jared Diamond has demonstrated.[20] The ancient library system in Alexandria, Egypt, built during the reign of Ptolemy II in the third century B.C.E., housed between 400,000 and 700,000 parchment scrolls. Theories about its destruction vary, but there is agreement that it contained the collected knowledge of civilizations in Africa and the Hellenic world and was used by scholars for centuries, while Europeans were mired in warring feudalistic monarchies steeped in superstitious beliefs that impeded scientific advances and spread ignorance like the black plague that engulfed it during the fourteenth century.

Pernicious diseases like bubonic plague and smallpox were contracted from animals or parasitic vectors of domesticated animals that were husbanded by Europeans and Eurasians. Fortunate to live in a region of the world that contained plants and animals that could be domesticated, early Europeans were able to develop an agrarian system that enabled them to create a surplus. With fewer people needed on farms to sustain the region's population, people began to move into cities to pursue other endeavors and for the safety and security of numbers.

Bringing people together in large numbers created social, economic, and political change as well as public health problems. To meet the needs of increasing populations, a division and specialization of labor evolved which facilitated the delivery of food and other necessities to the population. Bureaucratic structures were created to control and administer the productive process and people within enclaves and to maintain monarchical hegemony over the land and its inhabitants, first as a feudalistic system, then, as nation-states consolidated power and expanded into mercantilism, and ultimately evolving into capitalism.

But the aggregation of people in the confined spaces of villages, towns and cities provided an ideal milieu for the transmission of disease. The bubonic plague that spread through Europe in the mid-fourteenth century is estimated to have claimed the lives of nearly 100 million people, a quarter of the population of the continent at that time. While Europeans were wont to consider themselves superior to other cultures and civilizations, they had little concept of the germ theory at the time and blamed women and Jews for the spread of the scourge, sacrificing many of them on fiery piers to appease a supposedly wrathful God.

Some inhabitants of the pestilence survived because they developed immunity to the germs that ravaged their communities. The sad irony of this fact is that they and their descendants transmitted these diseases to indigenous populations as they traveled to new territories in search of fame, fortune, resources and markets for their homelands. Diamond contends that as much as 99 percent of the indigenous populations were decimated after first contact with Europeans in North, Central and South America, Australia, South Africa, and the Pacific Islands.[21]

The belief in the "White Man's Burden"—that Christian Europe was elected by God to rule the world—and the mercantilist and nascent capitalist pressure for new markets spurred by competition between the nation states of Spain, France, Portugal, Holland, and England, fueled the drive to colonize and exploit indigenous peoples. And yet, God-fearing pious Christians were forbidden to mistreat other human beings, and instead were to treat others the way they would want to be treated, as in the Golden Rule. This belief system created a moral conundrum for European Christians that was conveniently solved by defining indigenous peoples as lesser humans—lower on the phylogenetic scale of human evolution. In their haughty magnanimity they rationalized their exploitative encounters as part of a Divine plan for bringing the word of a merciful God to wretched heathens who would be doomed without their intervention.

The debate between de Las Casas and Sepulveda which captured the attention of Catholic clergy in the middle of the sixteenth century helps to elucidate this theological struggle. It is thought that prior to and even after the papal bull, *Sublimus Dei,* of Pope Paul III on June 2, 1537, which exhorted explorers not to enslave indigenous people but to convert them, many Christians did not believe indigenous people had souls. That perception was perhaps given impetus by the Papal Bull, *Inter Caetera,* of Pope Alexander VI on May 4, 1493, when he partitioned parts of the New World to satisfy his allies and declared, "Among other works well pleasing to the Divine Majesty and cherished of our heart, this assuredly ranks highest, that in our times especially the Catholic faith and the Christian religion be exalted and be everywhere increased and spread, that the health of souls be cared for and that barbarous nations be overthrown and brought to the faith itself." In addressing Spanish royalty, Alexander VI further refers to the travel of Columbus and other explorers and admonishes the kings and queens of Portugal and Castile:

> … the name of our Savior be carried into those regions, we exhort you very earnestly in the Lord and by your reception of holy baptism, whereby you are bound to our apostolic commands, and by the bowels of the mercy of our Lord Jesus Christ, enjoin strictly, that inasmuch as with eager zeal for the true faith you design and equip and dispatch this expedition, you[r] purpose also, as is your duty, to lead the peoples dwelling in those islands and countries to embrace the Christian religion; nor at any time let dangers or hardships deter you therefrom, with the stout hope and trust in your hearts that Almighty God will further your undertakings.[22]

While Indians were branded as heathens, shiftless, and at times difficult to control, the most pernicious stereotypes harbored by Europeans were about Africans who they compared to apes and monkeys. Always placed lower on the phylogenetic scale than white Europeans, Africans, from the time of first contact, were considered an earlier primitive version of "modern," intellectually superior Europeans. The simian label, along with dark complexion, was used to stigmatize Africans and other dark-skinned people. Unfortunately, the label has stuck through the centuries.[23]

HOW SCIENTIFIC RACISM BECAME FASHIONABLE

While a preference for whiteness can be apprehended 4,000 thousand years ago, formalized theories about the racial superiority of whites began to emerge in the seventeenth century. Gossett credits the French physician, Francois Bernier in 1684 with developing the first racial classification, but it wasn't until Blumenbach delineated racial categories of humans in 1775 that racial classifications began to gain traction among scientists as an attempt to explain phenotypical differences among groups of people around the world.

The European penchant for ascribing dark-skinned people to subordinate, inferior status on the phylogenetic scale of human evolution was bolstered by the writing of philosophers in the Renaissance and Enlightenment. These men variously depicted humans as incapable of creating social inequality in their natural state (Rousseau), designated Europeans as biologically (Voltaire) and intellectually (Locke) superior to primitives, and justified the expropriation of indigenous peoples' land and property (Hobbes).[24]

It was politicians, in their zeal to rationalize the rapacious plundering and subjugation of indigenous people, who helped to promulgate pseudo-scientific theories about the natural superiority of white Europeans over dark-skinned peoples. Later, they extrapolated these concepts into the twentieth century nightmare of Nazism, with its vision of the historical inevitability of Aryan ascendancy and ultimate domination of the world. God-fearing Christians' search for the moral justification of their greedy depredations of newly discovered lands received support from early crackpot physical type theories postulated on the European continent from 1600 to 1800.

From examining facial configurations in physiognomy propounded by Johann Kaspar Lavater and Johan Gaspar Spurzheim, to measuring cranial distortions in Franz Joseph Gall and George Combe's phrenology, and Cesare Lombroso's attempts to explain criminal behavior on the basis of inherited atavistic stigmata representative of primitive man, physical-type theories sought to classify people by biological characteristics and racial groups. They attempted to delineate superior and inferior species of humans along structural/physical/biological dimensions. Such theories were deterministic, which is to say that they held that human behavior was preordained and caused by biological traits. These traits were believed to be subject to scientific analysis and could serve as indices of behavior and intelligence. Almost without exception, the progenitors of these theories were (and continue to be) white males who invariably depict Africans, Asians, Latinos, and Native Americans as inferior in their intellectual development and capacity to be civilized according to normative white Eurocentric standards.[25]

Some elements of these theories have survived despite the fact that there is no scientific evidence to support them. Attitudes based on their pseudo-scientific conclusions continue to surface as evidenced in the remarks of Nobel Laureate, James Watson, co-discoverer of the molecular structure of DNA. In an interview in Britain's *Sunday Times* on October 17, 2007, the eminent scientist stated he was "inherently gloomy about the prospect of Africa," because "all our social policies are based on the fact that their intelligence is the same as ours—whereas all the testing says not really." Further, he averred that "there is no firm reason to anticipate that the intellectual capacities of peoples geographically separated in their evolution should prove to have evolved identically. Our wanting to reserve equal powers of reason as some universal heritage of humanity will not be enough to make it so."[26]

The primary contribution of physical type theories has been to frame the boundaries of racist eccentricities, at times unintentionally misleading scientists and the public, and at others purposefully distorting reality in an attempt to rationalize social inequality and the domination and exploitation of human beings. The institution of slavery conducted on a massive scale from the 1500s to the mid-1800s, helped to create a scientific, cultural, and moral framework for the rationalization of human bondage and subsequent attitudes about the genetic inferiority of blacks that persist today.

DARWIN'S CONTRIBUTION AND DILEMMA

One shining light that helped illuminate the way toward creating an enlightened understanding of the brotherhood of mankind was Charles Darwin, who was opposed to slavery and devoted his life to providing the scientific and intellectual framework for understanding the common origin of humanity. Darwin's contribution to science lay in his break with pluralist determinists who had conceived of the world as being populated by many diverse races of men. Biology, from their perspective, determined temperament and human behavior.

Darwin broke with this tradition by demonstrating that there is a unity in nature with all humans. Animals and plant life descended from a primordial origin. He believed that people and animals were not bound to their biological roots but adapt to their environment through evolution, the primary method of which was natural selection. In their attempt to adjust to the rigors of their environment, organisms evolve. Those developing the most effective mechanisms for survival pass on these adaptations to their offspring in what Darwin termed "survival of the fittest."

Darwin proved his theory by demonstrating the lineage of barnacles and pigeons, isolating unique traits which characterized their hereditary unified ancestry. One simple, yet clever experiment he employed helped to debunk the popular pluralist myth that life had multiple sites of origin around the world. It had been generally accepted that seeds soaked in salt water would become infertile. Darwin obtained a wide variety of seeds from friends and researchers around the world and soaked them in brine. To his amazement, the vast amount of them grew, and some varieties' germination and growth was accelerated by the solution. Most seeds fared well even after soaking for a month.

He then calculated the time it would take for the seeds to travel to distant lands by estimating the speed of ocean currents in the Atlantic and determined that a seed could travel 33 nautical miles a day and reach a distance of 1,300–1,400 miles in just 42 days, thereby demonstrating the feasibility and probability of the dispersal of life forms around the world. While Darwin and other scientists suspected the existence of an ancient primordial grand continent, today known as Pangea, there was little scientific evidence of its existence at the time he wrote. Today, scientists are able to use DNA and paleoanthropology along with sophisticated dating techniques to establish the validity of his theory.[27]

The pluralists of Darwin's age believed that man arose in different regions of the world and that some species of humans were genetically superior to others, most notably, white Europeans over Africans and Asians. This perspective was used to justify slavery and provided an ideological framework that undergirded the Southern Confederacy in its attempt to legitimize that institution. Historians Desmond and Moore even demonstrated a Confederate Civil War strategy which placed *agent provocateurs* in professional anthropological societies in England to cultivate pluralist perspectives and the dissemination of racist publications to rationalize and justify the Southern institution of slavery.

These materials depicted blacks as intellectually inferior to whites, depraved, uncivilized, and incapable of governing themselves. Whites were seen as the savior of Negroes, caring for them as benevolent masters. Without white intervention and protection, blacks would revert to primitivism and cannibalism. "'… what better destiny could God, in his merciful wisdom, have marked out for him than the one which he occupies under our institution of slavery?' Freed, he goes the way of the American Indians. Enslaved, he is saved. Faced by 'extermination or slavery', the latter, God's beneficent gift, was the black man's salvation."[28]

Darwin's thesis that all men had a common heritage and were related was anathema to the South and threatened to drive a stake into the very heart of the Southern justification for slavery. On his five-year voyage as a young researcher aboard the Beagle, he was able to see first hand the cruelty and inhumanity of the institution of slavery in South America and other occupied lands. Nevertheless, Darwin was a creature of his time, and though he believed in the brotherhood of mankind, he also considered Europeans as superior to aboriginal peoples.[29] Differences in culture and civilization were not the result of biology but environment, and that was a crucial distinction between his unitary theory of evolution and his adversaries who postulated biological determinist explanations which depicted different races of man at different stages of evolutionary capacity for development.

Although Darwin had worked out his concepts of evolution and natural selection earlier in his career, he waited twenty years before publishing his research in *Origin of the Species* in 1859. Even then he chose not to include information about humans, preferring instead to allow readers to deduce the implications of his research for mankind. The motivation to eschew a discussion about the evolution of man was apparently based on his desire to avoid a bitter controversy between him and pluralists led by Harvard University's Louis Agassiz.

In *The Descent of Man,* published in 1871, he addressed the issue head on and opened the door to racist interpretations by allowing that environment creates differing temperaments and moral behavior. Although Darwin saw blacks as biologically equal to whites, with the capacity for civilization and accomplishments inherent in all men, the application of the process of natural selection was used by pluralists and slavery apologists to legitimize social inequality. The contention that environmental circumstances create superior members of a species through natural selection led to the conclusion among some scientists and moralists that the races of man were also the product of selective breeding occasioned by natural forces. And, more than just nature was at work, for even Darwin noted that:

> At the present day civilized nations are everywhere supplanting barbarous nations, excepting where the climate opposes a deadly barrier; and they succeed mainly, though not exclusively, through their arts, which are the products of the intellect. It is, therefore, highly probable that with mankind the intellectual faculties have been gradually perfected through natural selection....[30]

Darwin went on to link the process of natural selection to the uniquely human propensity of caring for and allowing the propagation of inferior members of the species:

> With the savages, the weak in body or mind are soon eliminated and those that survive commonly exhibit a vigorous state of health. We civilized men ... do our utmost to check the process of elimination; we build asylums for the

imbecile, the maimed, and the sick; we institute poor-laws; and our medical men exert their utmost skill to save the life of everyone to the last moment. There is reason to believe that vaccination has preserved thousands, who from a weak constitution would formerly have succumbed to smallpox. Thus the weak members of civilized societies propagate their kind. No one who has attended to the breeding of domestic animals will doubt that this must be highly injurious to the race of man. It is surprising how soon a want of care, or care wrongly directed, leads to the degeneration of a domestic race; but excepting in the case of man himself, hardly any one is so ignorant as to allow his worst animals to breed.[31]

Even worse, Darwin assumed that the most able and fit young men were enlisted to fight in wars and died prematurely, leaving the poor and inferior members at home to propagate their kind:

A most important obstacle in civilized countries to an increase in the number of men of a superior class has been strongly urged by Mr. Greg and Mr. Galton, namely, the fact that the very poor and reckless who are often degraded by vice, almost invariably marry early, while the careful and frugal, who are generally otherwise virtuous, marry late in life, so that they may be able to support themselves and their children in comfort. Those who marry early produce within a given period not only a greater number of generations, but, as shown by Dr. Duncan, they produce more children. The children, moreover, that are born by mothers during the prime of life are heavier and larger, and therefore probably more vigorous, than those born at other periods. Thus the reckless, degraded, and often vicious members of society, tend to increase at a quicker rate than the provident and generally virtuous members.[32]

Darwin's contribution to understanding the biological forces of nature on the planet rank among the most significant scientific insight in history, namely that all life is related, natural selection causes species to change over time by adapting to the environment, and species are not immutable; they change over time. His desire to demonstrate the equality of all men was undermined by the application of natural selection to humans in what became known as Social Darwinism. As such, his theory was used to justify the very institution that he and his family had crusaded against: slavery.

One has only to read some of the comments of defenders of slavery to apprehend the tortuous logic utilized in defense of the indefensible. Their thinly veiled rationalization for protecting the most notorious form of chattel slavery in history revolved around pluralistic polygeneticist theories which held that there were multiple species of humans around the world. Further, these species were unequal in ability and potential, and the most advanced, sophisticated, and civilized species of man were light-skinned Europeans.

Concomitantly, disparaging references were made about dark-skinned peoples in Asia and especially Africa. They were, as we have seen, likened to apes and savages. Frequent references were made to their purported cannibalistic propensities and their lack of modern accoutrements of civilization. Indeed, it was said that nothing of value—science, inventions, and the arts emanated from Africa. Finally, and perhaps most insidious, was the contention that blacks were incapable of self-government and therefore whites were paternalistically assuming this responsibility, in essence caring for blacks who, otherwise left to their own devices, would revert to their barbaric state in nature, killing one another and starving for want of the necessary desire and knowledge to survive.

JEFFERSON'S JUSTIFICATION OF SLAVERY

The personification of these sentiments finds expression in the words of none other than one of the most influential supposedly egalitarian "Founding Fathers" of our nation, our third president, Thomas Jefferson. Jefferson owned slaves while penning the famous words of the Declaration of Independence, "We hold these truths to be self-evident, that all men are created equal, that they are endowed by their Creator with certain unalienable Rights, that among these are Life, Liberty and the pursuit of Happiness." In fact, from 1774–1826, 606 men, women, and children worked as slaves on his various landholdings in five Virginia counties.[33]

Reading his erudite *Notes on the State of Virginia,* one is impressed with the breadth of his intellectual abilities and the scope of his scientific acumen. He enumerates the varieties of animals and plants, the topography, climate, laws, and characteristics of the population in his state, variously writing in English, Spanish, French, Greek, and Latin. But his writing about human nature and the institution of slavery showed an ambivalence about the physical and mental status of blacks and Indians:

> It will probably be asked, Why not retain and incorporate the blacks into the State, and thus save the expense of supplying, by importation of white settlers, the vacancies they will leave? Deep-rooted prejudices entertained by the whites; ten thousand recollections by the blacks of the injuries they have sustained; new provocations; the real distinctions which Nature has made; and many other circumstances, will divide us into parties, and produce convulsions, which will probably never end but in the extermination of the one or the other race.[34]

It is as though he sensed the injustice of the institution but, as a land and slave owner, is unable or unwilling to break with the system. This becomes clear when he tried to rationalize the bondage of blacks by characterizing them as inferior to whites:

> The first difference that strikes us is that of color. Whether the black of the negro resides in the reticular membrane between the skin and scarf skin, or in the scarf skin itself; whether it proceeds from the color of the blood, the color of the bile, or from that of some other secretion, the difference is fixed in Nature, and is as real as if its seat and cause were better known to us. And is this difference of no importance? Is it not the foundation of a greater or less share of beauty in the two races? Are not the fine mixtures of red and white, the expressions of every passion by greater or less suffusions of color in the one, preferable to that eternal monotony which reigns in the countenances, that immovable veil of black which covers all the emotions of the other race? Add to these the flowing hair, a more elegant symmetry of form, their own judgement in favor of the whites, declared by their preference for them, as uniformly as is the preference of the oranootan for the black woman over those of his own species.[35]

Jefferson not only deprecates blackness, but slides into the popular myth of Africans consorting with apes to establish their lower position on the phylogenetic scale. Further, he avers that:

> They secrete less by the kidneys, and more by the glands of the skin, which gives them a very strong and disagreeable odor. ... They seem to require less sleep. ... They are at least as brave, and more adventuresome. But this may perhaps proceed from want of forethought, which prevents their seeing a danger till it be present. When present, they do not go through it with more coolness or steadiness than whites. They are more ardent after their female; but love seems with them to be more an eager desire than a tender delicate mixture of sentiment and sensation. Their griefs are transient. ... In general, their existence appears to participate more of a sensation than reflection. To this must be ascribed their disposition to sleep when abstracted from their diversions, and unemployed in labor ... Comparing them by their faculties of memory, reason, and imagination, it appears to me that in memory they are equal to whites; in reason much inferior, as I think one could scarcely be found capable of tracing and comprehending the investigations of Euclid, and that in imagination they are dull, tasteless and anomalous.[36]

Despite such negative evaluations of the intellectual capacities of African slaves, Jefferson seemed to inject a note of understanding, if not compassion, for them; but then continued to disparage their motivation and capacity to learn:

> Many millions of them have been brought to, and born in America. Most of them, indeed, have been confined to tillage, to their own homes, and their own society;

Yet many have been so situated, that they might have availed themselves of the conversation of their masters; many have been brought up to the handicraft arts, and from that circumstance have always been associated with whites. Some have been liberally educated, and all have lived in counties where the arts and sciences are cultivated to a considerable degree, and have had before their eyes samples of the best works abroad. ... But never yet could I find that a black had uttered a thought above the level of plain narration; never seen even an elementary trait of painting or sculpture. In music they are more generally gifted than the whites with accurate ears for tune and time, and they have been found capable of imagining a small catch. Whether they will be equal to the composition of a more extensive run of melody, or of complicated harmony, is yet to be proved.[37]

He then attempts to build a case of the natural inferiority of blacks by comparing them to white slaves in antiquity, despite the fact that the nature of slavery in the two time periods were vastly different and he knew it:

The improvement of the blacks in body and mind, in the first instance of their mixture with the whites, has been observed by everyone, and proves that their inferiority is not the effect merely of their constitution of life. ... Epictectus, Diogenes, Phaedon, Terence, and Phaedrus, were slaves. But they were of the race of whites. It is not their condition then but Nature, which has produced the distinction. Whether further observation will or will not verify the conjecture, that Nature has been less bountiful to them in the endowments of the head, I believe that in those of the heart she will be found to have done them justice.[38]

Ironically, he manages to rationalize blacks' supposed penchant for thievery:

That disposition to theft with which they have been branded, must be ascribed to their situation, and not to any depravity of the moral sense. The man in whose favor no laws of property exist, probably feels himself less bound to respect those made in favor of others. When arguing for ourselves, we lay it down as fundamental, that laws to be just must give a reciprocation of right; that without this, they are mere arbitrary rules of conduct, founded in force, and not in conscience; and it is a problem which I give to the master to solve, whether the religious precepts against the violation of property were not framed for him as well as his slave? And whether the slave may not as justifiably take a little from one who has taken all from him, as he may slay one who would slay him?[39]

And then, with a sense of acknowledgement about the moral conundrum that slavery has created:

That a change in the relations in which a man is placed should change his ideas of moral right and wrong, is neither new nor peculiar to the color of the blacks.

... The opinion that they are inferior in the faculties of reason and imagination, must be hazarded with great diffidence. To justify a general conclusion, requires many observations, even where the subject may be submitted to the anatomical knife, to optical glasses, to analysis by fire, or by solvent.[40]

After describing the innate inferiority of blacks, he tempers his argument with compassion:

How much more than where it is a faculty, not a substance we are examining; where it eludes the research of all the senses; where the conditions of its existence are various, and variously combined; where the effects of those which are present or absent bid defiance to calculation of great tenderness, where our conclusion would degrade a whole race of men from the rank in the scale of beings which the Creator may perhaps have given them.[41]

Yet, he catches himself and reverts once again to the conclusion that:

To our reproach it must be said, that though for a century and a half we have had under our eyes the races of black and red men, they have never yet been viewed by us as subjects of natural history. I advance it therefore as a suspicion only, that the blacks, whether originally a distinct race, or made distinct by time and circumstances, are inferior to the whites in the endowments both of body and mind. It is not against experience to suppose that different species of the same genus, may possess different qualifications. ...This unfortunate difference of color, and perhaps of faculty, is a powerful obstacle to the emancipation of these people. Many of their advocates, while they wish to vindicate the liberty of human nature, are anxious also to preserve its dignity and beauty. Some of these, embarrassed by the question, "What further is to be done with them?" join themselves in opposition with those who are actuated by sordid avarice only. Among the Romans, emancipation required but one effort. The slave, when made free, might mix with, without staining the blood of his master. But with us a second is necessary, unknown to history. When freed, he is to be removed beyond the reach of mixture.[42]

These fascinating passages give us a glimpse of the prevailing attitudes of white slave owners in early America. What is at once fascinating and tragic about Jefferson's remarks is that they reveal myths and stereotypes about blacks that persist to this day. Despite scientific discoveries from paleoanthropology, microbiology, and genetics, many whites believe, as did Jefferson, that blacks are intellectually inferior and incapable of contributing anything of value to our civilization. As Jefferson and others of his time, many whites still think that dark-skinned people are morally deficient, lazy, prone to thievery, incapable of rational thought, wracked by emotions, and ungovernable save by the imposition of white rules and laws that maintain a semblance of civilized behavior among them.[43]

Even more insidious is the belief, still existent, that "the stain" of black blood carries with it the threat of reducing white civilization through "mixing." Such beliefs resulted in a system of racial apartheid in the South and the ideological justification for Jim Crow laws that perpetuated social inequality. As we shall see, the persistence of racial stereotypes and racist behavior are reflected in a wide range of social, economic, and health disparities in the United States to this day, and they penetrate into classrooms through distorted Eurocentric curricula and teachers' stereotypical views about children of color.

PRESIDENTIAL VIEWS ABOUT BLACKS AND SLAVERY

Nor was Jefferson alone in these beliefs. Whether to justify the slave system because of its economic importance to the South (and parts of the North), or to salve their conscience in an attempt to rationalize the maltreatment of human beings as chattel, devoid of basic rights and freedoms—the very ones promised in the Declaration of Independence and the Constitution for white males—the ideological underpinning for racism that emerged full blown during the early years of our nation had a profound impact on the relationship between blacks and whites.

Twelve of the first eighteen Presidents of the United States were slave owners, and eight owned slaves while they were in office, including George Washington, "the father of our country." The same man, held up as a role model for our children, owned with his wife, Martha Custis, a rich widow whom he married, over 300 slaves. Unlike Jefferson, Washington never spoke out about slavery one way or the other. Also, unlike Jefferson, Washington's will freed the 124 men, women, and children who were his property (the rest being the property of his widow and outside the terms of the will). In fact, Washington also provided pensions to the older slaves on his Mt. Vernon plantation.[44]

Disparaging sentiments about the moral and intellectual faculties of blacks were not confined to our Founding Fathers. Even the "Great Emancipator," Abraham Lincoln, remarked during a debate with Stephen Douglas in 1858:

> I will say then that I am not, nor ever have been in favor of bringing about in any way the social and political equality of the white and black races—that I am not nor ever have been in favor of making voters or jurors of negroes, nor of qualifying them to hold office, nor to intermarry with white people; and I will

say in addition to this that there is a physical difference between white and black races which I believe will for ever forbid the two races living together on terms of social and political equality. And inasmuch as they cannot so live, while they do remain together there must be the position of superior and inferior, and I, as much as any other man, am in favor of having the superior position assigned to the white race. I say upon this occasion I do not perceive that because the white man is to have the superior position the negro should be denied everything.[45]

There is a long line of racist presidential slurs and unethical treatment of blacks and other ethnic minorities running through contemporary presidential administrations, as historian Kenneth O'Reilly illustrates in his analysis of the sordid politics that has preserved the white male aristocracy framed by the nation's founders.[46] Nourished by racist ideological theories that fueled popular white stereotypes about the inherent inferiority and moral degeneracy of dark-skinned people, a political climate stifling the development of progressive race relations cast a pall over the capitol for centuries, preventing the enactment of legislation ranging from outlawing lynching to the delivery of inexpensive and accessible comprehensive health care for all the nation's inhabitants.

The stereotypical characterizations about people of color, which we have outlined in this chapter, are inextricably linked to one of our nation's greatest educational conundrums, the achievement gap, which in the minds of some educators, explains differential rates of academic achievement and success between light and dark-skinned students. As we will see in the next two chapters, physical-type theories purporting to explain differences among the so-called races of man gave way to increasingly more sophisticated justifications of the existing social order based on supposedly innate differences in intelligence, all the while blaming the victims of social stigmatization and institutionalized discrimination for their underachievement and misfortune.

NOTES

1. Thomas F. Gossett, *Race: The History of an Idea in America*, New edition, N.Y.: Oxford University Press, 1997.

2. According to Gossett, the biblical account of the origin of the curse of Ham, Noah's son, stemmed from a passage in Genesis 9:24 wherein Ham is contemptuous of his drunken father lying naked. Noah's other sons averted their eyes from him but Ham did not. Noah was said to bless the descendants of his sons Shem and Japheth but cursed the descendants of Ham. Nothing in the Bible indicates that Ham and his son Canaan are black, and Gossett contended that this idea was inserted in the Babylonian Talmud between the second and sixth century C.E. Gossett, loc. cit., p. 5.

3. Tommy L. Lott, "Patriarchy and Slavery in Hobbes's Political Philosophy," in *Philosopher's on Race: Critical Essays*, Julie K. Ward and Tommy L. Lott, (eds.), Oxford, England, 2002, pp. 63–80.

4. Thomas Carlyle, "Occasional Discourse on the Negro Question," *Fraser's Magazine for Town and Country*, 40 (February, 1849), p. 536.

5. Jared Diamond, *Guns, Germs, and Steel: The Fates of Human Societies*, N.Y.: W.W. Norton, 1999, p. 78.

6. "Jeffrey Amherst and Smallpox Blankets: Germ Warfare Against American Indians," *http://www.nativeweb.org/pages/legal/amherst/lord_jeff.html*. Retrieved 11/26/09.

7. Quoted in Francis Moran III, "Between Primates and Primitives: Natural Man as the Missing Link in Rousseau's *Second Discourse*," in Ward and Lott, op. cit., p. 126. *Hottentot* was a perjorative reference to the Khoi Khoi ethnic group of present day Cape Town in the Republic of South Africa.

8. Cited in Peter Fryer, *Staying Power: The History of Black People in Britain*, London: Pluto Press, 1984, pp. 137–138.

9. "Sarah Baartman, at rest at last," *http://www.southafrica.info/about/history/saaarrtjie.htm*. Retrieved 11/26/09.

10. Sadiah Qureshi, "Displaying Sara Baartman," *History of Science*, 42, (2004): 233–257.

11. Bartololme De Las Casas, *A Brief Account of the Destruction of the Indies*, pp. 6–10. Found at: *http://manybooks.net/pages/casasb2032120321-8/0.html*. Released January 9, 2007 [Ebook #20321]. Retrieved: 11/28/09.

12. Ibid.

13. Ibid.

14. Pope Paul III---Sublimus Dei—On the Enslavement and Evangelization of Indians in the New World—1537," at: *http://www.catholic-forum.com/saints/pope0220a.htm*. Retrieved on 12/12/09. For a discussion of the dialogue between de las Casas and Sepulveda see: Bonar Ludwig Hernandez, "The Las Casas-Sepulveda Controversy: 1550–1551," at: *http://userwww.sfsu.edu/~eph/2001/hernandez.html*. Retrieved 11/27/09. See also Gossett, loc. cit., pp. 12–14, and Joe R. Feagin, *Racist America*, N.Y.: Routledge, 2000, pp. 71–72.

15. Ivan Hannaford, *Race: The History of an Idea in the West*, Baltimore: The Johns Hopkins University Press, 1996.

16. Ibid., p. 149.

17. Hannaford, op. cit. pp. 206–207. See also Gossett, op cit., pp. 35–39.

18. For one of the most comprehensive analyses of African slave databases see: David Eltis and David Richardson (eds.), *Extending the Frontiers: Essays on the New Transatlantic Slave Trade Database*, New Haven: Yale University Press, 2008; and for a fascinating genealogical database containing tens of thousands of the ancestors of African-Americans see: Afriquest at *http://www.africanheritage.com/afriquest_press_release.asp*.

19. Lisa A. Lindsay, *Captives as Commodities: The Transatlantic Slave Trade*, Upper Saddle River: Pearson Prentice Hall, 2008.

20. Jared Diamond, *Guns, Germs, and Steel*, N.Y.: W.W. Norton, 1999.

21. Ibid. p. 92.

22. "The Bull *Inter Caetera* (Alexander VI)," May 4, 1493 at: *http://www.nativeweb .org/pages/legal/indig-inter-caetera.html*. Retrieved: 12/12/09.

23. Even now, with America's first black president, derogatory caricatures and cartoons of Barack Obama and his wife appear in the popular press and the Internet. During his campaign for President Barack Obama was depicted as a Sambo on the cover of a box selling waffles, and shortly after being elected he was "memorialized" by a Greenwich Village, New York City bakery as a "Drunken Negro Head" cookie. As opposition to his stimulus package increased, the New York Post published a cartoon on February 18, 2009 which, despite the artist's and editor's denials, was widely construed as him being a crazed chimpanzee shot by police. Soon after, there surfaced images of him as The Joker and Adolph Hitler—satirical attempts to discredit his stimulus policies, but nevertheless thinly veiled racist caricatures. In November, 2009, the president's wife, Michelle, was characterized as an ape, once again demonstrating the racist inference that blacks are more simian-like and inferior to whites. Although many celebrities, including former president George W. Bush, have been scornfully caricatured, linking blacks to simians has an unmistakable racist implication, connoting stupidity, backwardness, and subhuman. There can be no doubt about the intent of such depictions from the comments of bloggers, e.g. "Get Obama out of office. He is a corrupt stupid jerk that has no right even running a soup kitchen. Kick his ass out of office and send him back to Africa. By the way, Michelle looks more like a rabid baboon." "Everyone should stop stressing—Barack Hussein Obama will not win a 2nd term—he is horrible. Unfortunately, we just have to wait. On second thought, export his stupid, racist ass out of our country. Get the ape wife and ape kids out, too." "What an insult to the Apes IMO." "BLACKS LOOK LIKE APES...FACT...GET OVER IT..." "Obama is a coward and his wife does look like an ape. This is not racist, just a fact. Put a picture of baboon or ape next to hers and it is pretty close!" *http://www.homelandstupidity.us/2009/11/25/offensive-michelle-obama-ape-picture-one-*. Retrieved 12/13/09.

24. Jean Jacques Rousseau: *The First and Second Discourses*, Roger D. Masters, (ed.), Judith R. Masters (trans.), N.Y.: Bedford/St. Martin's, 1969; Francois Marie Arouet (Voltaire), *Essai sur les moeurs et l'esprit des nations, 1756*, Ann Arbor: University of Michigan, 2009; John Locke, *An Essay Concerning Human Understanding*, P. Nidditch (ed.), Oxford: Clarendon Press, 1975; Thomas Hobbes, *Leviathan* 1660 (online at: *http://oregonstate.edu/instruct/phl302/texts/hobbes/leviathan-contents .html*). For a review of these perspectives see: Julie K. Ward and Tommy L. Lott, (eds.), *Philosophers on Race: Critical Essays*, Oxford: Blackwell Publishers, Ltd., 2002.

25. Franz Joseph Gall and Johan Gaspar Spurzheim, *Phrenology: And the Moral Influence of Phrenology*, Philadelphia: Carey, Lea, and Blanchard, 1835. George

Combe, *A System of Phrenology*, Boston: B.B. Mussey and Co., 1851 at *http://www .archive.org/details/systemofphrenolo00combuoft*. (Retrieved: 12/21/09); John Caspar Lavater, *Essays on Physiognomy*, Thomas Holcroft (trans.). London: Tegg and Co., 1878; Cesare Lombroso, *The Criminal Man*, Mary Gibson and Nicole Hahn Rafter (trans.), Durham: Duke University Press, 2006.

26. "Black people 'less intelligent' scientist claims," Times Online, October 17, 2007 at: *http://www.timesonline.co.uk/tol/news/uk/article2677098.ece?token =null&print=yes&ra*. Retrieved: 12/14/09.

27. For a discussion of Darwin's experiments see: Adrian Desmond and James Moore, *Darwin's Sacred Cause: How a Hatred of Slavery Shaped Darwin's Views on Human Evolution*, Boston: Houghton Mifflin Harcourt, 2009: 246–248.

28. L.S. McCord, quoted in Desmond and Moore, loc. cit. pp. 236-237.

29. Desmond and Moore, loc. cit.: 151.

30. Charles Darwin, *The Descent of Man and Selection in Relation to Sex*, N.Y.: D. Appleton and Co., 1871, p. 154.

31. Ibid. pp. 161–162.

32. Ibid., p. 167.

33. Monticello Newsletter, 16 (2) Winter, 2005, at *http://www.monticello.org/ press/newsletter/2005/winter/database_05w.pdf*. Retrieved on December 27, 2009.

34. Thomas Jefferson, *Notes on the State of Virginia*, new edition, Richmond: J.W. Randolph, 1853, p. 149.

35. Ibid., pp. 149–150.

36. Ibid., pp. 150–151.

37. Ibid., pp. 151–152.

38. Ibid., pp. 152–154.

39. Ibid., p. 154.

40. Ibid., p. 154.

41. Ibid., p. 154.

42. Ibid., pp. 154–155.

43. For other important documents of the proslavery era in the United States see: Paul Finkelman, *Defending Slavery: Proslavery Thought in the Old South, A Brief History with Documents*, Boston: Bedford/St. Martin's, 2003.

44. Dorothy Twohig, "'That Species of Property,' Washington's Role in the Controversy over Slavery," *The Papers of George Washington*, at: *http://gwpapers .virginia.edu/articles/twohig_2.html*. Retrieved on December 28, 2009.

45. Fourth Lincoln/Douglas debate, Charleston, Illinois, September 18, 1858. Roy P. Basler, editor, *The Collected Works of Abraham Lincoln*, Vol. 3, "Fourth Debate with Stephen A. Douglas at Charleston, Illinois," September 18, 1858, pp. 145–146.

46. Kenneth O'Reilly, *Nixon's Piano: Presidents and Racial Politics from Washington to Clinton*, N.Y.: The Free Press, 1995.

Chapter 4

Darwin's Descendants

Contemporary Scientific Racism

To such barbarian stocks belong many of the peoples of Asia, the American Indians, and the African negroes. The congenital barbarians have always been dangerous foes of progress.

—Lothrop Stoddard, *The Revolt Against Civilization:*
The Menace of the Under Man

A SAVAGE CENTURY

The decades since the United States was founded have seen the periodic reemergence of racist theories trying to justify the morally and scientifically indefensible: the stigmatization of the poor, the dispossessed, and dark-skinned people as intellectually and socially inferior to whites. Facile attempts to rationalize racism and the disparate treatment of people of color continue to emerge as the war against rationality and science goes on. New assaults on the sensibilities of society occur in vain attempts to explain differences in educational and occupational attainment and deviant behavior between whites and ethnic minorities by blaming the victims of discrimination rather than the insufficiency of societal institutions.

The twentieth century was marked by the most destructive wars in the history of mankind. Estimates vary, but it is safe to say over 65 million combatants and civilians, and perhaps as many as 85 million people died during the First and Second World Wars. Millions more perished from artificially created famines and genocide in the Soviet Union, Africa, and Asia. From the Turkish slaughter of the Armenians to Stalin's destruction of the Kulaks;

from the Korean conflagration to Vietnam and the genocide of Cambodia; across India and Pakistan to Nigeria, Ethiopia, the Congo, Angola, Uganda, and Rwanda; to ethnic cleansing in Yugoslavia and Darfur, humans have stereotyped their adversaries as "the other"—biologically different and inferior in some structural way.

We have seen that in the United States the system of slavery which provided the economic foundation for the colonies and early states was bolstered by an ideology that sought to justify the dominant position of whites over blacks and Native Americans. This was accomplished through the integration of theological scriptures and pseudo-scientific theories which depicted dark-skinned people as being morally and socially unfit to function in modern social systems.

THE IMPACT OF IMMIGRATION

The demise of physical type determinist theories in the eighteenth and nineteenth centuries, which tried to encapsulate the behavior of minorities for the purpose of rationalizing and justifying the white-dominated social order, did not spell the death knoll of racist thought. Toward the end of the nineteenth century and through the early decades of the twentieth, improvements in transportation and telecommunication facilitated the movement and interaction of people in unprecedented numbers. Social upheavals on the European continent kindled by the drive for equality and search for opportunities created an unprecedented stream of immigration to the United States.

Although there is widespread belief that the United States are being swamped by a horde of immigrants, the proportion of foreign born stands at 11.5 percent today compared to 15 percent in the early part of the twentieth century. In the past, the principal debarkation facility was Ellis Island in the harbor at New York City. Between 1892 when it opened, to 1924 when restrictive immigration policies curtailed the number of immigrants, 22 million people entered the United States through this portal. Forty percent of all United States citizens have a least one ancestor who was processed through Ellis Island.

These were heady times as the country was consolidating its westward expansion and the industrialization of the economy provided the impetus for relatively open borders. But then as now, there were some who viewed the influx of foreigners as a stain on the fabric of traditional white, Anglo-Saxon society. Such sentiments were fueled by the growing tradition of Teutonic, Nordic, Aryan, and Anglo-Saxon mythology in Great Britain, Europe, Scandinavia and, most significantly, Germany.

Adherents to this *Weltanschauung* believed in the natural superiority of Aryans and Anglo-Saxons. "People of the North"—descendants of the Vikings—were romanticized by poets, writers, and intellectuals of the late nineteenth and early twentieth century. Even Theodore Roosevelt and Henry Cabot Lodge were caught up and suffused by this *Zeitgeist* which resonated with old-line families who perceived the wave of dark complexioned immigrants from Italy, Greece, Russia, and other Slavic countries as an invasion and threat to their traditions.[1]

In times of great change, emotions may overcome reason and, despite the need for immigrant labor to fill industrial jobs, white aristocrats turned to racist theories that depicted immigrants as wanton profligates, debauchers, and moral degenerates who threatened the very values of traditional American society. Eugenicist/racist Lothrop Stoddard contended that immigrants, Bolsheviks, and the rising underclass threatened not only the establishment but also the future of civilization:

> Forward-looking minds are coming to realize that social revolutions are really social *breakdowns*, caused in the last analysis by a dual process of racial impoverishment—the elimination of superior strains and the multiplication of degenerates and inferiors. Inexorably the decay of racial values corrodes the proudest civilization, which engenders within itself those forces of chaos that will one day work its ruin.[2]

An even more popular read at the time was the nonfiction work of Madison Grant, a xenophobic racist whose writing reflected the hysteria of white Americans about the influx of immigrants into the country. Grant contended that heredity was the primary determinant of human behavior, and, of course, the Nordic Anglo-Saxons were the superior natural leaders:

> The great lesson of the science of race is the immutability of somatological or bodily characters, with which is closely associated the immutability of psychical predispositions and impulses.... the folly of the 'Melting Pot,' signified contamination of white Anglos by dark-skinned Alpines and Mediterranean's.[3]

Grant believed that immigration diluted the pure Anglo-Nordic strain of Americans:

> The danger is from within not from without. Neither the black, nor the brown, nor the yellow, nor the red will conquer the white in battle. But if the valuable elements in the Nordic race mix with inferior strains or die out through race suicide, then the citadel of civilization will fall from mere lack of defenders.[4]

Immigration posed a grave threat to American society and he scoffed at "hyphenated aliens in our midst upon whom we have carelessly urged citizenship." As white supremacists warn today, Grant predicted that continued immigration would be the death knell of the United States and concluded the preface to the fourth edition to his work with "Finis Americae."

Ironically, paranoia about the new immigrants even spread to psychiatrists who contrasted the new immigrants of the twentieth century with the older Anglo-Saxon arrivals. The newly arrived were depicted as "discordant elements," "other races," and "a serious menace" to the nation in contrast to the more "law-abiding" and stable "home-loving" older stock. The characterization of newly arrived immigrants from Eastern Europe took a more sinister turn when Dr. Sidney D. Wilgus, chairman of the Board of Alienists of the Lunacy Commission of New York, curtly labeled the recent immigration "unnatural" because it included many types of defectives: epileptics, nervous and insane persons, criminals, paupers, and alcoholics. He went further and specifically identified its undesirable ethnic groups: Jews, Italians, and the Slavs of Eastern Europe were "low grade" persons without achievement at home and destined for failure, poverty and institutionalization in America.[5]

OLD VERSUS NEW AMERICANS

Traditional "old Americans," those of English and Northern European lineage, were viewed as "the real Americans." As time passed and the Nordic, Anglo-Saxon, Aryan theme began to permeate Western European and American culture, pride in democratic institutions, which previously rallied Americans around the flag of a united nation, was replaced by racial lines. These lines began to delineate who were preferred immigrants and ethnic groups, and defined which groups were genetically superior or inferior.

The myth of white supremacy typified by blond-haired blue-eyed people from northern Europe was a recurrent theme from the late nineteenth through the twentieth centuries. As millions of immigrants from Eastern Europe landed in New York, and hundreds of thousands of Asians (principally Chinese and smaller numbers of Japanese) arrived on the West Coast, they brought with them different languages and customs, cultures that were perceived by "old line Americans" (white Anglo-Saxon Protestants) as threats to the status quo. Their presence challenged the balance of political and economic power. As they crowded into inner industrial cities in the North and mid-West, they vied with African-Americans and older immigrants for work. They often encountered opposition from labor unions determined to protect their members' jobs and living standards.

Restrictive immigration laws were passed because of the "yellow peril" in California. The Chinese Exclusion Act of 1882 prohibited immigrants from China from entering the United States for ten years. This provision was extended for another ten years by the Geary Act of 1892, which carried other onerous and discriminatory provisions such as requiring Chinese in the country to carry "certificates of residence" and "certificates of entry," which proved that they entered the country legally and had the right to remain. In the early years of the twentieth century, over 600 laws restricting Japanese participation in American society existed in California, according to historian Eric Saul.[6]

Antipathy toward the Japanese was heightened by the attack on Pearl Harbor on December 7, 1941. In February 1942, under Executive Order 9066 signed by President Franklin Roosevelt, over 110,000 Japanese, many of them American citizens, were forcibly relocated to ten detention camps in isolated parts of the western and central United States. This action led to the loss of property by the Japanese, who had to sell their homes and businesses in a matter of days or weeks, and was upheld by the United States Supreme Court.

Ironically, thousands of Japanese from Hawaii and these mainland camps volunteered to serve in a segregated unit, the 442 Infantry Regimental Combat Team that distinguished itself in WWII by being the most decorated unit in the history of the United States military. While not one subversive activity by people of Japanese ancestry was recorded during the war, it was not until 1988 that the United States government acknowledged its wrongdoing in this affair. In that year President Ronald Reagan signed HR442, which provided $20,000 for each survivor or family member (totaling $1.6 billion) in reparations for those interred.

Prevailing intellectual thought in the latter part of the nineteenth and early twentieth centuries reflected the theme of rugged individualism and self-reliance, extolling the virtue of individual initiative (the Horatio Alger mythology). This fit nicely with the Social Darwinism of Englishman Herbert Spencer and his American counterpart, William Graham Sumner. Along with the budding eugenics movement, associated with psychologist G. Stanley Hall, the first American to receive a doctorate in that field in 1878, this provided the impetus of a movement that gained power and prestige in the face of mounting demographic changes that were brought about by immigration.

There arose a jingoistic backlash against immigrants, much like the present antipathy toward Latinos. Darker-skinned non-Aryan or non-Anglo-Saxons were then, as now, defined as less motivated and less capable than lighter-skinned inhabitants. The eugenics movement attributed this to their innate biological inferiority, and the Social Darwinists castigated non-Aryans for deficient achievements, high amounts of deviant behavior, and poverty. The tradition of blaming the victim, that is, discriminating against people who are different from the majority and then referring to their misfortune as evidence of their inferiority, became ingrained in the spiritual psyche of the nation—a handy tool for avoiding critical analysis of systemic racism and institutional weaknesses which create and perpetuate social inequality.

"SCIENTIFIC RACISM" RENEWED

Not surprisingly, crackpot racist theories emerged in this period which attempted to justify the power and privilege of the wealthy "old line Americans," as well as American international and domestic adventures such as westward expansion and the Mexican–American and Spanish–American wars. Frenchman, Count Arthur de Gobineau, wrote a four-volume treatise designed to defend French nobility, *The Inequality of Human Races,* between 1853 and 1857 that provided an early justification for the Teutonic, Anglo-Saxon, Aryan position. He contended that all history and civilization were based on race, and, of course, the Aryans (whites) were the leaders destined to rule the yellow (Asian) and black (African) races. Their superior native intellect and morality, made them natural leaders and masters of groups of inferior people. Asians were depicted as passive while Africans (blacks, Negroes) as gluttonous, sensual, and stupid.[7]

There followed a succession of racist theories from the latter nineteenth century through the first few decades of the twentieth century, culminating in the most sordid chapter in the degradation of man based on mythological racial characteristics—the Nazi Holocaust. Although de Gobineau's work preceded Hitler's regime by 80 years, his writing influenced German composer Richard Wagner, who, in the 1880s, applied the Aryan mystique to Germany, elevating the German folk to higher plane where Teutons were destined for greatness. This theme permeates much of Wagner's music and was exuberantly heralded by the Nazis as they elevated the myth of Aryan supremacy in their drive to cleanse the world of inferior races, and in the process caused the deaths of 11 million Jews, Gypsies, Jehovah's Witnesses, gays, disabled Germans, and political dissidents from 1933 to 1945.

Wagner's son-in-law, Houston Stewart Chamberlain, was an Englishman who became a German citizen in 1916. He was a virulent anti-Semite with a penchant for positing the thesis that great men in history, including Jesus Christ, were blond-haired blue-eyed Aryans.[8] Together with de Gobineau, their ideas helped form the basis of twentieth century racist ideologies which, to this day, maintain that Aryans and Anglo-Saxons are racially superior to other ethnic groups and destined to rule the world.

EUGENICS AND THE ELITE

The early twentieth century saw the emergence and fascination with the concept of intelligence and eugenics. Sporadic physical-type theories were propounded to explain crime and deviant behavior. As late as 1939, Harvard anthropologist Ernest Hooten presented a study of over 17,000 people from ten states purporting to demonstrate the innate biological cause of crime:

> Certain theoretical conclusions are, however, of no little importance. Criminals are organically inferior. Crime is the resultant of the impact of environment upon low-grade human organisms. It follows that the elimination of crime can be effected only by the extirpation of the physically, mentally, and morally unfit; or by their complete segregation in a socially aseptic environment.[9]

Much attention was, however, focused on differences in intelligence because of the work of the German immigrant, Franz Boas, who is regarded as the father of cultural anthropology. Boas became a naturalized citizen of the United States and taught at Columbia University from 1896 until his death in 1942. He was a strong opponent of racial and physical-type determinist theories, arguing for the important role that culture played in influencing the path of human growth and the development of society.

Boas earned a doctorate in physics in Germany. It was on an expedition to Baffin Island in 1883 that his lifelong commitment to understanding the interaction between culture and society began. His work prodded anthropologists into studying and analyzing societies as independent observers without being shackled to religious, superstitious, or pseudo-scientific dogma that fostered ethnocentrism and imperiled objectivity. It was Boas who broke with the prevailing tradition that depicted indigenous peoples as racially inferior to whites. When he introduced his unbiased analysis, the racist veneer of previous white hegemony over the definition of what constituted civilization was peeled back to reveal it for what it truly was:

> What is the proof of the development of specialized hereditary capacities? Where is the proof that such capacities, if they exist, are recessive? How can it be shown that such specialized characteristics in selected mating will be bred out? Not a single one of these statements can be accepted.[10]

His incisive intellect helped launch a new era of scientific research in the social sciences. Among his most famous students were Ruth Benedict, Margaret Mead, Alfred Kroeber, and Edward Sapir. Nevertheless, the influx of immigrants and fear of change in the distribution of power were forces that contributed to the continuation of racist pseudo-scientific theories. Even as Boas attacked such works as ill-conceived and illogical, the seeds of hate and prejudice were spreading from the work of one of the most infamous purveyors of the Nordic/Aryan myth: Theodore Lothrop Stoddard, the same person Boas criticized in the comment above.

Born in Brookline, Massachusetts in 1883, Stoddard graduated from Harvard *magna cum laude* in 1905. He studied law at Boston University and earned a doctorate in history from Harvard in 1914. Stoddard's writing gave impetus to the "scientific racism" of the early twentieth century in the United States. He endorsed the eugenics movement through works that stoked the fires of racial hatred, provoking ethnocentric white supremacist beliefs that resonate to this day on internet web sites.[11]

In a wide array of books from 1914 through 1940, Stoddard promulgated his belief in the supremacy of the white race, and warned of the peril to white society through immigration, which brought inferior ethnic stock into contact with Americans of Nordic, old-line Anglo-Saxon heritage.

The progress of science also fortified white race-consciousness with its sanctions. The researches of European scholars identified the founders of our civilization with a race of tall, white-skinned barbarians, possessing regular features, brown or blond hair, and light eyes. This was, of course, what we now know as the Nordic type.[12]

He also professed that whites possessed a genetic strain of superiority and greatness and a natural camaraderie which impelled them toward unity in their goal of world supremacy:

> Particularly good were the effects upon the peoples predominantly of Nordic blood. Obviously typifying as they did the prehistoric creators of white civilization, Nordics everywhere were strengthened in consciousness of genetic worth, feeling of responsibility for world-progress, and urge toward fraternal collaboration.[13]

But Stoddard was perplexed by dissension and disputes among white nations. Such fraternal in-fighting allowed for the intrusion of "colored peoples" onto the world stage. He therefore supported birth control and eugenics as methods for stemming the assault on American society and the superiority and purity of Anglo-Saxons, and he spoke out in favor of restrictions on immigration, of which he was especially apprehensive:

> The subjugation of white lands by colored armies may, of course, occur, especially if the white world continues to rend itself with internecine wars. However, such colored triumphs of arms are less to be dreaded than more endearing conquests like migrations which would swamp whole populations and turn countries now white into colored man's lands irretrievably lost to the white world.[14]

The way for the white civilization to triumph in this cataclysmic upheaval was for Nordic, racially superior whites to unite. It was their destiny to preserve white heritage and civilization. He was distraught, however, by conflicts among white nations stemming from Pan-Germanism, Pan-Slavism, and selfish desires to gain control of resources. These trends were diversions that threatened white racial unity and impeded white progress toward their destiny of world domination, allowing the intrusion of "colored peoples" onto the world stage and their ascendancy over whites.

Thus, in the years preceding Armageddon [WWI], all the European Powers displayed a reckless absorption in particularistic ambitions and showed a callous indifference to larger race interests. The rapid weakening of white solidarity was clearly apparent.[15]

Stoddard was candid about his prescription for saving Nordic civilization:

> Civilization is not a cure but an effect—the effect of sustained human energy; and this energy, in turn, springs from the creative urge of superior germ-plasm. Civilization is thus fundamentally conditioned by race. In any particular people, civilization will progress just so far as that people has the capacity to further it and the ability to bear the correlative burden which it entails.[16]

Stoddard believed that Nordic peoples constituted a super race that would rule the world if they eliminated defective members by cleansing society of undesirables:

> The problem of race betterment consists of two distinct phases: the multiplication of superior individuals and the elimination of inferiors. These two phases of race betterment clearly require totally different method. The multiplication of superiors is a process of race building; the elimination of inferiors is a process of race cleansing.[17]

Further,

> Race cleansing is the obvious starting-point for race betterment. Here scientific knowledge is most advanced, the need for action most apparent, and public opinion best informed. . . . We now know that so-called "degenerate classes" are not sharply marked off from the rest of the community, but are merely the most afflicted sufferers from taints which extend broadcast through the general population. The "degenerate classes" are, in fact, merely the nucleus of that vast "outer fringe" of mental and physical unsoundness visible all the way from the unemployable "casual laborer" right up to the "tainted genius."

Degeneracy is thus a cancerous blight, constantly spreading, tainting and spoiling sound stocks, destroying race values, and increasing social burdens.

In fact, degeneracy not only handicaps society but threatens its very existence. Congenitally incapable of adjusting themselves to an advanced social order, the degenerate inevitably become its enemies—particularly those 'high grade defectives' who are the natural fomenters of social unrest.[18]

Such ideas were embedded in the loathsome Nuremberg Laws of 1935 that systematically destroyed democracy and civil rights in Germany, leading to the forced sterilization of hundreds of thousands of Germans—disabled, Jews, Jehovah's Witnesses, gypsies and political dissidents.

Despite his rhetoric, Stoddard was a pacifist. He was cool toward Nazism because it posed a threat to his grand theory of white racial supremacy by creating yet another internecine struggle among whites, further eroding their vitality and path to world hegemony. Nevertheless, traveling as a journalist, he met with Hitler and many leading Nazis shortly before the United States entered the Second World War and published *Into the Darkness*,[19] which was a naïve assessment of Nazi Germany and the scope, methods and intent of Hitler's Third Reich. Hitler was not only enamored with Stoddard's reasoning; he was also an avid fan of Madison Grant, the inveterate American racist and eugenicist.

For Stoddard, World Wars I and II were deviations from the natural order and course of history—digressions that prevented whites from achieving their preordained and rightful historical imperative—world domination. Reading his preposterous discourse on the natural superiority of the white race is a repulsive experience, exacerbated by the persistence of these ideas and his elevation to the status of folk hero by contemporary white supremacists. While some semblance of his perverse logic persists in the writing and pronouncements of race-baiters, and even slips into racist slogans and thought of some otherwise stalwart citizens and defenders of "the American way," we must learn from this sordid chapter in our history not to prejudge people on the basis of their physiology but, as Dr. King asserted, "on the content of their character."

NOTES

1. See the discussion of their views in Thomas F. Gossett, *Race: The History of an Idea in America,* N.Y.: Oxford University Press, New Edition, 1997, pp. 113–117.

2. Lothrop Stoddard, *The Revolt of Civilization: The Menace of the Underman,* N.Y.: Charles Scribner's Sons, 1922. Popular culture of the time also reflected such sentiments. See Jack London, *The Valley of the Moon,* N.Y.: The MacMillan Company, 1913, pp. 21–24, 154.

3. Madison Grant, *The Passing of the Great Race: Or the Racial Basis of European History*, Fourth edition, N.Y.: Charles Scribner's Sons, 1921. Originally published in 1914, p. xix.

4. Ibid., p. xxxi.

5. Leland V. Bell, *Treating the Mentally Ill.* N.Y.: Praeger Publishers, 1980, pp. 66–67.

6. Statement in film documentary, *Honor Bound.*

7. Arthur de Gobineau, *The Inequality of Human Races,* Adrian Collins, (trans.), N.Y.: G. P. Putnam's Sons, 1915.

8. Houston Stewart Chamberlain, *Foundations of the Nineteenth Century,* John Lees, translator, London: John Lane, 1911.

9. Ernest A. Hooten, *The American Criminal: An Anthropological Study*, Cambridge: Harvard University Press, Vol. 1, 1939, p. 309.

10. Franz Boas, "Review of the *Rising Tide of Color*," in *The Nation*, vol. 111, December 8, 1920, p. 656. Cited in Gossett, op. cit. p. 426. See also: Franz Boas, *The Mind of Primitive Man*, N.Y.: The MacMillan Company, 1911 and Franz Boas, *Race and Democratic Society*, N.Y.: J.J. Augustin, 1945.

11. E.g*., www.stormfront.org, www.aryan-nations.org, www.VDARE.com*; *www .natvan.com*.

12. Lothrop Stoddard, *The Rising Tide of Color Against White World Supremacy*, N.Y.: Charles Scribner's Sons, 1920, p. 199.

13. Ibid., p. 200.

14. Ibid., p. vi.

15. Ibid., p. 204.

16. Lothrop Stoddard, *The Revolt Against Civilization: The Menace of the Under Man*, N.Y.: Charles Scribner's Sons, 1922, pp. 2–3.

17. Ibid., p. 244–245.

18. Ibid., pp. 245–246.

19. N.Y.: Duell, Sloan and Pierce, 1940.

Chapter 5

Justifying the Indefensible

Rationalizing Domination and Exploitation

> The fact is, those illegal aliens are costing our economy $200 billion in depressed wages for working Americans. It is costing $50 billion a year in social and medical costs. And it's costing us, no one knows precisely how much, to incarcerate what is about a third of our prison population who are illegal aliens.
>
> —Lou Dobbs on "Democracy Now!" December 4, 2007

ANTI-IMMIGRANT HYSTERIA

The anti-immigrant hysteria and racism prevalent at the turn of the twentieth century is paralleled by similar themes and movements in the United States and the world today. Nativistic and nationalist movements led by demagogues on the right stereotype immigrants, especially dark-skinned people, as uncouth, illiterate, even primitive intruders whose culture and large families threaten to destabilize the existing social order (their status quo), mongrelize society, and destroy societal institutions.

Much of the venom of these malcontents is directed toward Muslims, Africans, and Latinos who have been the victims of housing, job, and educational discrimination as well as targets of hate crimes that have resulted in beatings and deaths.[1] The shadow of racism is long and casts a pall over our lives today. Observed physiological differences between dark-skinned people and whites are still used to link blacks to primitive, simian ancestors, as if lighter-skinned people had different origins. Then, as now, racists exaggerate physiological characteristics of dark-skinned people (thick lips, broad noses, curly hair), contending that these are atavistic traits.

This reasoning is then used to explain differences in cultural traditions and intellect. Everything from music, to artistic and scientific accomplishments is, in the minds of white supremacists, reduced to genetic differences. Taking the lead from the World War I intelligence studies and the eugenics movement, biological determinists of the twentieth and twenty-first centuries attempt to link the achievement gap in educational attainment between black and Latino students and their white and Asian peers to differing genetic abilities among the ethnic groups. Contemporary hate literature is replete with references to the cultural and intellectual inferiority of blacks and Latinos and the threat such groups pose to the "advanced" white civilization.[2] It is estimated that there may be as many as 60,000 hate web sites on the World Wide Web.[3]

As we have seen, these are specious arguments based on unscientific assumptions about human evolution. They are compounded by ignorance or denial of the role that white-dominated institutions and practices (notably racism and the exploitation of land and people) have played in denying dark-skinned people equal opportunities; blocking their upward mobility, and perpetuating their impoverishment to maintain whites' competitive advantages.

RACE AND INTELLIGENCE

A watershed development in the history of the way our society conceptualizes racial differences emerged serendipitously from an analysis of American soldiers' intelligence tests in World War I. Prior to the Great War, a young Frenchman by the name of Alfred Binet, who had been trained as a lawyer, became fascinated with the study of psychology. Although he had no formal graduate training in the field, he obtained a position in the Laboratory of Experimental Psychology at the Sorbonne in 1891. Three years later he became the director of the department.

Binet was respected for his research, which attracted a young graduate student, Theodore Simon, to work with him at the lab. Binet was asked by the French government to develop a means of predicting the academic success of school children. He and Simon created an intelligence test that asked children to perform simple commands and gestures, repeat spoken words and numbers, and identify objects in pictures and words. They conceptualized the idea of "mental age" which was based on the application of the scale to French school children.

Binet was cautionary in the use of the test and its implications. Although he believed heredity played an important role in intelligence, he noted that the results of his test were mediated by the environment as well as genetics, and test scores were malleable and variable, subject to factors which themselves change and could influence the outcome. Unfortunately, this was also the time of large scale migration and immigration and scientific racism, with its eugenics orientation.

In 1908, H.H. Goddard, a eugenicist, introduced the Binet-Simon scale in the United States in the hope of proving the natural superiority of the white race. Then, in 1916, Stanford psychologist, Lewis Terman, another biological determinist, took the Binet-Simon scale originally developed to test French school children and created the Stanford-Binet scale for the purpose of "curtailing the reproduction of feeble-mindedness and the elimination of an enormous amount of crime, pauperism, and industrial inefficiency."[4]

This story took an interesting turn when the United States Army asked psychologist Robert Yerkes to develop a test for screening recruits who wanted to serve in World War I. Never before had the military sought to screen so many young men. Over two million prospective soldiers were tested by the new Alpha (written) and Beta (oral) intelligence tests to determine their suitability for leadership and occupations in the military. Yerkes assembled a distinguished team to develop these tests in a special committee of the American Psychological Association on the Psychological Examination of Recruits. Among its members were Henry Goddard, Lewis Terman, and Walter Bingham, who, along with Yerkes, were eugenicists interested in preserving white racial domination and protecting it from the intrusion of "inferior" genes of immigrants.

The racists' and eugenicists' assumptions about the genetic inferiority of dark-skinned immigrants and the natural superiority of Nordic-Anglo people seemed to be confirmed by the intelligence test results. In general, white recruits of Nordic-Anglo ancestry scored higher than immigrants and blacks, but a closer examination of the data revealed some fascinating findings. White recruits in the South scored higher than black southern recruits, but northern blacks scored higher than southern whites. For example, literate blacks from Illinois had higher median scores than literate whites from nine southern states, and literate blacks from New York scored higher than literate whites from five southern states.

Members of the committee could have used these findings to demonstrate the importance of one's environment and education on intelligence test results, but they steadfastly refused, preferring to attribute discrepancies in their theory to, as Dr. Bingham contended, the greater admixture of white blood among blacks in the North and the migration of more intelligent blacks from the South to the North. Yerkes subscribed to these views and wrote a forward to Bingham's book, wherein he endorsed the conclusion that the tests proved the inferiority of blacks and immigrants "could be generally rated intellectually by the amount of Nordic blood in their veins."[5]

FEAR OF THE MASSES

Racists and eugenicists feared the intrusion of immigrants and growth of the African-American population in the United States. They believed they were physically and intellectually inferior to whites and were incapable of assimilating into American society and accommodating to western forms of government. To better understand their reservations, one has to consider the social and demographic changes that were occurring at home and abroad at the turn of the century.[6]

Changes in the world view which influenced man's understanding of himself, his relationships with one another, and the head of state or Sovereign progressed from superstitious beliefs to rational scientific empiricism in the eighteenth and nineteenth centuries. Philosophers Locke, Rousseau, Mill, and Bentham altered the traditional role of the governed and governor. The inviolable Hobbesian contract which invested power and responsibility in the hands of the monarchy could, from the perspectives of Enlightenment philosophers, be abrogated if the monarch was despotic and/or incapable of fulfilling his responsibility to his subjects.

Shocked by the American and French revolutions in the late eighteenth century, monarchs and ruling elites were jolted once again in 1848 when a series of revolts shattered Germany, France, the Austrian Empire, the Italian states, Denmark, and Poland. The threat of mob rule by lower social classes under the guise of democracy could spell disaster for ruling elites who had monopolized political and economic power for centuries. The industrial revolution, as Marx noted, dehumanized the world of work and alienated the very nature of man from society, turning him into a mechanical, instrumental object.[7]

Marx's idea of restoring harmony in the world of work and society was to create a revolution of the working class (proletariat) against the exploiting property owners and capitalists (bourgeoisie) and redistribute wealth and property based on individual needs. Critiquing the excesses of the industrial revolution with its attendant demographic changes—increasing population, urbanization, and the impoverishment of the working class—was not unique to Marx, but his call for the radical restructuring of society helped to fuel unrest among the working class and struck fear in the hearts of ruling elites.

Journalist Kenan Malik[8] contends that it was the wave of unrest among the lower classes throughout Europe in the mid-nineteenth century, along with post-Enlightenment ideas about the proper role of government, and the application of scientific empiricism and Social Darwinism, that led to the racial distinctions which depicted lower social strata of society on the European continent as racially inferior. While it is conceivable that such trends led to class antipathies abroad, this line of reasoning is not as relevant as the linear progression of the stigmatization of dark-skinned people, the commodification of Africans in the slave trade, and the dehumanization of dark-skinned and indigenous people which served to institutionalize racism in America.

The threat to the status quo posed by incipient working class calls for democratic reforms in politics and the economy along with the influx of immigrants from "less desirable" genetic stocks, provided the backdrop for the florescence of the eugenics movement in the United States at the turn of the twentieth century. Even when World War I intelligence test results raised questions over racist assumptions about the genetic intellectual inferiority of blacks, the eugenicists dismissed them by concocting absurd rationalizations for the results, such as alleging that northern blacks' higher intelligence test scores were the result of smarter southern blacks moving north.

Over the following decades social science research was able to establish the important role that environment plays in educational and testing outcomes. The landmark Supreme Court case, Brown vs. the Board of Education[9] was an official acknowledgement of the effects of the application of unequal resources on the educational opportunities and outcomes of African-American children. Research by psychologists Claude Steele and Joshua Aronson of Stanford University confirmed that minorities and women may underperform in educational settings because of preconceptions they have about their abilities.[10]

In a sense, minorities and women create a self-fulfilling prophesy with themselves as victims of society's stereotypes about them. Just like the little black children who choose white dolls as the pretty ones, they are caught in a web of fear and self-doubt—a false consciousness created by racists that intentionally distorts reality by substituting labels and symbols which nurture fear, suspicion, anxiety, and hostility and obfuscates reason and compassion. This is not to deny the fact that ability and motivation influence achievement. It is impossible, however, to ascribe absolute percentages to the nature/nurture, heredity versus environment calculus in the attribution of cause and effect in educational and occupational attainment in life. Yet, despite voluminous evidence to the contrary, racist, genetic theories purporting to explain disparities between whites and people of color continue to surface.

CONTEMPORARY RACIST THEORIES

Almost like clockwork, each decade sees the reemergence of a new treatise purporting to prove the genetic inferiority of dark-skinned people to whites, paralleling in many ways hysterical denunciations about the "wave of aliens swamping our society." More than a century after the heyday of "scientific racism," and the xenophobic anti-immigration movement that led to the passage of restrictive immigration laws and dubious psychological experiments to demonstrate, a priori, the intellectual deficiencies of minorities, we are again faced with determinist, racist, white supremacist screeds which are intellectually and scientifically indefensible.

While anthropologists and physiologists were attempting to rationalize social inequality by measuring heads and body parts and concocting theories about the genetic superiority of Aryans and Anglo-Saxons, the relatively new science of psychology embarked on a field of study that to this day baffles and astounds professionals and laymen alike: the science of human intelligence. Amazing physiological discoveries through brain imaging are helping us to understand thought processes, memory, and learning.

In spite of the growing evidence drawn from the fields of modern biology, anthropology, psychology, sociology, and cognitive neuroscience, which are defining physiological and environmental influences on human development and potential, the ghosts of the past miraculously reappear, resurrecting determinist theories and arguments that have been thoroughly discredited by modern natural and social sciences. For example, Professor J. Philippe Rushton, a psychologist at the University of Western Ontario in Canada, is a leading representative of contemporary racist physical type theory. His book, *Race, Evolution, and Behavior*[11] presents "evidence" demonstrating the genetic inferiority of Africans and African-Americans.

This transplanted Englishman has been writing articles, making presentations, and publishing books and pamphlets which purport to demonstrate that blacks have larger genitals, breasts, and buttocks than whites and Asians, and there is an inverse relationship between the size of these body parts and intelligence. Despite the magnitude of data he has accumulated to prove his case[12] he has not been able to persuade legitimate scholars and scientists that his work is meritorious.

Stanford biologist Mark Feldman described his work as "laughable," and University of Washington psychology professor David Barash wrote in a review "bad science and virulent racial prejudice drip like pus" from his book.[13] Today, Rushton self-publishes the book through his Darwin Research Institute founded in 1989 to "guarantee academic freedom for research on race differences." He contends that he was compelled to take this path after pressure from the academic community caused Transactions Publishers to pull his book and offer an apology.

Thousands of abridged copies are in circulation and interested readers can purchase copies in bulk from Rushton's web site. What they may not realize, in addition to his dubious scholarship, is that Rushton is the president of the

Pioneer Fund, founded by the late Harry Weyher, Jr. in 1937 to "advance the scientific study of heredity and human differences." Among grant recipients were the late William Bradford Shockley, who shared the Nobel Prize in Physics in 1956 for inventing the transistor. He is also credited with helping develop Silicon Valley. His admirers would rather forget his rabid racial eugenics in the latter part of his life (he died in 1989).

Shockley believed that the higher birthrate of African-Americans was detrimental to the United States and would, if left unchecked, spell genetic disaster for the nation because of what he believed was their lower intelligence. He advocated voluntary sterilization for people with IQs under a hundred. Although his position was unpopular, he had no compunction about parading around college campuses with a sign hanging from his neck indicating that blacks had average IQs fifteen points lower than whites.

Another grant recipient from the Pioneer Fund was Arthur Jensen, Professor Emeritus of Psychology at the University of California at Berkeley. In a much-criticized article in the 1969 *Harvard Educational Review*,[14] Jensen concluded that genetic factors were more important than environment in determining IQ. Foremost among the determinants of IQ were prenatal influences such as the nourishment of the mother and the child. Jensen later helped to popularize the concept of G or general intelligence factor which, he contended, was constructed on two levels of learning ability: level one, which related to rote memorization of simple facts and skills and was, he believed, equally distributed in the population; and level two, which involved complex reasoning and problem-solving, which he said was more prevalent among whites and Asians than African-Americans and Mexican Americans.

His work created a controversy among scholars, and the *Harvard Educational Review's* next issue was devoted entirely to rebuttals of his thesis. To his credit, he recommended that diverse styles of teaching should be integrated into classrooms to accommodate the different learning styles of children. We know today that many of the differences in educational achievement and test scores are the result of environmental factors beyond the control of students and their parents, such as teacher quality, methods and objectivity, distribution and allocation of resources, content and relevance of the curriculum, school climate and student culture, class size and composition, location of the school, economic status of the students and their families, and many other variables that confound what might seem to be a link between genes and intelligence.

Nevertheless, his thesis, though unpopular, catalyzed debate about race, intelligence, and heredity—a debate which was rekindled in the 1994 book *The Bell Curve* by the late Harvard psychologist, Richard Herrnstein, and sociologist, Charles Murray.[15] The book created an academic firestorm which led to a deluge of articles and books critiquing the authors' premise that intelligence is largely hereditary, cannot be appreciably influenced by educational opportunities such as affirmative action programs in schools, universities, and the world of work, and people with lower IQs account for more crime, deviant behavior, and poverty than the "cognitive elite," who are genetically suited to leadership and the accumulation of capital.

This argument is a sophisticated restatement of the eugenicists at the turn of the twentieth century. Indeed, passages of the book belie the "scientific" objectivism purportedly claimed by the authors' statistical analysis of data sets to establish their case—a case which they had already stated in earlier publications that revealed their intentions.[16] Their comments about the threat that immigrants and people with low IQs pose to the genetic stock of the United States are reminiscent of statements by Madison Grant and Lothrop Stoddard. Their contention that the higher reproductive rates of people with low IQs (African-Americans and Latinos) smacks of the kind of racist rhetoric that abounds today on white supremacist internet web sites.

Their solution for the salvation of the United States is to allow the cognitive elite to run society because they are better prepared for this task; and to simplify laws, regulations, and social interactions so the less well genetically endowed masses can participate and be mollified to avoid social unrest.

Cognitive partitioning will continue. It cannot be stopped, because the forces driving it cannot be stopped. But America can choose to preserve a society in which every citizen has access to the central satisfaction of life. Its people can, through an interweaving of choice and responsibility, create valued places for themselves in their worlds. They can live in communities—urban or rural— where being a good parent, a good neighbor, and a good friend will give their lives purpose and meaning. They can weave the most crucial safety nets together, so that their mistakes and misfortunes are mitigated and withstood with a little help from their friends.

All of these good things are available now to those who are smart enough or rich enough—if they can exploit the complex rules to their advantage, buy their way out of social institutions that no longer function, and have access to the rich human interconnections that are growing, not diminishing, for the cognitively fortunate. We are calling upon our readers, so heavily concentrated among those who fit that description, to recognize the ways in which public policy has come to deny those good things to those who are not smart enough and rich enough.

At the heart of our thought is the quest for human dignity. The central measure of success for this government, as for any other, is to permit people to live lives of dignity—not to give them dignity, for that is not in any government's power, but to make it accessible to all. That is one way of thinking about what the Founders had in mind when they proclaimed, as a truth self-evident, that all men are created equal. That is what we have in mind when we talk about valued places for everyone.[17]

What a fascinating utopia, run by intellectually superior citizens for the benefit of the less well genetically endowed. Huxley and Orwell's premonition reprised. A vision not unlike B. F. Skinner's in *Beyond Freedom and Dignity*[18] which called for the development of a technology of human behavior to regulate human desires and channel them into socially desirable activities—a society devoid of ethical considerations about the implications of manipulating people who willingly participate in their own enslavement. We're currently trying to recover from an economic collapse precipitated by the "cognitive elite" who applied their superior intellectual talents to raping the financial system of the United States and the world. Alan Greenspan, was not the only one with a "flaw in his equation." Intelligence encompasses more than test measurements—it also denotes wisdom, compassion, and ethics—something in short supply in "scientific" psychological evaluations of "superior people." Such ostensibly intelligent people have repeatedly brought this nation to the brink of catastrophe.[19]

No one disputes the difference in standardized test scores, IQ, academic success, income, and occupational attainment between whites and Asians compared to blacks and Latinos. What is disputed is causality, which is to say, there is a persistent, unremitting intellectual tradition from the time of the Englishman Francis Galton, Darwin's cousin, who coined the term eugenics in 1883,[20] to this day, which has attributed these differences to heredity, attempting to ascribe superior genetic endowment to whites, especially those of Nordic, Aryan, and Anglo-Saxon ancestry.

THE FALLOUT FROM RACISM

In light of recent discoveries about the distribution of common DNA among all humans, such propositions are not only specious, but ridiculous, and one should question the scholarship and intentions of people who continue to promulgate such theories. Ethnic groups around the world share 99.9 percent of the same genetic material. There is no evidence of any superior or inferior group; no support for the proposition that one particular group is smarter, faster, more cunning, adventurous, industrious, funnier, contemplative, morose, courageous, or naïve. Abilities and aptitudes are distributed among ethnic groups and differences within any group fall along a continuum from less to more on these and many other traits or characteristics.

To single our dark-skinned people and recent immigrants, now Latinos, at the turn of the twentieth century, Asians, southern and eastern Europeans, and a century earlier the Irish, as being genetically inferior to white Anglo-Saxon Nordics is, in light of scientific knowledge, false and absurd. Furthermore, the extent of admixture, or mixing of genes among ethnic groups, is increasing as mass transportation facilitates travel and migration around the world. In the United States, the fastest growing demographic segment of the population are people of mixed ancestry, multicultural background, now estimated to be over six million people. It is estimated that 30 percent of the genes of African-Americans are from white people. Did nature somehow shortchange them in the genetic lottery so they have test-taking and motivational deficiencies?

Of course there are significant differences in standardized test results and G (general intelligence) between Asians, whites, African-Americans and Latinos. The existence of these differences demonstrates the need for remedial education and affirmative action programs, and greater attention *to the environmental conditions that create these disparities*. Scientists have established that genetic differences among ethnic/racial groups are insignificant and do not explain variations in educational and occupational attainment. Teachers must be vigilant, guarding against the intrusion of fallacious ideologies, factual distortions, and convenient white supremacist theories into their perceptions of the ability of children of color. Unfortunately, our culture has assimilated these myths, and they all too frequently have a negative effect on the interaction and outcomes between teachers, administrators, students, and parents.

We should not be lured into simplistic determinist explanations evocative of Social Darwinism that attributed human misery to individual and group failings, overlooking the systemic roots of poverty and inequality that breed frustration, anger, educational and economic hardship, social pathologies, mental illness, and alienation. Despite evidence to the contrary, there is still considerable public support for the belief that intelligence and performance on standardized tests are genetically linked predictors of academic and occupational success. Because of this, misperceptions about the abilities, morals, and motivation of segments of our population persist and perpetuate stereotypes about them, relegating them to the status of inferior, second-class citizens.

The current infatuation with standardized tests, mandated by the Federal No Child Left Behind legislation to monitor student achievement, is an example of conceptually misplaced good intentions. It is predicated on a lack of understanding about social and environmental conditions that create and perpetuate the achievement gap between white and Asian students and blacks and Latinos. In their zeal to make a colossal educational system accountable, that great American experiment that provides tens of millions of students with compulsory free education, the framers and enforcers of the program relied on measurement techniques which have consistently revealed racial and ethnic disparities. This strategy not only reinforces stereotypes about the presumed genetic inferiority of black and Latino students, it stigmatizes schools, teachers, administrators, and parents for conditions that predated the legislation—conditions, the effects of which on academic achievement, were already known, and which will require fundamental changes in the way we educate our children and structure our society for the creation of a more equitable nation.

In our current educational system, wide-scale standardized testing of school children creates a self-fulfilling prophesy reinforcing labels that devalue, demean, and degrade students and teachers alike. Embarking on a testing crusade to demonstrate the existence of deficiencies in an educational system mired in the social inequality of resources is unnecessary. One can identify children and schools in need without resorting to stilted tests. A review of schools by census tracts shows the percentage of students on free and reduced lunches, and, sadly, the percentage of black and Latino students will yield similar results, sparing the annual $1.1 billion expense of testing which could be used to improve the quality of instruction in these schools.[21]

The association between educational attainment and income is strong and has been known for decades. It was part of the decision-making process in the Brown v. the Board of Education Supreme Court decision in 1954. Resurrecting the myopic strategy of standardized testing to illuminate educational disparities among ethnic groups is tantamount to utilizing racist theories purporting to explain differences in intelligence.

Of course differences exist, but the public and policy makers are fishing for a red herring when they focus on deficiencies in students' culture and motivation instead of on who is doing the teaching, the quality and methods of instruction, content of the curriculum, and available resources. We have created a closed loop system, rigged against minorities. They reject a system that is irrelevant and underfunded, and the system creates cultural barriers that predestine them to failure.

From its beginning, our society has institutionalized behavior and policies which benefit a white elite, while impoverishing dark-skinned people. Despite the necessity for their labor in vital industries such as agriculture, services (hospitality, hotels, sanitation, labor), and their growing advancement into higher paying higher status occupations and professions, large numbers of African-Americans and Latinos work under deleterious conditions for artificially depressed wages, while whites maintain hegemony over the more psychologically and financially rewarding jobs. By perpetuating inequality in education, whites are able to ensure that they will remove people of color as a competitive threat—a natural course of action given our societal emphasis on acquisitiveness and materialism.

Perhaps whites suspect that they could not maintain their lifestyle without the assistance of black and brown people, so they cling to Social Darwinist racist myths about the meritocracy, believing that they hold the higher intellectual ground by virtue of their biological superiority—that God and nature have endowed them with superior genes and ordained them to assume the mantle of leadership for the less genetically fit.

NOTES

1. See Amnesty International Report 2009, State of the World's Human Rights at *http://thereport.amnesty.org/*, and Human Rights Watch World Report 2009 at *www .hrw.org; http://www.splcenter.org/intel/intpro.jsp.*

2. See for example the web sites of Aryan Nations, *http://www.aryan-nations.org*, Vdare (named for the supposed first white child born in America, Virginia Dare) *http:// vdare.com*, the National Alliance/National Vanguard, *http:www.natvan.com*, Stormfront, *http://www.stormfront.org*, Imperial Klans of America, *http://www.KKK.net.*

3. See the discussion of racism on the internet in Jessie Daniels, *Cyber Racism: White Supremacy Online and the New Attack on Civil Rights,* Lanham, MD: Rowman & Littlefield, 2009. Daniels notes the difficulty in establishing the actual number of hate websites, which, she estimates range between 10,000 and 60,000. For an analysis of hate web sites see: The Intelligence Project of the Southern Poverty Law Center at: *http://www.splcenter.org/intel/intpro.jsp.*

4. Alfred Binet, *Human Intelligence* at: *http://www.indiana.edu/~intell/binet .shtml.* Retrieved: 1/9/10.

5. Thomas F. Gossett, *Race: The History of an Idea in America,* N.Y.: Oxford University Press, New Edition, 1997, p. 376.

6. Kenan Malik provides a fascinating chronological account of the cultural and philosophical changes that led to development of scientific racism and eugenics in his book *The Meaning of Race: Race, History and Culture in Western Society,* N.Y.: New York University Press, 1996.

7. Marx's best known critique of the capitalist system is found in his work *Das Kapital.* Volume one of four was published in 1867, but his *Economic and Philosophical Manuscripts of 1844,* and *The German Ideology,* written with Frederick Engels, are useful in clarifying his perspective. These works are available free on the internet.

8. loc. cit.

9. *Oliver L. Brown et al. v. the Board of Education of Topeka, KS et al.* 347 U.S. 483, 1954.

10. Claude Steele and Joshua Aronson, "Stereotype Threat and the Intellectual Test Performance of African-Americans," *Journal of Personality and Social Psychology*, 69 (5), November 1995, pp. 797–811.

11. Transaction Books, 1995, New Brunswick, N.J.

12. Recent editions of his book range to over 400 pages with charts and tables comparing measurements of different racial groups like the one enumerating differences in brain size that attempts to link this to IQ and "cultural achievements," "frequency of intercourse," "permissive attitudes," and personality types such as "aggressiveness," "cautiousness," "impulsivity," "self-concept," and "sociability."

13. "Academic Racism," *Intelligence Report*, Southern Poverty Law Center, Winter, 2006.

14. "How Much Can We Boost IQ and Achievement?" Vol. 39 pp. 1-123.

15. *The Bell Curve: Intelligence and Class Structure in American Life*, N.Y.: The Free Press, 1994.

16. Richard Herrnstein, *IQ in the Meritocracy*, Little, Brown and Company, Boston, 1973; Charles Murray, *Losing Ground: American Social Policy, 1950-1980*, Basic Books, N.Y.: 1984.

17. Ibid., p. 551.

18. N.Y.: Knoph, 1971.

19. See the excellent anthology of critiques of *The Bell Curve* in Bernie Devlin, Stephen E. Fienberg, Daniel P. Resnick and Kathryn Roeder, (eds.) *Intelligence, Genes and Success: Scientists Respond to The Bell Curve*, N.Y.: Springer, 1997. For a critique of racial disparities in test scores and the achievement gap see: Christopher Jencks and Meredith Phillips (eds.), *The Black-White Test Score Gap*, Washington, D.C.: The Brookings Institution, 1998.

20. *Inquiries into Human Faculty and its Development*, N.Y.: Macmillan, 1883.

21. The U.S. Department of Education provided $407.6 million to states to help defray the expense of testing in 2007–2008 academic year. Pauline Vu, "Do State Tests Make a Difference?" *Stateline.Org*, January 17, 2008, The PEW Center for the States.

Chapter 6

Why People Hate

No one is born hating another person because of the color of his skin, or his background, or his religion. People must learn to hate, and if they can learn to hate, they can be taught to love, for love comes more naturally to the human heart than its opposite.

—Nelson Mandela, *Long Walk to Freedom*

The key to understanding why there is so much social strife in the world is linked to some basic physiological and social psychological phenomena associated with being human. Research on the human genome continues to reveal amazing findings about genetic variation among people. As scientists unravel the mysteries of the DNA code, they are gradually uncovering information that will help to explain why some people are more prone to particular diseases such as types of cancer.

Although deciphering the genetic code with its billions of sequences offers much promise for the treatment of disease through the customization of drugs and preventive behavior, there is little likelihood that a gene for the disease of hate and prejudice will be discovered. Yet, hate and prejudice are human diseases that have caused untold suffering throughout history. Despite the beliefs of some philosophers and theologians, there is scant evidence to support the existence of a human nature and a biological basis for hate and prejudice.

While there may seem to be a universal tendency to denigrate and disparage one another, there is nothing innate in humans, no bad seed, which predisposes them to hateful behavior. And perchance, in some future time, scientists discover a gene that influences hate or prejudice, this would not mean that mankind is irreparably flawed and doomed, because humans, unlike most other animals, have the capacity for higher-level thinking. This function of our brain enables us to learn from previous experiences, interpret social phenomena, and adjust our behavior to different social situations.

THE BRAIN AND BIOLOGY

Our understanding of the human brain is far from complete, but scientists have determined that certain regions are affected by and react differently to threat. The "primitive" part of our brain, the area that is older in an evolutionary sense because it triggers behavior designed to maintain the viability of the organism in the face of threat, is called the limbic system. As you may imagine, behaviors emanating from this center, which encompasses the amygdala, the hypothalamus and the hippocampus located above the right and left temples and in the medial temporal lobe of the brain, are direct or preconscious, because they are reflexive and impulsive in response to threats to our safety.

The relatively new field of social cognitive neuroscience is exploring the relationship between brain physiology, function, and human behavior. Researchers are attempting to chart the human brain through imaging techniques to determine which centers are related to automatic processes, and what types of behavior are associated with regions of the brain linked to control and volition. New findings are being reported every day as neurobiologists and psychologists devise experiments and techniques designed to identify regions of the brain that affect various forms of human behavior. Evidence is accumulating that points to an interaction of biological and learned processes that influence such behavior as acceptance, rejection, and prejudice toward others.[1]

Even if negative predispositions are found to reside in one's genes, people are capable of overriding such tendencies through learning socially acceptable behavior. Conversely, anti-social behavior, like that found in gangs and hate groups, also reflects socially derived responses to group norms which pressure people to conform to the prevailing values and behavior of given situations. In other words, people have the ability to make choices—free will—or at least they possess the potential for thoughtful, reflective, ethical decision making that could override innate biological predispositions if they were found to exist.

THE ECONOMIC INCENTIVE FOR PREJUDICE

Of paramount importance to this discussion, then, is not the possibility of the existence of a biological basis of human behavior, but the identification of those conditions that may influence or predispose people to engage in anti-social actions. Below are some theories about why people hate, but there is one overriding fact that must be identified as a principal source of social pathologies in modern society—the pursuit of materialism.

Perhaps more than any previous time in history, the mantra of man is consumerism. The value of virtually all commodities has come to reside in their existential material manifestation, which is to say, their intrinsic worth lies not in their function per se but in their symbolic importance. It is not so much the utilitarian value that is prized in a commodity as the acquisition of the product or service itself. In the consumerist society things are valued, hoarded, and discarded, supplanted by newer things that ignite insatiable acquisitive desires that perpetuate the cycle of consumption ad infinitum.

In a society predicated upon using and consuming, competition for commodities transforms human relationships into competitive struggles for power and privilege—the quest to obtain, use, and consume merchandise as an end in itself, what poet Allen Ginsberg referred to as "shopping for images."[2] Even human relationships are perverted, wherein individuals become objectified products akin to commodities, manipulated toward the end of maximizing one's personal satisfactions. Everything and everybody succumbs to the *Zeitgeist*: buy it, use it, and feel good.

This consumerist ethos is marked by competition that feeds upon the population like a scourge across the land. Human relationships are reduced to instrumental relationships where people are not intrinsically valued for themselves but for what they can bring to interactions to satisfy the personal needs of the competing parties. As the environment and resources are threatened by degradation and scarcity, people are themselves perceived as threats in the competition for goods and services. There arises an ethic of insincerity that poisons relationships because everyone's motives are questioned and suspect.

The "ulterior motive" becomes the watchword of our time. No one can be trusted. People who look and behave differently are targeted as pariahs, deviants, and unfit members of society. Such attitudes are reflected in contemporary race relations in the United States where the majority white population stigmatizes minorities, especially people of color, segregates, profiles, and harbors negative stereotypes about them, and keeps large numbers of black and Latino young males in cages like animals.

The reasons for such retrograde behavior are rarely verbalized to shield the deeper apprehensions the white majority has about people of color. They fear competition arising from the quasi-liberated minorities who, bolstered by laws and benevolent policies such as affirmative action, are increasingly poised to scale the ladder of success in their quest of tantalizing commodities.

But minorities' covetous desires, which imitate those of the majority—financial security and wallowing in the trough of materialism—is the foundation from which hate springs. It is this similarity of means and ends that pits them against each other in their pursuit of pleasure, or what sociologist Philip Slater called "the pursuit of loneliness."[3] If people of color did not aspire to be upwardly mobile and seek the resources heretofore controlled by whites, they would not be perceived as threats to the existing social order—an order dominated not only in numbers but in power and privilege by whites since the formation of this nation

Depictions of people of color as animal-like sub-humans and immigrants as aliens can be seen as attempts to justify the dehumanization of people who are competitors in the consumer society. Fear of the "other," especially the dark-skinned "other," is deeply embedded in our social system. It originated, as we have seen, over 500 years ago when European nation-states began exploring and exploiting the world for economic profit. But now, as then, the drive to conquer, dominate, control, and disparage people with different cultures and skin color from the majority is intricately woven into the fabric of our society.

It is normal for humans to feel uneasy when being thrust into new surroundings, encountering people from different social and cultural backgrounds. But the complexity of our society, indeed, the increasing pluralism around the world expedited by technological innovations in transportation and communication, is bringing people from different backgrounds together more regularly and on an unprecedented scale causing friction between new and more established groups. Such tension occurred in the United States in the early years of the nation and at the turn of the nineteenth and twentieth centuries. Then, as now, there was widespread opposition to immigration. Social movements arose, depicting immigrants as undesirable and genetically inferior to the white majority.

There is urgency in identifying and allaying the white public's fears about competition and the genetic "suitability" of people of color, because our nation is undergoing a demographic revolution which will, in less than 40 years, create a new majority of African-Americans, Latinos, Asians, Native Americans, Pacific Islanders, and biracial people. Awareness of this social transformation intrudes into the consciousness of the white population and produces a variety of responses. Some whites welcome the change, others react stoically, accepting the inevitable, while still others, whose numbers are small but growing from exposure to malignant propaganda on the Internet, close ranks and resort to diatribes and invectives reminiscent of Nazi racism, which culminated in the extermination of eleven million people deemed inferior and socially undesirable.

FEAR, HATE, AND PREJUDICE

It is human and natural to fear the unknown. It is a primitive trait of our ancestors who were faced with all sorts of threats and challenges to their survival. From wild animals to inhospitable climatic changes, to unknown terrain encountered when foraging for food and shelter, to migrations to new territories where they encountered strangers, they developed an inner compass that became imprinted in their brains that helped defend them against the unknown. The limbic system evolved into this center of activities tasked with protecting the body from external threats. A fear-based flight or fight reaction emerged to prepare humans for unknown contingencies that could pose a threat to their existence.

This "Triple F" reaction persists in modern humans and produces physiological changes in the body as it prepares the individual for an encounter with the unknown. Epinephrine and norepinephrine are secreted from adrenal glands located on the top of the kidneys and pumped into the blood to increase the heart rate, blood flow to muscles and the brain, and convert glycogen to glucose in the liver. When faced with perceived imminent threat, the neck stiffens, back arches, muscles tense in the arms and legs, and breathing increases—which is known as the Startle Reaction.

Barring a continued challenge to the viability of the person, this reaction dissipates in a few seconds once the initial shock is processed by the brain and more conventional, socially acceptable methods of handling conflict and change are implemented. The Startle Reaction is a natural self-defense mechanism that is biologically based. It differs from social psychological states such as hate and prejudice, which are learned responses and centered in the more recently evolved and contemplative region of the brain called the cerebral cortex and the frontal lobes.

THE SOCIAL SIDE OF HATE

It is important to distinguish between primitive reflexive reactions in response to sudden changes in one's environment from encounters with strangers and people from different cultural and ethnic groups. The former are spontaneous, unplanned, emotionless responses to change, while the latter are the product of thought processes that may culminate in prejudice and hostility toward a group or individual deemed inferior, unworthy, or undesirable. It is understandable to fear what may initially be perceived as a threat to the viability of the organism, but hating someone or something is a manifestation of higher order thinking that encompasses a range of emotions, thought processes, and value judgments that transcend primitive reactions.

Hating is intentional, volitional. It is the result of individual decisions that culminate in value judgments that express affinity for or dislike of something or someone. It is an emotional learned behavior derived from adverse experiences, transmitted through significant others (family, peers, friends), or the media, and heightened and perpetuated by stereotypical distortions and misrepresentations of individuals and groups perceived as unwanted and inferior.

The German-born psychologist Erich Fromm wrestled with the concepts of ethics, freedom, volition, and hate because he was affected by the devastation wrought by the Nazi regime. Fromm, reared as an orthodox Jew, emigrated to the United States in 1934. He distinguished between *rational* or *reactive hate*, which is a person's hatred toward something or someone that threatens one's freedom or integrity; and *character-conditioned hate,* which is irrational hate to destroy or cripple life. Character-conditioned hate is a continuing readiness to hate "… lingering within the person who is hostile rather than reacting with to a stimulus from without." According to Fromm, "The hating person seems to have a feeling of relief, as though he were happy to have found the opportunity to express his lingering hostility. One can almost see in his face the pleasure he derives from the satisfaction of his hatred."[4]

While *reactive hate* can impair human interaction and relationships, negative initial reactions can be modified and assuaged, much like those which trigger the Startle Reaction syndrome in the primitive centers of the brain, once the source of fear is explored and understood. Character-conditioned hate, however, is a learned, conditioned response that carries with it a set of values and behaviors as well as definitions that categorize and classify an individual or group in a negative pejorative view of the world. It has an emotional connotation that is resistant to change. While it may seem counter-intuitive, it can function to preserve the moral integrity of the individual or group, what sociologist Franklin H. Giddings called "consciousness of kind."[5] These feelings were expressed in nineteenth and twentieth century nationalistic movements that united majority populations along the lines of linguistics, culture, and heritage while stereotyping minorities within and without as aliens and undesirables. This trend was epitomized by Nazi Germany and is operative today in the nativistic movements of white supremacist anti-immigration organizations in the United States, Europe, Russia, and Scandinavia.[6]

The work of Theodore Adorno helped explain why some people discriminate against minorities. He and his colleagues posit the authoritarian personality type characterized by conformity and allegiance to controversial beliefs, intolerance and aggression toward non-believers, insecurity, superstition, male-dominated chauvinism, stereotypical thought patterns and scapegoating. While the concept has some heuristic value, its validity was questioned in subsequent research.[7]

No one is born hating another person or group. Jews and Muslims don't emerge from the womb with a genetic predisposition to hate one another any more than do blacks and whites, or Indians and Pakistanis. The Triple F Startle Reaction, which arises from the limbic system, may precipitate an initial reactive/defensive form of hate, but it has no intrinsic emotive affiliative meaning other than the fear of newness and change linked to a possible threat to the integrity of the self. On the other hand, the constellation of attitudes, beliefs, values, and concomitant behavior surrounding character-conditioned hate are derived from learning. There is no reflexive genetic need to hate another person or group. Such emotions and values are learned products of our culture, and they can be unlearned.

A central tenet of this chapter is that societal pressures emanating from economic competition for scarce resources create conditions conducive to the definition of others as competitors and adversaries. This theoretical construct, if valid, is particularly insidious because it combines elements of rational and character-conditioned hate, creating a hybrid form of prejudice that engenders characteristics about "the other." These sentiments coalesce into communal expressions that may rationalize behavior leading to policies and laws that are detrimental to minorities and immigrants and inimical to the long-term interests of society.

In the classroom, and on school and college campuses, they have been the source of conflict ranging from taunting to bullying that have erupted into violent confrontations among teachers, staff, and students. The fact that approximately half the students in public schools are of color, representing cultures that vary from the traditional Eurocentric method of speech, dress, comportment, and other behavioral digressions from "the norm," challenges the suitability of current educational curricula and teaching methods, and calls for a re-assessment of our approach to education to make it inclusive of all students, not just the declining white majority.

NOTES

1. For an overview of the field of social cognitive neuroscience, see: Matthew D. Lieberman, "Social Cognitive Neuroscience: A Review of Core Processes," *Annual Review of Psychology*, 58, 2007, pp. 259–289.

2. Allen Ginsberg, "A Supermarket in California," *Collected Poems 1947–1980*, N.Y.: Harper Collins, 1984.

3. Philip E. Slater, *The Pursuit of Loneliness*, Boston: Beacon Press, 1970.

4. Erich Fromm, *Man for Himself: An Enquiry into the Psychology of Ethics*, London: Routledge, 2002, p. 215. Originally published in 1947.

5. Franklin H. Giddings, *The Principles of Sociology: An Analysis of the Phenomena of Association and of Social Organization*, N.Y.: Macmillan and Company, 1896.

6. An excellent analysis of these trends is contained in Kenan Malik's *The Meaning of Race: Race, History and Culture in Western Society*, N.Y.: New York University Press, 1996. For a review of anti-immigration hate groups in the United States see the web site of the Southern Poverty Law Center at *www.intelligencereport.org*. Also, Kenneth S. Stern, *A Force Upon the Plain: The American Militia Movement and the Politics of Hate*, N.Y.: Simon and Schuster, 1996; Jeffrey Kaplan (ed.), *Encyclopedia of White Power: A Sourcebook on the Radical Racist Right*, Lanham, MD: Rowman & Littlefield Publishers, 2000; Howard J. Ehrlich, *Hate Crimes and Ethnoviolence*. Boulder, Colorado: Westview Press, 2009.

7. Theodore Adorno, et al., *The Authoritarian Personality*. New York: Harper and Brothers, 1950.

Chapter 7

Surviving White Culture

It is a peculiar sensation, this double-consciousness, this sense of always looking at one's self through the eyes of others, of measuring one's soul by the tape of a world that looks on in amused contempt and pity. One ever feels his two-ness, an American, a Negro; two souls, two thoughts, two unreconciled strivings; two warring ideals in one dark body, whose dogged strength alone keeps it from being torn asunder.

—W.E.B. Dubois, *The Souls of Black Folk, 1903*

While the demographic composition of the United States has undergone dramatic changes in the last few decades because of the increased diversity of our population, we should not assume that the attainment of notoriety, status, and recognition by some people of color negates the harsh reality of desperation and defeatism that permeates the lives of many. President Clinton's comments to a group of clergy in a White House gathering in 1998 were prescient: "In fifty years we know what we're going to look like, but we don't know what we're going to be like."

Even a superficial review of research yields the incontrovertible conclusion that people of color are widely discriminated against in this society (and others) on the basis of their skin tone. This finding is consistent across education, income, and class lines. It is painfully obvious in the residential segregation that has led to monochromatic neighborhoods in the nation's inner cities, job discrimination that has consistently contributed to a black unemployment rate double that of the white, educational experiences that have created and perpetuated an achievement and graduation gap between Asian and white students compared to blacks and Latinos, and disparities in health care that create morbidity and mortality rates for people of color far in excess of white rates, even controlling for social class (income, education, and occupation). Racism also plays a significant role in the way people of color are treated in the criminal justice system. They have higher rates of incarceration than whites, and their sentences are longer for the same crimes that whites commit.

A WORLD OF FALSE HOPES AND PROMISES

For people of color, even when they "make it," they often find themselves isolated at the top, surrounded by a sea of white faces who are either naïve about interacting with them or reticent about having a person of color equal to or higher than them in the pecking order. The old adage spoken by blacks, that to make it in America you have to work twice as hard as whites, still has traction. As journalist Ellis Cose[1] illustrated through interviews with "successful" African-Americans, one of the key dimensions of "making it" in a white-dominated society eluded them—acceptance. Novelist Philip Roth demonstrated in *The Human Stain* that color runs deep in a society obsessed with whiteness.[2] The darker the skin tone, the greater the difficulty being accepted by the dominant white majority.

Even people of color have been co-opted into a racist mindset that mimics the white supremacist ideology. Naïvely brainwashed into self-loathing by the dominant white Eurocentric culture, some try to lighten their skin, straighten their hair, and surgically alter facial appearances to approximate a European ideal of beauty that eludes them.

Whites, too, are manipulated by corporations, treating their bodies like commodities that can be bought and sold, discarded like clothes in the quest of an ideal that pushes reality beyond the boundaries of human variation. How ironic it is to hear white women longing for curly hair, and white sun-bathers competing for "best tan on the beach," using lotions and machines that damage their skin in a vain quest for the pigment that some of their black and brown brothers and sisters would gladly swap for their pallid complexion. Having power, however, allows whites to engage in such frivolous pursuits because they know their actions are mere digressions from a white Eurocentric norm that keeps people of color outsiders in an elusive quest for dignity and respect.

Though rational self-assured people of color aren't interested in changing their complexion by using skin lighteners, there is a market for these products, just as white women are prodded into purchasing billions of dollars of facial creams, rejuvenating lotions, Botox injections, and surgery to reduce wrinkles and regain a youthful appearance. Shampoos made to make the hair look flaxen and silky, straight or curly, wavy and undulating are featured in pictures splashed across television screens and the pages of magazines. They adorn billboards offering the promise of allure and attractiveness to heighten one's sexual desirability in the competition for that special mate who will be unable to resist the "Madison Avenue" look.

As the Dove Evolution Beauty campaign revealed, these models are part of a cruel hoax that fosters a false consciousness in women by creating a demand for looks that few people can attain:[3] having hair that shines so bright you need sunglasses to look at it, and skin so soft and wrinkle-free that it makes newborns look old. The goal of these corporations is to create an illusionary model based on scarcity and competition. A state of needs and demand for something that can never be attained is a salesman's paradise where goods can be developed and transformed through stylistic changes that pique the human penchant for commodities which can never be satiated. In the course of attempts to satisfy the insatiable, one group is pitted against another to obtain the increasingly unobtainable in a world filled with racial and class inequalities and antagonisms punctuated by depleting and mal-distributed resources. Sadly, teenage girls and women of color are two groups that are exploited through this "Madison Avenue" manipulation.[4]

But men, too, are not immune from this manipulation. How can one forget Malcolm X's description of "conking" (straightening) his hair by putting lye on his scalp and covering his head with a plastic bag while enduring excruciating pain for the sake of having "good hair."[5] Later, after becoming racially aware and autonomous, he recalled how demeaning and degrading the experience was. Yet, from the time of Madam C. J. Walker, in the early part of the twentieth century to the present, a mind-boggling array of hair and body products have been marketed to people of color to assist them in their quest for the unattainable Eurocentric image—one that eludes whites as well.

Madam Walker, the inventor of the straightening comb, parlayed her products into an empire and became America's first black millionaire, employing 10,000 women when she died in 1919.[6] Today's beauty products account for $34 billion in annual sales. Annual expenditures by African-Americans on health and beauty aids are 11.2 percent higher than all other ethnic groups and accounted for $9.5 billion in 2008.[7]

Women of color spend three times more on hair maintenance than white women, accounting for 30 percent of total hair product sales in the United States.[8] Sociologist Adia Harvey Wingfield puts the figures even higher, with black women spending $8.7 billion on hair relaxers in 2002 and $46.7 billion on ethnic hair care products and services sold and performed in salons a decade ago.[9]

Even the "My Black is Beautiful" campaign with its premise to "celebrate the diverse collective beauty of African-American women and encourage black women to define and promote their own beauty standard—one that is an authentic reflection of their indomitable spirit," has been co-opted for profit.

"Recognizing that beauty and self-confidence are intrinsically linked, 'My Black is Beautiful' is designed to ignite and support a sustained national conversation by, for, and about black women; the way they are reflected in popular culture and serve as the catalyst for a movement that affects positive change."

What noble objectives, but coming from Proctor and Gamble with ads for Pantene, Olay, Definity, and the Cover Girl Queen Collection on the bottom of the Manifesto page, one questions its sincerity and motivation. Beauty is big business. If black consciousness among African-American women leads to a rejection of Eurocentric standards of beauty, then the promotion of varying conceptions of blackness can be used to tap the African-American market, creating new, tantalizing models that can be dangled in front of women of color in their quest for recognition, self-confidence, and respect.

Our culture influences our choices and these affect race relations. Our market-driven ethos of materialism imperils social interaction. It adversely affects relationships between whites and people of color because it places human relationships on the shopping block where all groups compete for scarce commodities.

In our society, even children learn early that everything has a price. When basic human needs such as food, clothing, shelter, education, and health care are commoditized and regulated by a marketplace controlled by corporations whose bottom lines drip with glitz and greed, sincere human relationships become expendable in the rush to maximize self-interest.

Life becomes a matter of survival of the fittest where everyone is pitted against all in a never-ending struggle to obtain resources made scarce through marketing strategies that promote them as desirable, necessary, and priced as exclusive or bargains, depending on the targeted audience. While the product, price, and pitch may vary, the message is the same. A variety of strategies are used to convince the public that they should be independent, self-confident, and respected, all the while herding them like sheep into the consumption of goods and services that are not only superfluous but detrimental to their own lives, inimical to society's well-being, and degrading to the environment.

The latest fad to be subordinated to our culture of consumption is the "Green Revolution," which has people jumping over one another to purchase items that are reusable—to leave a lighter imprint on the environment. While public outrage and concern over our deteriorating environment is commendable and warrants direct action, little is being said or done about the real causes of environmental degradation: population growth and consumerist culture. In fact, the United States has yet to ratify the Kyoto Protocol, signed by over 180 nations, because it imposed requirements on signatories that would limit the production of greenhouse gases and, in the Bush Administration's perspective, stifle our economy (in its headlong rush to pollute the world).[10]

When people are forced to compete over basic human needs, and living becomes an extension of commoditization, life is reduced to a bazaar where everything is for sale at the "right" price. In such a social system, competition suffocates collaboration and sincere, meaningful relationships become suspect as people scramble for the satisfaction of their personal needs for survival. Manipulation of one another for these ends becomes standard operating procedure, acceptable and expected. As this ethic of insincerity pervades society, trust is sacrificed.

Human relationships become compartmentalized, regimented, and above all, instrumental. People view each other as objects to be manipulated—commodities used to maximize one's own needs and gratification in the quest for survival and comfort. Friends, even relatives, cannot be trusted, and professionalism and oaths of allegiance to one's country, employer, and clients are violated as if the words were little more than ethereal epithets mouthed by mythical deities in a make-believe world.

Can one blame anybody for being suspicious of the motives and intentions of people who commit acts of terror in schools, homes, and workplaces? Who violate the trust of employees and squander their retirement? Who rip off investors and charities in Ponzi schemes designed to prey on the greedy impulses nurtured by society? Who pledge secrecy and then divulge intimate details and pictures about business associates, employers, and lovers? Who swear oaths about upholding professional standards and knowingly falsify audits and flaunt ethics? Who pledge to provide the highest quality of care to clients and patients and deny them equal service and treatment based on their gender, sexual orientation, income, religion, ethnicity, or color?

In such a society, dominated by white Eurocentric traditions of beauty and culture, with a tradition of demonizing people of color for centuries, the alien "other" not only carries with it the stigma of being different, an outsider, but makes it easier for whites to dehumanize "them." They are viewed not only as inferior, but interlopers in the quest for elusive goods and services. In a word, they are the competition. In the zero-sum game that envelops everyone in the quest for fame and fortune, people of color are, by tradition and definition, unworthy and unwelcome contestants.

LEARNING TO HATE ONESELF

Most whites learn early in life that people who are different are deficient. Rodgers and Hammerstein's musical, *South Pacific*, written half a century ago is still apropos: "You've got to be carefully taught." Prejudice and racism are not genetically produced attributes of human nature; they are learned attitudes and behaviors, carefully constructed to preserve a system of power and privilege designed by whites over five hundred years ago.

The consequences of the tyranny of white supremacist ideology can be devastating. They are manifested in the internalization of racist beliefs and stereotypes that depict people of color as biologically and intellectually inferior to whites. The culture of whiteness in our society dominates the social and psychological landscape. It pervades what we see, read, and hear. It is omnipresent. Despite cultural intrusions of other ethnicities with their images, music, food, clothes, and myriad stimuli, white Eurocentric culture remains the standard against which all others are compared. It is what is thought to be desirable and acceptable, worshipped, and tantalizingly promised as attainable if one plays by the rules established by white society in schools and the community.

This cruel hoax has been used by white society to mislead and misdirect the energy and enthusiasm of people of color as they sought, often vainly, to capture the gold ring of the good life of materialism. The editorial pages of newspapers are replete with columns by conservative black pundits extolling the virtues of white society, decrying the failures of dysfunctional people of color, blaming their brothers and sisters for being victims, while they ignore the social system rigged against them.

For example, Shelby Steele, a leading conservative African-American writer and Senior Fellow at the Hoover Institution at Stanford University, launched a diatribe against affirmative action by noting inaccurately:

> Affirmative action has always been more about the restoration of legitimacy to American institutions than the uplift of blacks and other minorities. For 30 years after its inception, no one even bothered to measure its effectiveness in minority progress.
>
> But fortunately race relations in America are not much driven by the courts. We argue over affirmative action and disparate impact because we don't know how to talk about our most profound racial problem: the lack of developmental parity between blacks and whites. Today a certain contradiction runs through black American life. As many of us still suffer from deprivations caused by historical racism, we also live in a society where racism is simply no longer a significant barrier to black advancement—a society so sensitized that even the implication of racism, as in the Henry Louis Gates case, triggers a national discussion.

We blacks know oppression well, but today it is our inexperience with freedom that holds us back almost as relentlessly as oppression once did. Out of this inexperience, for example, we miss the fact that racial preferences and disparate impact can only help us—even if they were effective—with a problem we no longer have.[11]

Such writing, while it may appeal to the white majority, is full of contradictions and half truths. For example, although discrimination against people of color is still widespread, a considerable body of research reveals that it has had a salutary impact on affirmative action on women and minorities.[12] It is ironic that Steele's twin brother, a Stanford University psychologist, has become well-known for demonstrating how stereotypes perpetuate racist and sexist beliefs about presumed inferior intellectual abilities of women and minorities.[13]

Fortunately, most people of color recognize such doubletalk for what it is—political pandering for the sake of ingratiation and self-promotion, and they have not altered their allegiance to the Democratic Party. The 2008 Republican National Convention held in Minneapolis/St. Paul had just 36 African-American delegates—two percent of the total. But history teaches us that political alliances are fickle and can become expendable if they interfere with the white power structure.

Historian Ira Katznelson[14] demonstrated how ephemeral and tenuous were northern Democrats' commitments to improve the lives of African-Americans in the face of pressures by their southern colleagues to maintain Jim Crow culture and white hegemony over blacks in the South during the New Deal. Vestiges of laws and policies enacted then find expression in contemporary policies and legislation retarding equality and progress among African-Americans today.

The mind-numbing effects of white cultural domination are even more pernicious on children of color. Living in a society dominated by white images, even when alternative images and heroes are presented, such as musicians, movie stars, and athletes, children learn what is desirable, what is the standard against which they and everyone else will be compared, who has the resources and power to make things happen, and who really controls things. The proverbial "man" is not black, but white. Despite protestations to the contrary, they know who really has the juice.

One of the most devastating examples of the effects of white dominance on the psyche of children of color was demonstrated through the studies of psychologists Kenneth and Mamie Clark in the 1940s. Presenting plastic dolls of different colors to black children three to seven years old revealed that a majority of the children preferred white dolls. Even more troubling was their finding that many of the black children more closely identified with the white dolls and whiteness than with their own ethnic group. When asked to color in figures of boys and girls according to their own color, many dark-complexioned children colored the figures white or yellow.

The Clarks' research was used by the NAACP Legal Defense Fund in the historic *Brown vs. the Board of Education of Topeka* case in 1954 which led the Supreme Court to conclude that segregation was damaging the self-esteem of black children, and that prejudice, discrimination, and segregation were causing black children to develop a sense of inferiority and self-hatred. The Court concluded that "separate but equal" educational facilities were "inherently unequal."[15]

In the years following the Brown decision African-Americans made significant inroads into white society, but the balance of power and insidious domination of Eurocentric images remained, continuing its negative intrusion into the lives of black children, diminishing their self-esteem and deadening their enthusiasm. In 1985 another husband and wife team of African-American psychologists, Darlene Powell-Hopson and Derek Hopson reported similar findings to the Clarks when they replicated their doll experiment. Black children preferred white dolls in response to positive attributes such as good, smart, and pretty 65 percent of the time compared to 67 percent of the time in the Clarks' experiment. In 40 years there was virtually no change in the results. The Hopsons demonstrated, however, how positive comments about the black dolls reversed the initial selections of the children.[16]

In 2005, Kiri Davis, a 16-year-old African-American high school student created a national furor with her documentary film *A Girl Like Me*, which explored standards of beauty imposed on African-American girls by white dominated society. In a replication of the doll experiment, Davis found 16 of the 21 African-American children preferred the white doll when asked to select the "nice doll." Aside from black teenagers discussing the negatives associated with black physiological characteristics and their relatives' attempts to obtain lighter skin through bleaching, one of the most depressing moments of the film occurred when, after repeated negative associations with black dolls, Davis asked a child to select the one that looked like her. Reluctantly, almost surreptitiously, the child pushed the black doll forward.[17]

Philosopher George Yancy dissects the negative impact of a white-dominated society on African-Americans' sense of self. Their behavior and motivation are constantly scrutinized by an uncomprehending and disbelieving white population that is often incapable of acknowledging their worth and existence because, as philosopher Linda Martin Alcoff notes, whiteness is the measure of man in our society. This is the essence of white privilege.[18]

Africans, as philosopher Michelle Wright demonstrates, have, for more than three centuries, been relegated to the status of "the other"—being considered as outsiders, primitive, lacking free will, and the ability to govern themselves. It was the European tradition which cast blacks as different, even subhuman, in the work of Hegel, Kant, de Gobineau, and other pre- and even post-Enlightenment philosophers that led to stereotypes, which persist into modern time.[19]

In September 2009, I showed the Kiri Davis video to a group of nearly all-white teachers at a high school in New Jersey. The student body was composed of 85 percent African-Americans and had a graduation rate so low that some people in the community were suggesting that it be closed. A white woman who taught parenting in a health class eagerly affirmed its relevance to the students in the school. "We have animated dolls that the girls take home to care for. All of them are white except two black dolls. No one would take the black dolls home—not the white girls or the black girls. We had to counsel a black girl for six weeks until we got her to the point where she would accept the black doll."

A white middle-aged teacher then expressed amazement at that reaction and confessed that she couldn't fathom the behavior of the black teenagers in the film. "I never heard of the idea of blacks 'passing.'" The next day an African-American teacher said she never thought she would hear anyone openly discuss human's African origins in this way in her school and was incredulous about her colleague's remarks.

The school had 460 students and recorded 3,265 referrals to the principal's office for discipline the previous year, averaging 42.3 referrals per faculty member, with 414 out of school student suspensions and 28 for ten days or more. Four of the teachers accounted for nearly 800 discipline referrals. The youthful principal knew of the cross-cultural conflict between some of his older white staff and the young students of color, but he was reluctant to use the "nuclear option" of inviting them to retire. I had just concluded a presentation and found one of the teachers in his office admonishing him about the evils of my perspective. Considering the negative implications of leaving culturally inept and unqualified people in the classroom, wouldn't it be logical to explore ways of reducing the damage they are doing to our youth and the future of our nation?

BLAMING THE VICTIMS

Stereotype threat, a form of internalized racism, is a useful concept which helps us understand how imbalanced our culture has become. It explains why members of despised and stereotyped groups often embrace dominating negative conceptions of themselves. Psychologists have demonstrated the power of this concept in their study of African-Americans taking standardized tests. When the test was described as diagnostic, the students performed poorly because they subconsciously adhered to racial stereotypes about their intellectual inferiority. Without that admonition their performance was higher.[20]

Our society takes underperformance as evidence of inferiority and labels the victims of social stigma as deficient. In actuality, it is the persistence of a racist social milieu that reinforces negative images that become self-destructive and inimical to the mental and physical well-being of disadvantaged groups. We blame the victims for their deprived status even though it is thrust on them by a social system that, though purportedly fair and colorblind, contrives against them.[21]

Perhaps it was the continued degradation and dehumanization of African-Americans, especially women, that led Proctor and Gamble to create the "My Black is Beautiful" campaign. Recognizing that 71 percent of black women felt they were portrayed more negatively than women of other ethnic groups, P&G launched the movement to empower African-American women to establish their own standard of beauty. Of course, P&G stands ready to assist with a line of products designed exclusively for them.

Whites, too, are racism's victims. We don't need to periodically rediscover racism in our society. There is abundant evidence that testifies to its existence and effects on people of color. Aside from guilt-laden arguments that characterize them as uncaring oppressors with the morals of fruit flies, tangible societal ramifications emanate from the social and psychological deprivation of people of color.[22]

Think about the vast untapped resources that our society would have if people of color (and women, the differently-abled, GLBTs, religious, and ethnic minorities) were treated fairly with regard to educational and occupational opportunities. The magnitude of their contributions in the labor market is inestimable. What inventions and discoveries could be made if they were given equal access to the opportunities that white males have? Could there be a cure for cancer or diabetes? New forms of energy? What impact would their productivity have on our economy, such as tax revenue, consumption, and investments? How would the creation of wealth and equal opportunities affect government expenditures in Medicaid, food stamps, subsidies for education? What would be its impact on our criminal justice system?

Certainly, we could all benefit from the compassion and experiences of people of color in our society. If black and Latino children were nurtured to raise their aspirations, how would this affect unemployment and underemployment rates? Creating opportunities for oppressed groups of people is, in the end, a self-serving mission that would enhance the quality of life of everyone in society. The trick is to convince dominant whites that it is counter productive to perpetuate a two-tiered system of power and privilege that favors them at the expense of a growing multitude of "others." What prevents us from doing this? Why, in the face of such logic, do prejudice, discrimination, and racism persist? And what kind of school climate exists when teachers don't understand or value the diversity in their classrooms? When they are afraid of their students and dread going to work? When they put in the hours and go through the motions, pretending and masquerading to be doing work so vital to the well-being of society?

NOTES

1. Ellis Cose, *The Rage of a Privileged Class,* N.Y.: HarperCollins, 1993.

2. Philip Roth, *The Human Stain,* N.Y.: Vintage, 2001.

3. See the Dove Evolution video which exposes the manufacture of beauty at: *http://www.youtube.com/watch?v=hibyAJOSW8U.*

4. See: "Beauty at Any Cost: The Consequences of America's Beauty Obsession on Women and Girls," 2008, *http://www.ywcatriangle.org/pdf/ Beautypercent20atpercent20Anypercent20Cost.pdf.* Retrieved: 3/25/09. For insight into the world of beauty and African-American women see: Ingrid Banks, *Hair Matters: Beauty, Power, and Black Women's Consciousness,* N.Y.: New York University Press, 2000; Adia Harvey Wingfield, *Doing Business with Beauty: Black Women, Hair Salons, and the Racial Enclave Economy,* Lanham, Md.: Rowman & Littlefield Publishers, Inc., 2008.

5. Alex Haley, *The Autobiography of Malcolm X,* N.Y.: Ballantine Books, 1964, pp. 52–55.

6. See Wingfield, loc. cit., p. 33.

7. "Black Gold, Part II: Health and Beauty Categories are Untapped Mines in the African-American Market," Hunter-Miller Group, Inc., *Marketing Snapshot,* Issue 22, December, 2003; "Ethnic Hair, Beauty, Cosmetics in the United States, 2008," *TF Market Research. http:www.alacrastore.com/storecontent/markintel/ PACKAGED_Facts-59036979.*

8. Kendra Hamilton, "Embracing 'Black is Beautiful'—African-American Involvement in Fashion Industry, and Consumer Spending on Apparel and Beauty Care Products," *BNET Business Network,* January 4, 2001.

9. Wingfield, op. cit. p. 36.

10. At a United Nations international conference on climate change held in Copenhagen in December, 2009, the countries could not reach an accord and agreed to continue discussions for another year. For reports and information on the conference go to: *http://unfccc.int/2860.php.*

11. Shelby Steele, "Affirmative Action is Just a Distraction," *The Washington Post,* July 26, 2009 at: *http://www.washingtonpost.com/wp-dyn/content/article/2009/07/24/ AR2009072402090.html?sid=ST2009072403325.* Retrieved 2/01/10.

12. For reviews on this point see: Barbara Bergmann, "The Continuing Need for Affirmative Action," *Quarterly Review of Economics and Finance*, 39, no. 5, pp. 757–768; Harry J. Holzer and David Neumark, "Assessing Affirmative Action," *Journal of Economic Literature*, 38, September, 2000, pp. 483–568; Harry J. Holzer and David Neumark, "What Does Affirmative Action Do?" *Industrial and Labor Relations Review*, 53, no. 2, pp. 240–271; Francine D. Blau, Marianne A. Ferber, and Anne E. Winkler, *The Economics of Women, Men and Work*, Englewood Cliffs: Prentice-Hall, 2002; Terry H. Anderson, *The Pursuit of Fairness: A History of Affirmative Action*, N.Y.: Oxford University Press, 2004; Harry J. Holzer and David Neumark, eds., *The Economics of Affirmative Action*, London: Edward Elgar, 2004.

13. Claude Steele, "Thin Ice: 'Stereotype Threat' and Black College Students," *The Atlantic Monthly*, August, 1999, pp. 44–54.

14. Ira Katznelson, *When Affirmative Action was White*, N.Y.: W.W. Norton, 2005.

15. See: Kenneth B. Clark and Mamie P. Clark, "Emotional Factors in Racial Identification and Preference in Negro Children," *Journal of Negro Education*, vol. 19, #3 (Summer 1950): 341–350; Kenneth B. Clark, *Prejudice and Your Child*, Second edition, Boston, Beacon Press, 1963.

16. Darlene Powell-Hopson and Derek Hopson, *Different and Wonderful: Raising Black Children in a Race-Conscious Society*, N.Y.: Prentice-Hall, 1990.

17. The documentary is available at: *http://video.google.com/videoplay?docid= 1091431409617440489&ei=ge0S5yCJIz-qALe9oCzCw&q=Kiri+davis+a+girl+ like+me&hl=en#*. On May 25, 2010, CNN ran a story on the Anderson Cooper Show about a similar experiment which yielded similar results using pictures of different color dolls. See: *http://www.cnn.com/2010/us/05/18/doll.study.parents/index.html*.

18. George Yancy, *Black Bodies, White Gazes*, Lanham, Md.: Rowman & Littlefield Publishers, Inc., 2008. See especially his discussion of Toni Morrison's *The Bluest Eye*, N.Y.: Holt, Rinehart and Winston, 1970, for the negative impact of dominant whiteness on the African-American psyche in chapter 6 "Desiring Bluest Eyes, Desiring Whiteness: The Black Body as Torn Asunder."

19. Michelle M. Wright, *Becoming Black: Creating Identity in the African Diaspora*, Durham, N.C.: Duke University Press, 2004.

20. Claude Steele and Joshua Aronson, "Stereotype Threat and the Intellectual Performance of African-Americans," *Journal of Personality and Social Psychology*, 1995, 69:797–811.

21. See William Ryan, *Blaming the Victim*, N.Y.: Vintage Books, 1976.

22. See for example Benjamin P. Bowser and Raymond G. Hunt, *Impacts of Racism on White Americans*, (eds., second edition), Thousand Oaks, Cal., Sage Publications, 1996, and Nathan Rutstein's formula for transcending these negative effects in *Racism: Unraveling the Fear*, Washington, D.C.: The Global Classroom, 1997.

Chapter 8

You Have to be Carefully Taught

Learning about Race and Racism

What good fortune for those in power that the people do not think.

—Adolf Hitler

ECONOMIC MYOPIA

White skin gives white people advantages over people of color, but sometimes they are even willing to forego societal and personal benefits for the
sake of keeping power. Rather than educate, train, hire, and promote people
of color, treating them on an equal footing with white men and women, public
schools, universities, and the corporate world cling to myths and stereotypes
about them. They are depicted as lazy, indolent, violent, less ambitious, and
intellectually inferior to whites. Even when their own economic interests
are threatened, whites persist in perpetuating policies that enforce racial disparities in education and health care, lending and housing, incarceration, and
commerce. The paucity of people of color in positions of power and influence
in the nation's businesses and political institutions testifies to the enduring
discrepancies that signify discrimination in our society.

To many whites in positions of power, it matters little that people of
color possess the same genetic material as they do, or that they have been
reared in the same capitalist ideology which extols the virtue of consumption and materialism. The extremes to which such power plays can go
came to light in one of the most competitive areas of our culture: professional football. Marlon Briscoe was an All-American African-American

football player at the University of Omaha. Briscoe had been an outstanding quarterback in college, but no African-American had broken the color barrier at that position when he was drafted by the Denver Broncos in 1968.

The Broncos wanted Briscoe to play cornerback, but he managed to get a tryout at quarterback in training camp. Broncos' management labored under the mythology which questioned black leadership ability and denied him the opportunity to play quarterback until their starter, Steve Tensi, was injured. Briscoe was tapped as his replacement and improved the team's performance over the previous season, playing in eleven games, including seven starts, setting a Broncos' rookie quarterback record of 14 touchdowns, and finishing second in the ballot for rookie of the year.

Assuming he had secured the position, he returned to Omaha to complete coursework for his undergraduate degree when he received a call from his cousin who lived in Denver. He was shocked to learn that the team had signed a quarterback from Canada and was having quarterback meetings in the off-season without him. Briscoe never played the position again.[1]

Maybe it's progress or symptomatic of our times, but forty years later another black quarterback, Michael Vick, was resurrected from ignominy by the Philadelphia Eagles after serving 18 months in prison for running a dog fighting ring. Though fan sentiment was running against his reinstatement in the National Football League, Eagles management chose to offer him a two-year contract starting at $1.6 million for his first season with a $5.2 million option for the second year.

In this case, the profit motive trumped indignation. Public opposition to Vick's rehabilitation was ironic, given the fact that dozens of NFL players have been arrested for felonies, many multiple times. One analysis counted 308 arrests of NFL players between 2000 and 2007 with convictions, diversions, and fines in 68 percent of the cases. Fifty of the players were multiple offenders including two players with five arrests, two with four, and twelve with three. The most common charges were drunken driving (32 percent), fights, assaults and disorderly conduct (21 percent), domestic violence/violence against women (17 percent); drug-related offenses (13 percent) and gun-related incidents (8 percent).[2]

A *Washington Post* study of felony charges against NFL players in 2006 revealed similar findings including arrests for possession of concealed firearms, aggravated assault, resisting arrest, discharging a firearm, vandalism, trespassing, fleeing and eluding a police officer, and reckless driving.[3]

Here's how one of my African-American undergraduate students viewed these events:

Two years ago my favorite athlete, Michael Vick, was arrested and charged with animal cruelty. To me this really showed me how racist our society is. Vick and some friends had a dog fighting ring that resulted in some dogs getting hurt or even executed, and this caused Vick to have to go to prison. I don't feel as if him going to prison was about the dogs. I feel like the only reason he was incarcerated was because he was a successful black man. People run dogs over all the time and nothing is done about it, but because this is Michael Vick the judge felt as if this were some heinous crime.

White people go hunting and kill all sorts of animals and are never charged with no kind of crime. The whites actually have television shows, commercials and all sorts of achievements that promote the killing of animals, but nobody seems to have any problems with this. I've been in places where white people had deer heads mounted on their walls glorifying what they've killed, but I don't see any of them going to prison or jail. This young man had to spend two years of his life behind bars for crime that happens everyday by opposite races and are not penalized.

—Darius Travis

While Vick's case was unique because no NFL player had served such a lengthy prison sentence and returned to play, the public's outrage over his abuse of animals in the light of violence perpetrated against women, other citizens, and police officers by his peers causes one to wonder whether race played a role in the decisions of owners and the public's treatment of him. This paradox was accentuated by the comparatively minor punishment meted out to Ben Roethlisberger, the white quarterback of the Pittsburgh Steelers, for alleged sexually assaulting a 21-year-old woman in a Georgia bar in March 2010—the second such allegation against him in two years (a six-game suspension for the 2010 NFL season reduced to four if he undergoes counseling).

The lack of public discourse about racism makes it difficult to gauge whether this was the case, or for that matter, countless other incidents which people of color assume are racist while whites ignore or disdainfully label them as "playing the race card." There is, however, abundant evidence of racism and exploitation of black athletes in professional sports.[4] Black athletes in other countries have had to endure humiliating public displays of racism. Dark-skinned soccer players have been jeered, called monkeys, pelted with bananas, and screamed at by monkey-imitating fans throughout Great Britain and the European continent. FIFA, the international regulatory agency for soccer, enlisted the support of professional players to suppress racial slurs and violence through an anti-racist campaign that has had some success. A more effective measure both there and in the United States would be to limit fan access to alcoholic beverages.

EVERYDAY RACISM

The scars that racism leaves are indelibly etched on the psyches of its victims, just as sexual discrimination, homophobia, ableism, and all the other -isms that warp our lives, spread anger, fear, discontent, and self-loathing, and sometimes explode into violence against others and ourselves. Everyday racism, the kind expressed in casual affairs that reflect rudeness and crudity, or behavior which can be interpreted as insensitive and uncaring can be shrugged off by dominant whites as an aberration or overreaction by people of color who are overly sensitive, because they do not have to live with the continued barrage of petty insults hurled in their face each day.[5]

When it comes to defining behavior as racist, a chasm exists between whites and people of color in their perception of motives and intent. Many people of color assume white behaviors are intentionally demeaning and dehumanizing while whites profess their innocence and disbelief of such accusations. This situation creates individual and social paranoia because, with the exception of blatant hate crimes, the victims of everyday racism are often uncertain about the true cause of the unwanted behavior. They are left, based on prior experience and assumptions about the dominant culture, to presume white culpability.

After studying personal journals about racial events recorded by over 600 white college students at 30 schools around the United States, sociologists Leslie Houts Picca and Joe Feagin concluded that many whites discuss racial matters in racially mixed situations differently than when they are exclusively with whites. Drawing on concepts enunciated by sociologist Erving Goffman,[6] they contend that whites have front stage (disingenuous politically correct) and backstage (candid racist) ways of communicating and behaving that reflect the fractured race relations in the United States.[7]

Since the FBI began collecting hate crime statistics in 1990, there have been noticeable trends with occasional spikes like that following the 9/11 terrorist attack on New York City. In recent years the number of reported hate crimes in the United States, according to data submitted voluntarily by police departments around the nation, has been averaging around 7,500 annually. But in 2005, the Bureau of Justice Statistics of the United States Department of Justice reported results of household interviews with over 20,000 people which indicated the number of annual hate crimes approximated at nearly 200,000.[8]

These self-reported events may be subject to varying interpretations. What one person perceives to be an insult may be another's definition of a hate crime. We can never know the complete circumstances surrounding these situations, but perception is reality. Clearly, many Americans believe that they have been victimized because of some particularistic characteristic they possess, the color of their skin, their ethnicity, religion, physical appearance, sexual orientation, and myriad other factors. The sheer number of these purported offenses, most revolving around race, is indicative of a pervasive discontent roiling the fabric of American society, and this unrest is increasingly finding expression in negative, even racist sentiment against President Obama.

Looking at disparities between whites and people of color inevitably presages the question why whites do not take more dramatic action to improve dark-skinned peoples' substandard health care, inferior education, and job discrimination; why they refuse to live near them; and why many whites advocate and tolerate putting large numbers of young black and brown men in cages. Attorney General Holder may have hit the nail on the head—in their complacency about or habituation to racism, to business as usual, have whites become so inured to discrimination that they no longer see or recognize it, or just don't care?

THE MORAL VACUUM

Dante wrote that "The darkest places in hell are reserved for those who remain neutral in times of moral crisis." Holocaust survivors will tell you that they have the most contempt for bystanders, those individuals who stood by while their fellow human beings' lives were ripped apart. In acts of genocide, as in war itself, the enemy is depicted as inferior, even subhuman. Is that the way whites think about people of color? If so, how did this mindset arise? And what other factors might have contributed to the treatment and conceptualization of people of color as a group that should be viewed with anxiety, suspicion, repulsion, and denigration?

What is revealing is whites' adherence to centuries-old myths about their natural superiority and the subhuman characteristics of people of color. Genetic similarities among people are still superseded by color because the tenets of white supremacy permeate the minds and spirits of residents, white and black alike. From our earliest states of cognition we are bombarded with a vast array of physical and mental stimuli that perpetuate color inequality through the forced internalization of white European characteristics of beauty and behavior which, in turn, become normative standards. The most powerful methods of perpetuating this white racist hegemony are through the domination of the media that envelops our psyches in a cascade of images that reinforce white superiority.

From fairy tales to comics, magazines to books, radio to movies, we are taught that what is white is right and desirable. Conversely, white controlled and dominated media reinforce and perpetuate a cycle of tyranny which demeans and debases that which is different from the dominant culture. It matters not that whites account for less than a sixth of the world's population, or that billions of dollars are generated through entertainment (sports, videos, music, intellectual works) by people of color; entrenched white standards are still understood to be normative. Other styles are looked to as escapes, amusement, digression, alternatives—but at bottom, aberrations and deviations, much as minstrel shows and contemporary black comedians, musicians, and athletes demarcate the bounds of acceptability for the dominant white culture.[9]

Whites are also captives to their materialistic culture, which emphasizes conformity and consumption over cooperation and collaboration. We are all pawns, players in a game whose outcome has been preordained based on skin color and class. From the time we become aware of our environment, the rules of the game are taught to us by our parents, relatives, and friends and reinforced through the media.

"Don't do that!" "Don't go there!" "Don't play with him!" "Don't trust them!" A society that teaches to distrust one another's motives and intent creates an ethic of insincerity and a culture of disingenuousness. The optimal working assumption that governs human relationships is the phrase "getting one over" on somebody. People are simultaneously obsessed and parallelized by the prospect of being manipulated for the satisfaction of someone's personal agenda. In this environment, human relationships are up for grabs creating an enormous market of things and ideas that are ritually and daily prostituted in a world that places commodities and things above feelings. Lasting personal relationships have the permanence of evaporating snowflakes.

Consumerism trumps caring and compassion, and in the struggle to perpetuate one's own and class advantages, the poor and dispossessed, who are disproportionately people of color, are relegated to and kept in a disadvantageous position. The perpetuation of racism and poverty is fundamental to a capitalist system that preys on the less fortunate in a climate of mutual distrust and competition.

In such a climate, myths and stereotypes depicting and denigrating "the other" as intellectually inferior, rapacious, predatory, animalistic, and subhuman flourish as the tyranny of these concepts justify the status quo. In such a predatory social system, on the socioeconomic ladder leading to upward mobility, the residents of each rung fear upward mobility from the one beneath, for their progress threatens to displace them. That is why the concept of trust becomes a victim of materialism and competition—superfluous, unimaginable, expendable, and even burdensome.

Simple, protective phrases come to dominate our thinking about the people around us, especially people who do not look or sound like us. They are the "aliens" among us, the different ones who are not to be associated with or trusted. Sociologists Debra Van Ausdale and Joe Feagin provide insight into how early the indoctrination process begins. Children in a day care center for three and four year olds were observed: "Carla, a three-year-old child, is preparing herself for resting time. She picks up her cot and starts to move it to the other side of the classroom. A teacher asks what she is doing. 'I need to move this,' explains Carla. 'Why?' asks the teacher. 'Because I can't sleep next to a nigger,' Carla says, pointing to Nicole, a four-year-old Black child on a cot nearby. 'Niggers are stinky. I can't sleep next to one.'"[10]

The message of distrust and manipulation is so pervasive that it not only applies to minorities, but whites as well, creating a culture of disbelief reinforced by outrageous offenses and miscarriages of justice perpetrated by psychopathic and sociopathic personalities (Columbine, Virginia Tech, John Benet Ramsay, Timothy McVeigh, 9/11, the aftermath of Hurricane Katrina, Bernard Madoff, the financial collapse of 2008, the BP oil spill of 2010). These teach us to distrust one another, but especially to fear and loathe "the others" among us whose very presence threatens our social status, financial security, and the status quo because they want a piece of our pie.

DEMONIZING LATINOS

The increasing number of hate groups in the United States, now estimated near a thousand by the Southern Poverty Law Center, has been fueled by the influx of Mexicans who account for 55 percent of undocumented workers in the country. But contrary to the rhetoric spewed on hate web sites, these immigrants, like most before them, have come in search of a better life through jobs, not welfare. Yet, government agencies and even presidential candidates refer to them as aliens. To his credit, John McCain chastised some of his jingoistic colleagues for overlooking immigrants' humanity in their zeal to send them home.[11]

Unfortunately, many Americans fail to see new immigrants as fellow human beings. A national representative public opinion poll of 1,038 people conducted in October 2009 by CNN and the Opinion Research Corporation showed how deeply distrustful and resentful the majority was of this new minority. When asked how much discrimination Latinos were experiencing in getting good paying jobs, 57 percent said a lot or some, yet in 1990, 67 percent gave those responses. Nearly one in five respondents assumed that an unknown Latino man or woman in their neighborhood were here illegally. These responses are more intelligible when we consider the low reported rates of interaction the respondents had with people from other ethnic groups—54 percent said they had little or no contact with Latinos, a third had similar limited experiences with blacks, and 54 percent reported little or no interaction with Asians.[12]

While the American public has been fed a steady diet of misinformation about the impact of the new wave of Latino immigration on our society, scholars are generally in agreement that, prior to the economic collapse of 2007–2009, it did not lead to higher unemployment among the native-born population. In fact, Latinos often took jobs in industries such as agriculture, meat processing, construction, leisure and hospitality, and manufacturing that were unfilled. Between 2000 and 2004 there was a positive correlation between the increase in the foreign-born population and the employment of native-born workers in 27 states and the District of Columbia, accounting for two-thirds of all native-born workers. The share of foreign-born workers in the workforce of a state was not related to the employment rate of a state, and no evidence was found that poorly educated immigrant workers between the ages of 25–34 adversely affected their American counterparts.[13]

The economic downturn of 2007–2009 had a dramatic negative effect on the employment rate of Hispanic workers causing an increase in their unemployment from 5.1 percent in the fourth quarter of 2007 to 8 percent in the fourth quarter of 2008 compared to an unemployment rate increase for all persons from 4.6 percent in the fourth quarter of 2007 to 6.6 percent in the fourth quarter of 2008. African-Americans remained the only major racial group with double digit unemployment rates—11.5 percent in the fourth quarter of 2008.[14]

As the recession worsened in 2009 the national unemployment average reached 10.2 percent while the black unemployment rate surged to 15.6 percent, with the Hispanic rate reaching 12.7 percent compared to the white rate of 9.3 percent and Asians at 7.3 percent. While the unemployment rate for college graduates was lower overall for both blacks and whites, the white rate of 4.3 percent was 1.5 percentage points lower than black college graduates' rate of 5.8 percent. The racial unemployment rate gap was particularly pronounced between white high school graduates, 9.1 percent, compared to black high school graduates at 15 percent. Congresswoman Maxine Waters of California attributed these disparities to racism: "We don't like to talk about it, but there's still discrimination in our society. Black college graduates can't get professional jobs as easily as whites. We have blacks disguising their voices on the telephone or trying to hide their blackness in responding to job announcements. It's real."[15]

Latinos weren't faring well during the recession. The Southern Poverty Law Center, one of the nation's preeminent civil rights organizations, released a report in 2009 detailing the deplorable treatment low income Latinos were receiving in the South. Noting that the region is the home of the fastest growing population of Latinos in the nation, the report documented widespread hostility, discrimination, and exploitation toward them.

They are routinely cheated out of their earnings and denied basic health and safety protections. They are regularly subjected to racial profiling and harassment by law enforcement. They are victimized by criminals who know they are reluctant to report attacks. And they are frequently forced to prove themselves innocent of immigration violations, regardless of their legal status.

This treatment—which many Latinos liken to the oppressive climate of racial subordination that blacks endured during the Jim Crow era—is encouraged by politicians and media figures who scapegoat immigrants and spread false propaganda. And as a result of relentless vilification in the media, Latinos are targeted for harassment by racist extremist groups, some of which are directly descended from the old guardians of white supremacy.[16]

Journalist Kenan Malik described a similar dehumanizing process on the European continent nearly two decades ago, where immigrants were socially, psychologically, and institutionally relegated to second class citizenship, even labeled as unfit and inferior. Faced with the rising tide of immigrants from the Middle East and developing African nations, a wave of anti-immigrant hysteria, similar to the situation in the United States today, rolled across England, France, the Netherlands, and Scandinavia, fed by myths, stereotypes and misinformation, and eventuating in policies and laws designed to suppress immigrants and their "alien" culture.[17]

In our culture of disbelief, where images come to dominate our visions of one another and money is the measure of one's success, people who have the "goods" are labeled as desirable and worthy, while the less successful are disparaged and denigrated as failures. Social Darwinism, the legacy of the English sociologist Herbert Spencer, is alive and well and lies within the psyche of every man, woman, and child reared in a society that extols the virtues of meritocracy—where brotherhood and sisterhood are preached on Sundays but racism, sexism, ableism, and homophobia are practiced during the week.

Ideas have a powerful impact on culture, even when they are fallacious. As Joseph Goebbels, Hitler's Minister of Propaganda declared, "If you tell a lie big enough and keep repeating it, people will eventually come to believe it." The foundation of the origin of race is built on lies, half-truths, and misconceptions.

Some of the myths and stereotypes that are used to justify white privilege and racism are expressed in jokes and stereotypes about people of color. They influence our interactions and impede social justice. While they may bring a chuckle or knowing nod among whites (and even people of color) sometimes the line of decency and probity is crossed, as radio host Don Imus learned in 2007 when he made a disparaging remark about black women on the Rutgers University basketball team.

There are demons that swirl around in our heads—the ones that were put there by our families, friends, and society. These ideas cause us to question and doubt strangers, friends, and colleagues of another hue. Their existence challenges our self-concept and mocks our protestations about fairness and equality. In schools, as society, they are a disease that infects the minds of students and staff causing self-doubt, inhibiting learning, fracturing relationships, leading to conflict and academic failure. Educators must strive to reverse the negativity which emanates from the false consciousness that engulfs students of color in a shroud of stereotypes preventing them from becoming productive members of our society. Our final chapter offers suggestions for improving the prospects of all students and society through dialogue and community service.

NOTES

1. Personal communication with Marlon Briscoe. Also, see: "The Field Generals," *http://www.fieldgenerals.com/press-aol.htm*; William C. Rhoden, *Third and a Mile: The Trials and Triumphs of the Black Quarterback*, N.Y.: ESPN Books, 2007, chapter four.

2. See: *http://www.nbaboards.net/index.php?showtopic=2429&mode=threaded& pid=14618*.

3. See: *http://www.washingtonpost.com/wp-srv/sports/nfl/longterm/2006/nfl _chart_12162006.html*.

4. See John Hoberman, *Darwin's Athletes*, Boston: Houghton Mifflin, 1997, and more recently William C. Rhoden, *Forty Million Dollar Slaves*, N.Y.: Crown Publishers, 2006.

5. See Annie S. Barnes, *Everyday Racism*, Naperville, Ill.: Sourcebooks, Inc., 2000, for examples of these insults.

6. *The Presentation of Self in Everyday Life*. N.Y.: Anchor Books, 1959.

7. Leslie Houts Picca and Joe R. Feagin, *Two-Faced Racism: Whites in the Backstage and Frontstage*, N.Y.: Taylor and Francis, 2007. In a similar approach, Eduardo Bonilla-Silva constructed a typology of white methods of conversing about race that mask their feelings. See his *Racism Without Racists: Color-Blind Racism and Racial Inequality in Contemporary America*, Third edition, Lanham, MD.: Rowman & Littlefield Publishers, 2010.

8. Caroline Wolf Harlow, "Hate Crime Reported by Victims and Police," Bureau of Justice Statistics, Special Report, U.S. Department of Justice, Office of Justice Program, November, 2005, NCJ 209911.

9. See John Harvey's unique history of blackness and its influence on fashion in *Men in Black*, Chicago: The University of Chicago Press, 1995. For interesting analyses at the way language and symbols affect our perceptions of one another see: Bob Blauner, "Talking Past Each Other: Black and White Languages of Race," *The American Prospect*, 10, 1992:55–64 and Wayne Martin Mellinger, "Postcards from the Edge of the Color Line: Images of African-Americans in Popular Culture, 1893–1917," *Symbolic Interaction*, 15, 1992, pp. 413–433.

10. Debra Van Ausdale and Joe Feagin, *The First R*, Lanham, MD.: Rowman and Littlefield Publishers, 2001, p. 1. Cf. Shankar Vedantam's explanation for such phenomena in children, which he ascribes to hardwiring biological impulses in *The Hidden Brain*, N.Y.: Spiegel and Grau, 2010.

11. On April 23, 2010, Arizona governor Jan Brewer signed the nation's toughest bill on illegal immigration into law which actually delegates authority to law enforcement to detain people suspected of being illegally in the United States. The law makes it a crime for failing to carry immigration documents. Ironically, Senator John McCain, in a tough re-election battle, endorsed the law. See *www.nytimes.com.*

12. CNN Opinion Research Corporation Poll, October 16–18, 2009.

13. Rakesh Kochar, "Growth in the Foreign-Born Workforce and Employment of the Native Born," PEW Hispanic Center, Washington, D.C. August 10, 2006. See also Roger Lowenstein, "The Immigrant Equation," *The New York Times Magazine*, July 9, 2006: 38–43, 69–71; Daniel Altman, "Shattering Stereotypes about Immigrant Workers," *The New York Times*, June 3, 2007: 4.

14. Rakesh Kochar, "Unemployment Rose Sharply Among Latino Immigrants in 2008," PEW Hispanic Center, Washington, D.C. February 12, 2009.

15. David Goldman, "Black Unemployment 'A Serious Problem,'" CNN Money, December 4, 2009 at: *http://money.cnn.com/2009/12/04/news/economy/black _unemployment/index.htm.* Retrieved on 12/10/2009.

16. Mary Bauer, *Under Siege: Life for Low-Income Latinos in the South*, Southern Poverty Law Center, April, 2009, Montgomery, Alabama, p. 4.

17. Kenan Malik, *The Meaning of Race: Race, History and Culture in Western Society*, N.Y.: New York University Press, 1996.

Chapter 9

Thinking about Race

We can at least try to understand our own motives, passions and prejudices, so as to be conscious of what we are doing when we appeal to those
of others. This is very difficult, because our own prejudice and emotional
bias always seem to us so rational.

—T.S. Eliot

It can be difficult, even painful, to write about or question our motivation and
judgment of people of color, even risky lest we be misinterpreted as inveterate racists or foolishly naïve. Yet, to avoid revealing the scars that racism has
left on our personalities and society would be a disservice to ourselves and
others who have to wrestle with the same questions and conflicts. Hopefully,
readers may find some enlightenment and solace in the words that follow, and
will join us on the journey toward creating an inclusive society.

A LIFE LESSON

There's a story about a little boy who grew up in a northeastern city not
unlike many large urban cities around the nation. It had a diverse population
with a large black inner city surrounded by nearly all-white suburbs. The
urban ghetto teemed with life but its streets were strewn with litter and lined
with dilapidated houses. Some white folks said that the blacks preferred to
live there amidst the squalor, but the little boy wondered why anyone would
choose those conditions over the neat rows of homes with their green lawns
and tall trees where he lived.

Summer days were hot and unpleasant in this city, and the little boy would watch the black children gleefully swimming and diving in city pools through the windows of his family's car as it sped through the inner part of the city. But he never said a word. He just watched and listened and absorbed the sights and sounds like a sponge—ingesting and digesting words, ideas, and information.

He was three years old before he spoke his first word. It had something to do with food because eating was his favorite pastime. You could tell by his girth that he didn't miss any meals. And his parents encouraged him by flying in heaping spoons of food on make-believe airplanes. Around that time he put his first sentence together. It was a request that not only reflected his fondness for another favorite activity, but symbolized the power of learning and its relationship to prejudice: "Let's go see the jigaboos in the water."

Those words could have been uttered today virtually anywhere in this country—even at a country club in Pennsylvania. But they were not. They were my words, my first sentence, spoken in 1947, when I lived in Newark, New Jersey. And despite enormous progress made in race relations, more than half a century later, this nation and I are still wrestling with their implication.

Nobody is born a bigot. Stereotypes and prejudice are learned responses to differences. We all have personal preferences and tastes and some may even have genetic linkages such as preferences for sweets, but there is no genetic predisposition for skin color, ethnicity, or social class. These categories of human genetic and social variation are social constructs—created by humans. The only power and significance they have are what we bestow on them.[1]

For example, what did you think the little boy looked like? Was he light- or dark-skinned? What color was his hair? Was he the "All-American" blonde boy with blue eyes depicted in the Norman Rockwell paintings of the time? What does an All-American child look like today?

WHITE POWER/WHITE DOMINANCE

The images that are conjured up in response to these questions will depend in part on your life experiences and ethnic background. But the sheer weight of the dominant culture with its emphasis on white as normal will, even in the case of people of color, often evoke images of stereotypical blonde- or red-headed children. The power of the white-dominated society reverberates through the lives of everyone who resides here—black, brown, yellow, red, or white. Its reach is inescapable. Its effect may be deadening and demeaning.

The doll experiments reveal how the dominant white culture affects the lives of children of color in the United States. Despite the passage of time and significant advances made by African-Americans in our society—entertainment, sports, politics, business, education, science—vestiges of these attitudes remain and intrude into the psyches of all residents regardless of color and ethnicity. When Kwame Ture (Stokley Carmichael) coined the term "Black Power" in the '60s, black writers and activists like H. Rap Brown, Eldridge Clever, Amiri Baraka (Leroi Jones), and the Black Panther Party stood defiantly against traditional white values and domination, and they were labeled as communists and anarchists and targeted by law enforcement.

The Black Power movement reached an epiphany in the 1968 Summer Olympic Games protest of John Carlos and Tommie Smith, when they raised their clenched hands in a black power salute and show of solidarity on the dais as they received their medals for the 200 meter race. What disturbed whites most of all was the growing audacity of blacks to protest vestiges of Jim Crow traditions in the South and de facto discrimination elsewhere. An isolated act of defiance might be tolerated, but the civil disturbances that rocked cities across the nation that year, as well as the assassinations of the Reverend Dr. Martin Luther King, Jr. and Robert Kennedy threatened to turn the stable world of Jim Crow on its head and disrupt the balance of white power.

White people cannot fully comprehend what it means to be black, Latino, Asian, Native American, or multiracial in a society that equates whiteness with beauty and normality, and dark skin with ugliness and deviance. They know that, if given a choice, they would choose to remain white because of the negative stereotypes that permeate our culture and affect peoples' lives.

Writers have explored the negative impact associated with blackness in our culture as expressed through language.[2] Special attention has been directed to children's literature because it provides the foundation from which stereotypes about people of color emanate.[3]

Racist stereotyping about peoples' names has been found to affect the job prospects of African-Americans. A study by Bertrand and Mullainathan at the Business School of the University of Chicago revealed that resumes with white-sounding names sent in response to help-wanted ads in Boston and Chicago newspapers received 50 percent more callbacks for interviews than African-American sounding names.[4]

Conversely, a study of the possible economic consequences of black names by Fryer and Levitt concluded that while there has been a dramatic increase in the number of children, especially African-American girls, with black names in recent years, there was no significant negative impact on the economic status of black Americans. "With respect to this particular aspect of distinctive

Black culture, we conclude that carrying a black name is primarily a *conse-quence* rather than a cause of poverty and segregation."[5] Nevertheless, these researchers acknowledged that callback rates might be adversely affected by applicants' names, and there is, as they document, voluminous research dem-onstrating discrimination against African-Americans.

While some whites make disparaging remarks about black names, they fail to recognize that the novelty of African-American names is representative of creativity, and, in a sense, rebellion against traditional white culture. Casting off slave names for variants of traditional names and, later, during the Black Power movement of the '60s, the Africanization of names, is not only a sign of defiance but independence from white culture, and that is what offends some whites who view blacks as subservient appendages of "their" society. If blacks and other people of color were free to compete equally with whites—if the playing field were leveled—who would care for their children, sick, and elderly? Grow and cook their food and clean their homes? Take away their rubbish and clean their restaurants and offices?

There is little doubt that white males dominate the world of work and per-petuate their preferred position in the labor force. Michael Luo's anecdotal piece in the *New York Times* was an attempt to demonstrate the persistence of racism surrounding African-American names and black job candidates' resumes as impediments to employment.[6] A recent representative national study of social networks among 2,525 people currently or previously employed found that the "good old boy" network dominated by white males is alive and well. The researchers demonstrated that white males receive sub-stantially more information about potential jobs than women and minorities. White males have significantly more social capital—contacts and influence in the world of work—than women and people of color. Individuals with all white males in their social networks received 75 percent more job leads than people with no white males in their social networks, and the more influential they were, the greater the number of contacts and opportunities they had to learn about jobs and pass the information along. People for whom English was not the primary language received 60 percent fewer job referrals.[7]

In a similar vein, economists studying 1,500 managers in a large retail firm with 700 stores and 100,000 frontline employees in the United States found that the race of the manager affected the racial composition of people being hired. African-Americans were less frequently hired by whites, Latinos, and Asians, and Latinos tended to hire fewer whites than white managers. These hiring patterns were especially pronounced in the South. This behavior serves to perpetuate employment and income disparities between whites and people of color and will continue to disadvantage women and minorities in the world of work.[8]

CHALLENGING WHITE DOMINANCE

Most whites have never considered the implications of creating a true meritocracy where people of color, women, religious and sexual minorities, and the differently-abled are free to obtain the education and skills that would allow them to compete on an equal footing with them and sell their labor at realistic market values. Keeping these groups subservient not only makes life for the white majority comfortable and convenient, it is also inexpensive. When prominent people of color challenged the structure of white society their patriotism was questioned, they were exposed to ridicule, their careers ruined, or, worse, they were assassinated.

Confronting racism and classism led blacks like sociologist and social critic W. E. B. Du Bois; actor, singer, and athlete Paul Robeson; and diplomat, United Nations official and Nobel Peace Laureate Ralph Bunche, to flirt with socialism and communism in their struggle for civil and human rights. Du Bois was chastised in part because he supported bringing the case of African-Americans before the United Nations in Geneva in 1947—a move supported by the Soviet Union to embarrass the United States.

Bunche and Du Bois were also opposed to nuclear weapons at the height of the Cold War which pitted the United States against the Soviet Union in a nuclear armaments race. Calls for disarmament at a time of Red Scare paranoia were perceived as unpatriotic by the military and political power elite, but all three of the men were champions of social justice and outspoken critics of poverty, racism, and lynching, which made them enemies of the status quo. Similar allegations of being a communist fellow traveler were hurled at the Rev. Dr. Martin Luther King, Jr., and he was harassed by the FBI, especially when he spoke out against the Vietnam War.

These men, and organizations such as the NAACP, were put under enormous pressure by politicians and the United States government for advocating fair and equitable treatment of African-Americans, the destruction of Jim Crow in the South, and de facto segregation in the North. Aligning themselves with attempts to pass liberal declarations in the United Nations such as the Genocide Convention, the Covenant on Civil and Political Rights, and the Covenant on Economic, Social, and Cultural Rights, which guaranteed universal health care, housing, employment, and education, cast them as traitors and un-American in the eyes of racists and conservatives who sought to maintain blacks in a subordinate economic and social position to perpetuate white superiority and diminish the possibility of black competition.

As heiress Mary Pillsbury Lord, successor to Eleanor Roosevelt heading the American delegation at the United Nations Commission on Human Rights said, such policies as those contained in the United Nations Declaration of

Human Rights with "its emphasis on the guarantee of social and economic rights like work and free medical care was at variance with U.S. ideals."[9]

THE GULF IN RACIAL ATTITUDES

Despite progress, black Americans and Latinos are still behind the social and economic eight ball. After all the debate and hand wrenching attendant upon affirmative action, the gap between them and whites remains more like an insurmountable chasm. Worse still, social scientists Paul Sniderman and Thomas Piazza found, in their analysis of national representative public opinion surveys, that affirmative action programs evoked racist attitudes among whites, and the mere mention of the term was enough to produce negative responses.[10] Sociologist Eduardo Bonilla-Silva's work confirms the persistence of such values despite a shift from overt to latent rationalizations among whites who claim to be non-racists or what he terms "color-blind racists."[11]

Whites' negative attitudes about blacks and other dark-skinned people haven't changed over the years. A report by the Gallup organization showed deep divisions in support for affirmative action based largely along racial lines. While 50 percent of Americans supported the concept of "affirmative action for racial minorities," 72 percent of blacks were in favor compared to 49 percent of whites.[12] Lawrence Bobo's research, however, indicates that white and non-white attitudes about affirmative action may overlap. Whites may actually acknowledge the utility of such programs. Although the acceptance or rejection of the principle is largely race based, blacks for and whites against, attitudes can be modified through logic and dialogue.[13]

In fact, white attitudes toward people of color still reveal a disturbing tendency to stigmatize, denigrate, and distrust them. A *Washington Post*–ABC News telephone poll conducted in 2008 of a random sample of 1,125 adults prior to the election of Barack Obama, found that nearly half of all Americans believe race relations are in bad shape, and 30 percent of the respondents acknowledged feelings of racial prejudice. Whites and blacks held different perspectives about the state of race relations, with over 60 percent of blacks rating race relations as "not so good" or "poor" compared to 53 percent of whites.[14]

Shortly before the election in 2008, an Associated Press/Yahoo! News Poll of 2,227 adults conducted with Stanford University revealed that more than a third of white Democrats and Independents had negative attitudes toward blacks, describing them as "lazy" and "violent." Nearly a quarter (22 percent) of white respondents considered blacks "boastful," and almost a third (29 percent) thought they were "complaining," while 13 percent referred to

Pre conceived notions

them as "lazy" and 11 percent as "irresponsible." A third of white Democrats agreed with the statement that "if blacks would only try harder, they could be just as well off as whites."[15]

This poll also used a measurement technique called "affect misattribution," which flashed faces of people of different ethnicities on respondents' computer screens and asked them to rate neutral images associated with them as pleasant or unpleasant. The widely used Implicit Association Test (IAT) is a similar computer-assisted face recognition analysis designed to measure subliminal affinities for and against people of different colors. Since its introduction on the World Wide Web in 1998, over 4.5 million demonstration tests have been conducted with the IAT. Research on this instrument reveals strong affinities for members of one's own ethnicity/color and mild to moderate disaffection for members of others. Between 75 and 80 percent of whites and Asians show an implicit preference for whites over blacks.

Although most people are unaware of these biases, their existence appears to be pervasive, affecting even the creators of the project, despite protestations of being unbiased. More importantly, over 200 published scientific research studies have confirmed that implicit biases predict behavior. From friendliness to interaction and evaluations on the job, people higher in implicit bias have been shown to evince greater levels of discrimination. Researchers have concluded that implicit biases vary from person to person and are modified by one's environment and experience.[16]

How wide the gulf is between black and white attitudes was visible during the summer and fall of 2009. With the background of the faltering economy creating tension among whites and diverse ethnic groups in competition for jobs and resources, President Obama attempted to engage the nation in a dialogue about health care. Demonstrations throughout the country featured angry white protestors who chastised Obama administration representatives and legislators, ostensibly over the expanding federal debt, government intrusion into their lives, and socialism.

Tea Party protests were conducted in numerous cities, and on September 14, 2009, as many as a million angry protestors marched in Washington, D.C. to vent their anxiety and frustration with a system they contended had gone horribly wrong. Some people carried guns and knives to the demonstrations to assert their constitutional Second Amendment right. Others brandished signs that depicted the president as a cannibalistic medicine man, Adolph Hitler, the Joker from Batman, and a variety of other nefarious characters like Marx and Lenin.[17]

Columnists debated the implication of the crude caricatures and the intent of the protestors. Liberals tended to view them as disgruntled, while conservatives saw the protests as broad-based mainline criticisms of a shallow, socialistic government ideology that was bankrupting the nation. Former President Jimmy Carter linked the protests to racism, while former President Bill Clinton demurred, contending that a fringe group of protestors may be racist, but the majority were sincerely aggrieved by the political process that they believed was unresponsive to their views.

While we may never know the true intent of the protestors, one thing was evident throughout the debate: African-Americans and whites held diametric positions. Blacks overwhelming viewed the protests as racist, while whites, even those opposed to the demonstrators, preferred to rationalize the demonstrations as legitimate. Once again, the duality of the nation's legacy of color was reaffirmed as both "sides" continued to talk past one another.

This break down in communication between majority and minority group members may lie at the heart of the disproportionate rates of suspensions and expulsions of African Americans and Latinos in the nation's schools. The principal reason for such disciplinary action is defiance and insubordination. While we are not attempting to rationalize or condone students' disruptive behavior, it is conceivable that some of these discipline problems emanate from misunderstandings and cultural differences between white teachers and children of color. Looking at the pattern of disciplinary action in two school districts (one in New Jersey and one in Florida), I found that more than 80 percent of the discipline referrals were attributable to less than 10 percent of the teachers.

Administrators and educators should make every attempt to identify teachers and staff who have disproportionately high rates of disciplinary actions, ascertain if students who are being disciplined are disproportionately of color, and engage their staff in conversations about the challenges they are facing and their methods of dealing with them. Preferably, (as we will see in chapter 17) candid discussions about challenges posed by children of color and ways of improving their academic success should be conducted on a regular basis among staff so they can share their successes and pool their knowledge and resources. A comprehensive cultural diversity initiative should also be integrated into every campus and classroom incorporating multicultural materials and lesson plans as well as anti-bullying activities. The Southern Poverty Law Center's *Teaching Tolerance* magazine, web site (*www.tolerance.org*), and Teaching Diverse Students Initiative are excellent and available at no cost to teachers. So, too, are the materials and lesson plans at PBS.Kids. The Early Childhood Research Institute on Culturally and Linguistically Appropriate Services collects and describes intervention resources that have been developed across the nation for children with disabilities and the impact of culture on child development at *http://clas .uiuc*. The IRIS Center web site at Vanderbilt University gives teachers

PDF files they can use in their classroom to improve understanding and cultural sensitivity at: *http://iris.peabody.vanderbilt.edu/activities/index .html#DIVERSITY*. The Awesome Library (*http://www.awesomelibrary.org/ Classroom/Social_Studies/Multicultural/Multicultural.html*) is a web site with information, activities, lesson plans, and resources about multicultural education.

Resources such as these abound, but Boards of Education, superintendents and principals must demonstrate their support of such endeavors by making specific policy statements and holding staff accountable for implementing multicultural materials. This approach may encounter difficulty because of the enormous focus on teaching to standardized tests to achieve Adequate Yearly Progress (AYP) as mandated by No Child Left Behind. There is, however, voluminous research demonstrating the beneficial effects of implementing multicultural materials in the classroom on the academic success of children of color as well as white students.[18]

There are many paths to academic success. Creativity, initiative, and diversity do not conflict with the goal of preparing today's students for the pluralistic society and global world they have inherited.

NOTES

1. For more stories and insights about the perceptions of racism on whites see: Karyn D. McKinney, *Being White: Stories of Race and Racism*, N.Y.: Routledge, 2005.

2. Robert B. Moore, "Racist Stereotyping in the English Language," in Paula S. Rothenberg (ed.), *Racism and Sexism: An Integrated Study*, N.Y.: St. Martin's Press, 1988: 269–279.

3. See: The Council on Interracial Books for Children for further research, recommended books and guidelines for selecting non-stereotypical reading for children, and the Southern Poverty Law Center's publication *Teaching Tolerance* and other free teaching materials for children accessible at: *www.tolerance.org*.

4. Marianne Bertrand and Sendhil Mullainathan, "Are Emily and Greg More Employable than Lakisha and Jamal? A Field Experiment on Labor Market Discrimination," MIT Department of Economics Working Paper No. 03-22, May 27, 2003.

5. Roland G. Fryer, Jr. and Steven D. Levitt, "The Causes and Consequences of Distinctively Black Names," *The Quarterly Journal of Economics*, 119, no. 3, August 2004: 801.

6. Michael Luo, "In Job Hunt, College Degree Can't Close Racial Gap," *New York Times*, December 1, 2009: A1, and Michael Luo, "'Whitening' the Resume," *New York Times*, December 6, 2009: wk 3.

7. Steve McDonald, Nan Lin, and Dan Ao, "Networks of Opportunity: Gender, Race, and Job Leads," *Social Problems*, 56, August 2009: 385–402.

8. Laura Giuliano, David I. Levine, and Jonathan Leonard, "Manager Race and the Race of New Hires," *Journal of Labor Economics*, 27 (October 2009): 589–631.

9. Cited in Carol Anderson, *Eyes Off the Prize: The United Nations and the African-American Struggle for Human Rights, 1944-1955*, N.Y.: Cambridge University Press, 2003: 237. This is an excellent analysis of the civil rights movement in the United States and its involvement with attempts to create a human rights agenda at the United Nations. Compare the cases of W. E. B. Du Bois, Ralph Bunche, and Paul Robeson, see: W. E. B. Dubois, *Autobiography of W. E. B. Du Bois: A Soliloquy on Viewing My Life From the Last Decade of Its First Century*, N.Y.: International Publishers, 1968; *Ralph Bunche* by Brian Urquhart, N.Y.: W.W. Norton and Company, 1998; Paul Robeson, *Here I Stand*, Boston: Beacon Press, 1958, and Martin B. Duberman, *Paul Robeson*, N.Y.: Alfred Knoph, 1988.

10. Paul M. Sniderman and Thomas Piazza, *The Scar of Race*, Cambridge, Mass.: Harvard University Press, 1993.

11. Eduardo Bonilla-Silva, *Racism Without Racists*, Third edition, Lanham, MD: Rowman & Littlefield Publishers, Inc., 2010.

12. Jeffrey M. Jones, "Race, Ideology, and Support for Affirmative Action," in Alec Gallup and Frank Newport, Editors, *The Gallup Poll 2005: Public Opinion*, Lanham, MD: Rowman & Littlefield, 2006, pp. 314–315.

13. Lawrence Bobo, "Race, Interests, and Beliefs about Affirmative Action: Unanswered Questions and New Directions," *American Behavioral Scientist*, 41, 1998, pp. 985–1003.

14. Jon Cohen and Jennifer Agiesta, "3 in 10 Americans Admit to Race Bias," *Washington Post,* Sunday, June 22, 2008:A01.

15. Ron Fournier and Trevor Tompson, "Poll: Racial Views Steer Some White Dems Away from Obama," *http://www.facebook.com/topic.php?uid=2255675352&topic=5554.*

16. General Information, Project Implicit at *http://projectimplicit.net/generalinfo.php.*

17. For a glimpse of these demonstrators and their depiction of President Obama go to: *http://www.dailymail.co.uk/news/worldnews/article-1213056/up-million-march-US-Capitol-protest-Obama-spending-teaparty-demonstration.html.*

18. Research has demonstrated that culturally responsive lessons that connect materials with students' experiences, respect the legitimacy of their culture, teach students to value all cultures, and incorporate a diversity of learning styles has a positive effect on student learning and achievement. See: G. Ladson-Billings, *The Dreamkeepers: Successful Teachers of African-American Children,* San Francisco: Jossey-Bass, 1994; M.B. Ginsberg and R. J. Wlodkowski, *Creating Highly Motivating Classrooms for All Students: A School Wide Approach to Powerful Teaching and Diverse Learners,* San Francisco: Jossey-Bass, 2000; G. Gay, *Culturally Responsive Teaching: Theory, Research, and Practice.* N.Y.: Teachers College Press, 2000; P. M. Cooper, "Does Race Matter? A Comparison of Effective Black and White Teachers of African American Students," in J. J. Irvine (ed.), *In Search of Wholeness: African American Teachers and Their Culturally Specific Classroom Practice,* N.Y.: Palgrave, pp. 47–66; W. G.Demmert and J. C. Towner, "A Review of the Research

Literature on the Influences of Culturally Based Education on the Academic Performance of Native American Students," Final Paper. Portland, Oregon: Northwest Regional Educational Laboratory, 2003; R.W. Doherty et al., "Five Standards and Student Achievement," *NABE Journal of Research and Practice*, 1, 2003, pp. 1–24; O. Lee, "Equity for Linguistically and Culturally Diverse Students in Science and Education: A Research Agenda," *Teachers College Record,* 105, 2003, pp. 465–489; C. Kilman, "Learning Lakota," *Teaching Tolerance*, 30, Fall, 2006, pp. 28–35. The work of the Banks' at the University of Washington is acknowledged as formative in helping teachers value and include diverse materials in their classes. See: James A. Banks and Cherry A. McGee Banks, *Multicultural Education: Issues and Perspectives,* Sixth edition, Hoboken, N.J.: John Wiley and Sons, 2007. Sonia Nieto at the University of Massachusetts is also renowned for her contributions to this field. See: Sonia Nieto and Patty Bode, *Affirming Diversity: The Sociopolitical Context of Multicultural Education*, Fifth edition, N.Y.: Allyn and Bacon, 2007.

Chapter 10

Teaching about Inclusivity in Schools

> But token days are not the ebb and flow of life. They ease our feelings of
> regret about the way things have to be for the remainder of the year. They
> do not really change the way things are.
>
> —Jonathan Kozol, *The Shame of the Nation*

Perhaps even more important than corporate diversity initiatives are training programs for teachers and administrators in the nation's schools. With over 99,000 public schools and over 50 million students, 40 percent of them children of color (African-American, Latino, Asian, Pacific Islander, Native American, multi-racial) and a panoply of religious minorities ranging from Buddhist to Muslim, Wiccan to Christian, Jewish to atheist; today's students represent a mind-boggling array of pluralism. The fastest growing ethnic segment of students is Latinos, who comprise 20 percent of children in grades K–12. Unfortunately, school children are being taught by an increasingly aged population of nearly 7 million people, many of whom are white middle-class women inadequately prepared to interact with children from different cultural backgrounds.

Nearly three-quarters of teachers in the United States are female. Only 8.4 percent are non-Hispanic blacks, 5.5 percent are Hispanic, 2.9 percent are Asian and 0.5 percent are American Indian or native Alaskan. The average age of teachers in the United States is the mid-40's.[1]

DIVERSITY AND TEACHER TURNOVER

Despite the overt diversity in the nation's schools, research indicates that they are more segregated today than before the 1954 United States Supreme Court *Brown v. Board of Education* decision.[2] Inner-city school districts, like

Newark, Philadelphia, Detroit, Washington, D.C., Chicago, and Los Angeles, are overwhelmingly black and Latino while surrounding suburban districts are virtually all white.

Because of the dearth of teachers of color, many teachers in inner city schools are white, young, inexperienced, and ill-prepared to interact with children from different cultural backgrounds. Older, more experienced teachers with seniority choose to work in middle and upper class white schools where students are more compliant, resources more available, parents are more supportive, and working conditions more agreeable. For some teachers, working conditions may be a euphemism for avoiding interacting with black and Latino students.

Younger teachers may enter the profession filled with enthusiasm and idealism, but when confronted with the enormity of the challenges they and their students face, they bail out. They quickly find they are powerless to solve the multiple problems of the children they encounter. From reading and writing to math and science, inner city students are often far behind their suburban white counterparts.

Many inner city children lack family structures and supports that undergird middle class white students in their quest for an education. Simple activities that have been shown to make dramatic differences in student preparedness and academic success such as parental reading on a daily basis are often absent—as well as the books, magazines, and newspapers found in middle- and upper-class homes.

New teachers find that teaching ethnic minorities and poor white students requires far more than the Eurocentric pedagogy they were inculcated in and were supposed to pass on. The list of challenges to teaching in inner city schools includes diminished resources; widespread discipline problems (teachers in some districts spend over 50 percent of their time on classroom management); lack of administrative support; rigid Eurocentric curricula that may seem irrelevant to students from different cultural backgrounds; enforced emphasis on teaching to standardized tests required by the federal No Child Left Behind law; malnourished, abused, and neglected children; and violence on campus.[3]

From July 1, 2005 through June 30, 2006, there were 35 school-associated violent deaths in elementary and secondary schools in the United States. In 2005–2006, 78 percent of the nation's schools experienced one or more violent incidents of crime, 17 percent experienced one or more serious violent incidents, 46 percent experienced one or more thefts, and 68 percent experienced some other type of crime. During the 2003–2004 school year, eight percent of secondary school teachers and six percent of elementary school teachers reported being threatened with injury or physically attacked by a student, and a greater percentage of teachers in city schools reported being threatened or attacked than teachers in suburban, town or rural schools (10, 6, and 5 percent respectively).[4]

Young, inexperienced teachers figure out that their job description includes being a social worker, surrogate parent, nutritionist, paralegal, disciplinarian, counselor/psychologist, and friend ... and they can't meet these demands. They find that their expectations of the job are radically different from the reality of their work.

In a middle school in central Florida with 1,400 students and 6,500 discipline referrals to the principal in a single year, a new African-American teacher remarked to me, "They didn't prepare me for this in college. I've never seen violence like this before." At a high school not far away, the principal confided that there had been 2,500 referrals to his office in a two week period—in a school with 2,000 students.[5]

Nor surprisingly, 30 percent of new teachers leave within the first three years of starting, and 50 percent in the first five years. Richard Ingersoll, an expert on teacher turnover, contends that the "best and brightest" young teachers, those with the highest SAT and National Teacher Exam scores are the most likely to leave.[6] The cost of this exodus is estimated to be nearly $5 billion annually.[7]

A report by the Harvard Civil Rights Project[8] revealed that the teaching labor force in the United States was becoming segregated, and white teachers, though the majority, were least likely to have much experience with racial diversity. They were categorized as "remarkably isolated." It should not be surprising then that racially and culturally insensitive teachers may have more difficulty relating to culturally diverse students. A tragic outcome of this syndrome was reported in a nationally representative study of teachers which found that only 11 percent of them said they were very confident about achieving success for hard-to-reach children by the end of the school year.[9]

THE PROBLEM OF DISPROPORTIONALITY

Too often, teachers under duress resort to traditional defensive measures in dealing with students who seem defiant and insubordinate. There can be little doubt that the extraordinarily high numbers of African-American and Latino children suspended, expelled, and relegated to special education programs where they languish is related to the clash between culturally ill-equipped white teachers and students who do not present themselves in the preconceived subservient middle-class manner.[10]

Researchers who focus on this phenomenon, referred to as disproportionality in special education programs, contend that decisions to assign minority children to these programs "reflect a set of societal beliefs and values, political agendas, and historical events that combine to construct identities that will become the official version of who these children are."[11] These researchers referred to the warehousing of black and Latino students in special education programs as "a travesty" and "unconscionable." A National Academy of Sciences study concurred, stating that the high incidence of disabilities is nearly impossible to distinguish from students' culture and the context of their schools.[12]

Conversely, the number of black and Latino students in gifted programs is notoriously low and has been attributed to their poor performance on standardized tests used for qualification into these programs. As we have seen, the use of standardized tests to evaluate children from cultural backgrounds different from the Eurocentric tradition may itself be indicative of racial discrimination.

The relegation of large numbers of African-American and Latino students to special education courses along with their high drop out and low graduation rates impedes their academic success. Although the percentage of students of color enrolled in colleges and universities has been increasing, there is still a wide enrollment gap between whites and Asians versus African-Americans and Latinos, especially men. The percentage of females versus males enrolled is significantly higher for each ethnic group.

In 2004, 43 percent of whites 18 to 24 were enrolled in college or universities compared to 32 percent of African-Americans and 25 percent of Latinos. White females comprised 45 percent of the enrollees compared to 38 percent of males. African-American women accounted for 37 percent of the enrollees compared to 26 percent of black men, and Latinas comprised 28 percent of the enrollees in colleges and universities compared to 22 percent of Latino men.[13]

In 2007, only 18.5 percent of African-Americans 25 and over had a four-year college degree compared to 31.8 percent of whites.[14] These figures are more disturbing considering that lifetime earnings vary greatly by educational attainment. A U.S. Census report revealed that high school graduates could expect to earn $1.2 million over forty years compared to $2.1 million for bachelor degree recipients, $2.5 million for masters degrees $3.4 million for doctorates, and $4.4 million for people holding professional degrees.[15]

STRESS FOR STUDENTS AND TEACHERS

By reviewing these facts we are not trying to excuse students from rude, crude, offensive, and criminal behavior. But it is conceivable that some of the defiance and insubordination evinced by students may be misinterpreted by teachers. Some offensive behavior may even be manifested by students because of naivety, condescension, disrespect, ignorance, and obliviousness on the part of teachers who do not know or, in some cases, do not care about working with children who have been stereotyped as losers before they enter school.

For their part, teachers leave the profession for a variety of reasons—getting other jobs, lack of resources, stultifying working conditions, poor supervision, rigid rules and regulations, and student violence directed at them or other students.[16] Teaching in inner city schools is not only challenging but stressful.[17] The stress and negative undercurrent associated with color and cultural conflict are never far below the surface of interactions between teachers, administrators, and students. Disagreements arise over language, dress, and comportment, and regularly play out in physical and psychological struggles pitting young against old, child against child, and innocent against biased.

Even so-called integrated schools are often far from the goal of providing students with opportunities to interact with peers from different cultural backgrounds. In reality we have created segregated-integrated campuses where middle and upper class whites rarely encounter children of color in their classes because of contemporary schemes ostensibly created to provide talented students with alternatives to traditional educational experiences. So we have gifted, honors, advanced placement, International Baccalaureate, college prep, fundamental, and magnet school opportunities with an overwhelmingly white student clientele, leaving the traditional program to languish as creative and enthusiastic teachers opt for the better (more compliant) white students. In some schools the traditional students are stigmatized by the supposedly superior students in special programs. It is not uncommon to have a multi-tiered school with different subcultures surrounding the types of students enrolled in specific curricula. Children realize that the pecking order inside school mirrors life in their communities with status distinctions, discrimination, and white privilege.

The profusion of charter schools and the refusal of advocates of school vouchers to abandon the concept threaten to further gut the public school system. By channeling resources to charter and private schools they are contributing to the resegregation of students' educational experiences. Siphoning off white students into specialized curricula with a paucity of children of color and sending black students to fundamentalist Christian schools is reducing opportunities for diverse public school experiences. Research on charter schools and voucher programs questions the quality of these experiences for students.[18]

In the case of Florida, three separate court decisions held that state's voucher program was an unconstitutional conflict between church and state. These decisions did not deter then-Governor Jeb Bush from creating a system of vouchers financed by tax-deductible corporate contributions. With 25,000 students and 1,000 private schools, 80 percent of them faith-based, the state's $3 billion deficit might prove debilitating for traditional public schools. And the benefits of a parallel privatized education system are dubious. Investing in such alternative educational activities was found to provide no academic advantages for students over their traditional schools.[19]

LOW GRADUATION RATES

The large volume of fights and injuries in classrooms and on school grounds are only the more visible manifestation of the disease of racism. Even more traumatic are the innumerable insults, studied indifference, and fear which characterize relationships between and among teachers, administrators, and students. Such attitudes are expressed in the tens of thousands, even millions of students who are referred for disciplinary action, suspended, or expelled each year. They are casualties of a nation that is still trying to come to terms with color and diversity. Many of these children—black, brown, red, and white—leave school in search of more congenial and ostensibly productive places.

The high school graduation rate for students in the United States, that is, the percent of students who complete high school with their peers in four years, is about 70 percent. This means that 1.3 million students fail to graduate each year or 7,200 drop out every day, but the numbers are far worse for children of color. While slightly over three out of four (76.1 percent) of white students graduate on time, only 55 percent of Latinos and 51 percent of African-American students do.[20] Even the figure for white students is not good in an age of high-tech specialization, but the sad fact is that black and Latino boys' graduation rates are even lower, less than forty percent in some large urban districts. This situation is not only unacceptable but unconscionable. It is correctable *if* we prioritize attracting and training qualified teachers and administrators to our educational institutions—people who are enthusiastic, committed, and comfortable working with students from diverse backgrounds. They *must*, however, be provided with the resources necessary to perform their work. Both of these conditions are necessary prerequisites for improving the academic success of all of our students.

THE CHALLENGE OF DIVERSITY TRAINING

In an attempt to improve interaction and communication between students and staff and the quality of the educational experience for all participants, school districts offer training in a variety of workshops ranging from conflict resolution and cultural competency to peace initiatives and understanding the culture of poverty. Many of the obstacles preventing the successful outcome of these experiences parallel those in the corporate sector. There is no nationally accepted and recognized professional certification organization that provides a standard curriculum, methodology, and theoretical framework to equip diversity trainers with empirically based knowledge, techniques, and a professional code of ethics. Consequently, people who enter the field have a wide range of experiences, education, skills, deficits, and social and political agendas. The training experience is often uneven. Trainers' approaches vary from traditional boring lecture formats to "touchy/feely" sensitivity encounter sessions that engage participants in a variety of physical and psychological activities designed to evoke empathy for oppressed groups.

Although corporate and educational diversity trainers may utilize similar techniques, much of their repertoire is derived from on-the-job experiences. These may be ill-conceived because they are not based on empirical and theoretical pedagogy. Some trainers have a penchant for assuming workshop participants are culturally naïve and incompetent—an issue no doubt prompted by the use of the phrases "cultural competency," "sensitivity," and "inclusivity" in workshops. Compounding this perspective may be the use of exercises that may be perceived as degrading or humiliating by participants, many of who are already defensive because they perceive the training as unnecessary from their white privileged vantage, or even punishment emanating from an incident unrelated to their own work. Activities designed to evince personal feelings may be threatening because participants risk revealing details about themselves that could be used against them by group participants or their employers.

Defensive teachers compelled to attend what may seem like remedial work, may resist, much as their corporate counterparts do. This resistance may take the form of overt hostility to the trainers through disparaging remarks, aloofness to the workshop, grudging compliance to requests for participation, sabotage of exercises, and, in some instances, grievances filed through unions, management, and even civil suits alleging infringement and violation of rights.

Teachers are an especially difficult group to train because they often perceive themselves, by virtue of their education and experience, to be more knowledgeable about the nuances of their job than trainers who come to the situation as outsiders. Some of this resentment may be the product of their work environments where students perceive them as omniscient, and they, in turn, perceive students as empty vessels in which they pour information, what Brazilian educator Paolo Freire derisively calls "education banks."[21] Suddenly, they are required to participate in training that may connote or even presuppose their inadequacy, and they recoil and resist.

Even more disconcerting are the beliefs harbored by some teachers about the supposed innate inability of children of color to master the material. Raised in a society steeped in social inequality and racist assumptions about the inferiority of people of color, they cannot conceive of the necessity for training designed to improve the academic success of students who they perceive to be socially, psychologically, and biologically incapable of achieving academic success on a par with their white peers. As social critic, bell hooks, notes "… it was obvious to every black student in these predominantly white schools that our teachers did not really believe we were as capable of learning as white children did. Smart black children were deemed exceptional. We were often viewed as 'freaks of nature' by racist white teachers and by those rare, caring white teachers who were nonetheless influenced by the white-supremacist idea that black folks were never as smart as white folks."[22]

The milieu of white privilege may also impinge on teachers' perceptions of themselves and impede the effectiveness of diversity training. Believing that their personal perception of reality, the Eurocentric curriculum, their methods of teaching, and their expectations about students' learning are universally accepted, they enter diversity workshops armed with the perception that they do not need to change their style of teaching because it is superior to others. They do not recognize or accept the need to adapt. In the face of conflict they utilize standard discipline—admonitions, berating, referrals, and suspensions. As hooks observed "Understanding the degree to which class privilege mediates and shapes perceptions about race is vital to any public discourse on the subject because the most privileged people in our nation (especially those with class power) are often the most unwilling to speak honestly about racist biases."[23]

Diversity training under these conditions becomes like a visit to the dentist. Fearful, apprehensive, and resistant, teachers scramble to avoid what they perceive is an unnecessary intrusion into their sacrosanct world—a world of privileges withheld from many of their students. Suffused with lamentations of guilt and denial, their response to such training is less than enthusiastic. Engaging in workshops offered by trainers whose primary credentials are their gender, ethnicity, and on-the-job experience, it is little wonder that outcomes have been underwhelming.

In a literal sense, it is difficult to assess the outcomes of training workshops because few trainers employ sophisticated methods of assessment, preferring instead qualitative evaluations utilizing open-ended questions gauging participants' perceptions of their experience. While such information is an important component of the evaluative experience, it should be augmented by empirical scales of attitude and behavioral change over time to measure whether the training has had a lasting effect on participants' attitudes, beliefs and behavior. This cannot be determined from socially desirable responses that may mask respondents' prejudices captured at a single point in time through open-ended questions.

Just as important as learning how to appreciate the diversity of one's students is learning about one's peers, and this, too, should be an objective of diversity training in corporations and schools. In a society devoid of trust, where people hide their emotions from one another because they fear being manipulated by disclosures, there can be little collegiality and a dearth of camaraderie. Every co-worker is seen as a potential rival, an obstacle to one's personal path to success. Every student who is different, who resists the embracing milieu of conformity to rules and regulations, who challenges the system through wit, criticism or creativity, or whose very presence evokes anxiety because they are different, may be viewed as obstructionist—insubordinate, defiant, non-compliant.

Rather than engage one another as peers and reach out to students from different cultures, teachers seek refuge in rules and regulations that perpetuate the status quo and protect them from intrusions that threaten their modus operandi. First discussed by economist Thorstein Veblen at the turn of the twentieth century,[24] sociologist Robert Merton referred to this behavior in organizations as a trained incapacity—being fit for an unfit fitness, which is to say, they have become habituated to performing their jobs in the same way for so long that they are incapable of recognizing and accepting change.[25]

It now becomes evident why schools and workplaces are seething with employee dissatisfaction and discord. The magnitude of cultural conflict and change wrought by the infusion of diverse students and workers threatens to disrupt the status quo and catapult teachers (co-workers and supervisors) out of their cultural comfort zone. Faced with this reality, thousands of teachers are taking early retirement. A report by The National Commission on Teaching and America's Future estimated that one-third of the nation's experienced teachers could retire in the next four years, half within a decade.[26] Hopefully they will be replaced by more culturally aware and responsive people.

NOTES

1. Schools and Staffing Survey (SASS), U.S. Department of Education, National Center for Education Statistics, Public School Teacher Data File, 2003-4 Table 19; "Facts for Features," U.S. Census Bureau, "Back to School: 2007–2008," CB07-FF.11, June 14, 2007; "Facts for Features," U.S. Census Bureau, "Special Edition: Teacher Appreciation Week (May 2–8), CB04-FFSE.06, April 22, 2004; Hope Yen, "Hispanics One-Fifth of K-12 Students," USA Today, March 5, 2009; also see: *http://www.usatoday.com/news/education/2009-03-05-minority-demographics_N.htm.*

2. See the research of Gary Orfield at the UCLA and Harvard University Civil Rights Project; John Charles Boger and Gary Orfield (eds.). *School Resegregation: Must the South Turn Back?* Chapel Hill: University of North Carolina Press, 2005; Jonathan Kozol, *The Shame of the Nation: The Restoration of Apartheid Schooling in America,* N.Y.: Crown Publishers, Inc., 2005.

3. In 2008 nearly 900,000 children were confirmed to be victims of abuse or neglect in the United States. American Humane, "Newsroom Fact Sheets," available at *http://www.americanhumane.org.*

4. U.S. Department of Justice, Office of Justice Programs, Bureau of Justice Statistics, "Indicators of School Crime and Safety: 2007," *http://www.ojp.usdoj.gov/bjs/ abstract/iscs07.htm.* Retrieved: 4/13/09; Dinkes, R. Cataldi, E. F., and Lin-Kelly, W. (2007). *Indicators of School Crime and Safety: 2007* (NCES 2008-021/NCJ 219553. National Center for Education Statistics, U.S. Department of Education, and Bureau of Justice Statistics, Office of Justice Programs, U.S. Department of Justice, Washington, D.C.: iv–v.

5. H. Roy Kaplan, *Failing Grades,* Second edition, Lanham, Md. Rowman & Littlefield Education, 2007.

6. Richard Ingersoll, "Revolving Doors and Leaky Buckets," in Carl Glickman, ed., *Letters to the Next President,* N.Y.: Teachers College, 2004, pp. 141–147.

7. Alliance for Excellent Education, "Teacher Attrition: A Costly Loss to the Nation and States." Issue Brief, Washington, D.C., August, 2005. Available at: *http:// www.all4ed.org/publications/TeacherAttrition.pdf.*

8. Erica Frankenberg, "The Segregation of American Teachers." Cambridge, MA. Civil Rights Project of Harvard University, 2006.

9. Steve Farkas, Jean Johnson, and Ann Duffett, "Stand By Me: What Teachers Really Think About Unions, Merit Pay and Other Professional Matters," N.Y.: Public Agenda, 2003.

10. See: Daniel J. Losen and Gary Orfield (eds.), *Racial Inequity in Special Education,* Cambridge: Harvard Education Press, 2002; and B. Harry and J. Klingner, *Why Are So Many Minority Students in Special Education?* N.Y.: Teachers College Press, 2006.

11. Harry and Klingner, loc. cit., p. 7.

12. M. Suzanne Donovan and Christopher Cross, *Minority Students in Special and Gifted Education,* Washington, D.C.: National Academy Press, 2002.

13. "Status and Trends in the Education of Racial and Ethnic Minorities," National Center for Education Statistics, U.S. Department of Education, Institute of Education Sciences, September 2007, Indicator 23, at: *http://nces.ed.gov/pubs2007/ minoritytrends/.*

14. *The State of Black America, 2009,* p. 33.

15. Jennifer C. Day and Eric C. Newburger, "The Big Payoff: Educational Attainment and Synthetic Estimates of Work-Life Earnings," Current Population Reports, U.S. Bureau of the Census, July 2002.

16. See research on teacher turnover by Richard Ingersoll, "Why Do High-Poverty Schools Have Difficulty Staffing Their Classrooms with Qualified Teachers?" Report

prepared for: Renewing Our Schools, Securing Our Future: A National Task Force on Public Education, A Joint Initiative of the Center for American Progress and the Institute for America's Future, November, 2004, and Jonathan Kozol, loc. cit.

17. Cf. Jonathan Kozol's work, *Savage Inequalities: Children in America's Schools,* N.Y.: Crown Publishers, Inc., 1991.

18. "Evaluation of the Public Charter Schools Program." Policy and Program Studies Services. Final Report, 2004. U.S. Department of Education, Document #2004-08. Washington, D.C.: SRI International. Available at: *http://www2.ed.gov/ rschstat/eval/choice/pcsp-final/finalreport.pdf.*

19. "Expanding Florida School Voucher Program is a Bad Idea," *St. Petersburg Times,* February 18, 2010. Found at: *http://www.tampabay.com/opinion/editorials/ expanding-florida-school-voucher-program-is-a-bad-idea/1074013.* In April 2010 Governor Charlie Crist signed a bill authorizing an expansion of the voucher program to include 70,000 students.

20. "Diplomas Count, 2009: Broader Horizons: The Challenge of College Readiness for All Students," *Education Week and the Editorial Projects in Education Research Centers,* June 9, 2009.

21. Paolo Freire, *Pedagogy of the Oppressed,* Myra Bergman Ramos, trans. N.Y.: Continuum, 2000.

22. bell hooks. *Teaching Community: A Pedagogy of Hope,* N.Y.: Routledge, 2003, p 69.

23. hooks, Ibid., p. 30.

24. Thorstein Veblen, *The Theory of the Leisure Class,* N.Y.: Macmillan, 1912.

25. Robert K. Merton, *Bureaucratic Structure and Personality,* The Free Press: Glencoe, Ill., 1957.

26. Thomas G. Carroll and Elizabeth Foster, "Learning Teams: Creating What's Next?" National Commission on Teaching and America's Future. Washington, D.C., April 2008.

Chapter 11

Corporate Diversity and the Cost of Color

In lieu of scientific research, we are offered speculation and conjecture, self-congratulatory theories from whites who have never been forced to confront the racial stereotypes routinely encountered by blacks, and who—judging themselves decent people, and judging most of their acquaintances decent as well—find it impossible to believe that serious discrimination still exists. Whatever comfort such conjecture may bring some whites, it has absolutely no relevance to the experiences of blacks in America.

—Ellis Cose, *The Rage of a Privileged Class*

WHITE THOUGHT AND PRIVILEGE

While sociological, psychological, and philosophical theories about the origin and persistence of racism are fascinating, they have been and continue to be challenged, even ridiculed, as speculative and unproven. There is, however, concrete evidence of how and why racism occurs and its effects on people of color. In the following chapters this evidence is presented to demonstrate the continuing negative effects of racism and discrimination in the United States.

How do you quantify the hurt and harm a black or Latina child feels when she's not called on because her teacher can't pronounce her name, or favors children with traditional white names who look, sound, and act like her own children and grandchildren? How do black, Asian, and Hispanic workers feel when supervisors and co-workers intentionally or unintentionally mispronounce their names or joke about their ethnicity? Sometimes, empiricism misses the mark.

On April 9, 2009, in a hearing before a Texas House Elections Committee about voter identification, Texas State Representative Betty Brown suggested to Ramey Ko of the Organization of Chinese Americans, that Asian Americans should consider changing their names because they're too hard to pronounce. "Rather than everyone here having to learn Chinese—I understand it's a rather difficult language—do you think it would behoove you and your citizens to adopt a name that we could deal with more readily here?"

The message communicated to victims of this racist behavior is that one group, dominant whites, are the standard by which other groups are gauged. Whites are the model everyone should emulate. They are more highly prized and valued than others. Once again, people of color are left wondering whether they should participate in this game. If they don't, they are labeled as lazy, unreliable, incorrigible, insubordinate, undependable, misfits, and complainers; or worse, playing the race card. Whites set the rules and force others to abide by them. Deviations are labeled as aberrant and punishable, but compliance does not ensure success or recognition.

Racism takes a psychological toll on everyone as it stultifies non-whites' self-concepts and reinforces white privileges which inflate their own importance. When whites assume that the playing field is level, they mistake slogans for reality, believing everyone has an equal opportunity to a quality education or job, as if standards of fairness were equally applied. Non-whites are culturally castigated as slothful, lacking initiative, and being psychologically ill-equipped to achieve at the level of whites. Such sentiments are in our literature, jokes, music, television, and motion pictures. They permeate our culture—it's like the air you breathe, this mixture of myths and stereotypes that deaden the brain and poison human relationships.

Whites, however, cling to these *shibboleths, using them to justify their opposition to remedial programs such as affirmative action, which many refer to as reverse racism. They prefer to blame the victim instead of looking within themselves and at dysfunctional societal institutions that perpetuate failure. When whites exhort people of color to pull up their bootstraps and climb aboard the gravy train, it's like challenging a boxer to fight with one hand tied behind him.

Yet, some of the most pernicious pronouncements against people of color, especially African-Americans, have come from members of the same ethnic group. Leading these self-deprecating African-Americans is Ward Connerly, the nation's foremost opponent of affirmative action. Coming from a deprived background, orphaned at four, raised by his grandmother who was on welfare, Connerly, a self-made millionaire, attributed his success in a

*Password for ancient isreal, people can't pronounce it right and they know youre a spy.

60 Minutes interview with Mike Wallace to those sacrosanct American values of hard work and individual initiative, something he contended Latinos and blacks lacked. Not only did he deny that the United States was racist, he also denied his heritage. When Wallace referred to him as African-American he replied "I'm not African-American. I was born here. I haven't been to Africa. I'm not going there."[1]

The process of assimilating is different for people of color than other ethnic minorities because of their pigmentation. Whites have established criteria that define nonwhites as being unequal and inferior—an incredible conclusion given historical facts that establish Africa as the locus of earliest human civilization and the springboard of all humanity. Despite this, white supremacist ideological perspectives are predicated on myths of white superiority to justify white dominance over people of color.

One of the paradoxical characteristics of white privilege is the inability or refusal of whites to acknowledge its existence. The myths that spawned white privilege are derived from white supremacist beliefs in the natural superiority of lighter-skinned peoples over darker ones. They are deeply ingrained in the minds of children—black and white—around the world. Put there by our parents, siblings, friends, and peers, they are reinforced through the media. They perpetuate status and class distinctions that give whites access to goods, services, respect, and deference that are denied, withheld, or grudgingly given to people of color.[2]

From financial transactions like having ready access to credit, mortgages, loans, and check cashing privileges to freedom of movement such as the ability to live or travel wherever one chooses, to benefiting from common standards of decency and respect when one shops, dines out, or encounters strangers, whites, despite their protestations to the contrary, are treated differently than non-whites in our ostensibly color-blind society.

In their zeal to prove their tolerance of other ethnic groups, whites are often heard to say "I don't see color." Such pronouncements are not only disingenuous but insensitive, for that is the first thing one person notices about another, especially a person of color in a white majority society. In an attempt to demonstrate acceptance of difference they inadvertently insult people of color by negating their uniqueness and ethnicity.

Trying to establish themselves as non-racist, they negate the humanness of the other, and assume, from a white-privileged vantage, that such sentiments will be welcomed, when in fact they are seen as naïve, even crude generalizations that demean, belittle, and attenuate one's humanity. Such statements are frequently uttered by white teachers about students of color, who they feel uncomfortable with and may even fear, disproportionately recommend for special education programs, and subject to more frequent and harsher

He did not know what he did not know

discipline than white students, while they scramble to teach in predominantly white suburban schools.[3]

PROVING THE CASE OF RACISM: THE MYTH OF CORPORATE DIVERSITY INITIATIVES

An enormous body of literature produced by scholars and non-profit organizations, such as the National Urban League and the United States Government testify to the existence of the lingering effects of white privilege to the detriment of African-Americans and other people of color in this country. Federal and state government organizations have been created to investigate complaints filed by people who believe they have been discriminated against. There is voluminous case law confirming the existence of racial discrimination and, consequently, laws that prohibit it.

In an average year approximately 80,000 complaints are filed with the Federal Equal Employment Opportunity Commission (EEOC). Half of these are based on claims of bias experienced by people of color at the hands of white employers or co-workers. The recession which began in 2007 precipitated an increase in the number of complaints. In 2008 the EEOC reported a 15 percent increase to 95,402, which was the highest number since it began keeping records in 1965. The largest increase (29 percent) involved claims of age discrimination, and the increase in retaliation claims was second. Allegations of racism accounted for nearly 35,000 complaints.

Some cases are so blatant and of such scale that they can only be attributed to concerted efforts to stigmatize and mistreat people of color. In 1989, several white managers of Captain D's seafood restaurant in the Florida Panhandle filed a class action suit against the parent company, Shoney's restaurant chain. They alleged that the chain systematically avoided hiring black employees, routinely assigned them to menial jobs out of the sight of white patrons, and prevented African-Americans from obtaining management positions. These policies were enunciated by the CEO of Shoney's, Ray Danner, one of the 500 wealthiest people in the United States, and the darling of the corporate community, supposedly for his management acumen.

In court documents it was revealed that, among other discriminatory actions, the job applications of black employees had the "O" in Shoney's blackened to alert staff that the applicant was African-American. When confronted with the evidence Shoney's prudently settled out of court for $132.5 million with the 21,000 claimants, and Danner reportedly paid $65 million of it.[4]

One of the most illuminating cases of corporate racism accidentally came to light in 1994. Prior to its merger with Chevron in 2001, Texaco was one of the oldest and largest oil companies in the world. In June 1994, a discrimination law suit was brought against Texaco by six African-American employees on behalf of 1,500 other black employees. That August, a Texaco executive secretly recorded two other executives in a meeting discussing the suit and their intent to destroy relevant case documents. The tape of this conversation was released in November of that year by the plaintiff's attorneys and played on a segment of ABC's *Nightline* hosted by Ted Koppel.

As the racist dialogue played, the contrite CEO of Texaco, Peter Bijur, squirmed uncomfortably before the camera. Confronted by the transparency of the conversation, Bijur was cajoled by Koppel into agreeing to resolve the suit. He had little choice in the face of a looming boycott by the NAACP and a stock loss of over $800 million following the revelation of the tape. The suit was settled for $176.1 million dollars.

While the size of these settlements may be unique, there is no end to similar cases. The list of corporations that have been convicted and settled discrimination cases reads like a "Who's Who of the Chamber of Commerce." Virtually every one has a noble sounding mission and vision extolling their commitment to equal opportunities and valuing a multicultural workplace. Many corporations provide diversity training, celebrate ethnic and religious holidays, and have human resource specialists tasked with developing programs that promote tolerance, understanding, and mutual respect among employees. In fact, the author of the Texaco statement on fairness and valuing diversity was one of the principals involved in the attempt to conceal relevant information from the plaintiffs in the case.

All large and mid-size corporations have mission statements that acknowledge the value of having a work environment that promotes equal opportunities and diversity. Most routinely offer and require employees to participate in some form of training designed to improve staff interaction, tolerance, and understanding of cultural differences. Many corporations have workers' councils and diversity groups that provide activities aimed at enriching the lives of employees. They celebrate different religious and ethnic holidays, everything from Hispanic Heritage Week (October) to Black Emphasis (History) Month (February, which some African-Americans are quick to point out is the shortest month of the year), to Women's History Month (March), and religious holidays ranging from Chanukah to Christmas and Kwanza (but rarely the Eid, observed by followers of the second largest religion in the world, Islam, at the end of the holy month of Ramadan).

They invest large sums of money and spend countless hours in staff training to enlighten employees about the positive ways they can improve their interaction with people who are different on the job and with customers and clients, as well as the negative implications of discrimination in the workplace. Judging by the large number of complaints filed each year with the EEOC and the size of the settlements, it's apparent that management's first priority for engaging in diversity initiatives is to avoid or mitigate racial and religious bigotry and the legal consequences emanating from it. Creating a congenial respectful workplace is tangentially related to dodging class action suits, although the effects of such programs would benefit both objectives if they worked.

Indeed, corporations' "diversity initiatives" are long on the legal dos and don'ts and short on activities designed to create more humanistic work environments. Even when well-conceived diversity programs are initiated, they are often inadequately funded, understaffed, and poorly implemented. It's almost as if management initiates such programs to be politically correct.

For some corporations, diversity training is viewed as a kind of organizational inoculation against prejudice—as if their employees could be vaccinated against bigotry. They fail to realize that diversity programs must become an ongoing integral part of the organization, and hold staff accountable for implementing affirmative action policies. Staff turnover, local, national, and international current events, changing mores, age, ethnic and religious variations among staff, clients, and customers all warrant continual and revised diversity initiatives that involve every level of the organization. Even so, according to a study of 708 corporations reported in the *American Sociological Review,*[5] corporate diversity training programs are ineffective methods for moderating bias and increasing hiring of women and minorities in management.

How and why do outrageous violations of human dignity persist in the world of work? Publishing and mouthing self-serving statements about equality and valuing differences, and compelling employees to attend training for a few hours or even days, can hardly supplant a lifetime of attitudes, beliefs, and behaviors that are reinforced by dominant cultural values that perpetuate negative images and stereotypes about people of color and other marginalized groups (women, differently-abled, religious and ethnic minorities, and GLBTs). Embracing diversity may be a great public relations gambit, and even sit well with juries and judges overseeing discrimination cases, but it cannot eradicate the centuries of denigration, suspicion, and distrust engendered by a system that pits each worker against every other for the satisfaction of basic human needs.

It is revealing that the people in charge of such activities are, for the most part, women and ethnic minorities, while the path to corporate power and status does not emanate from the Human Resource Department. Perhaps it is a measure of corporate commitment to the principle of organizational equality to relegate women and people of color to programs that are expendable.

Equal Rights Amendment : Never Passed

Nevertheless, *Diversity Inc.*, a leading publication that chronicles corporate diversity efforts, consistently demonstrates that corporations with balanced diversity programs are more financially successful than their reluctant counterparts.[6] Ironically, many of the companies, including Johnson & Johnson and AT&T, rated number one and two on the 2009 list of the "top 50 companies" for diversity initiatives, have been sued for violations against minorities. Apparently, as research indicates, litigation or its threat pays off for women and minority workers.[7]

AFFIRMATIVE ACTION AND THE RESIDUE OF POWER

The concept of affirmative action arose from an acknowledgement of historical inequities perpetrated against women and people of color. It first appeared during the Kennedy administration in 1961 and was later promulgated by President Johnson and incorporated in the Civil Rights Act of 1964. Implemented through President Johnson's Executive Order 11246 to apply to Federal contractors, it was, in principle, supposed to redress traditional inequities for women and minorities in the workplace, educational institutions, and the business community by requiring employers with government contracts to give preference in hiring to these groups over white males.

Volumes have been written about the social, psychological, and financial impact of this policy. Over the half century that it has been in existence, public furor has not abated, with whites, especially white males, vociferously opposing it and people of color in favor. It has ruined political careers and touched off fights and riots. This, despite the fact that white women have been the largest beneficiaries of affirmative action and the balance of power and privilege still resides in the hands of white men.

Although the nation has its first president of color, there have been only four African-Americans serving in the United States Senate since Reconstruction: Edward Brooke of Massachusetts and Carol Moseley Braun, Barack Obama, and Roland Burris, all of Illinois. In the U.S. House of Representatives, there were 42 African-Americans serving in 2009. There have been only two African-American justices on the U.S. Supreme Court: Thurgood Marshall and Clarence Thomas, and only four women—Sandra Day O'Connor, Ruth Bader Ginsburg, Sonia Sotomayor, and Elena Kagan.

The lack of political clout of Hispanics is also evident. There is only one Latino Senator, Robert Menendez of New Jersey, and just 27 Latino members of the House of Representatives, despite the fact that Latinos constitute the largest minority group in the country.

African-Americans have fared better at the local level. Prior to 1967, no major city in the United States had a black mayor, but the Civil Rights movement led to greater voter registration and political activity among blacks. According to the National Conference of Black Mayors, by 2009 there were 641 black mayors in the United States including Detroit, Atlanta, Philadelphia, and Newark. Yet, there have only been three black state governors since Reconstruction: Douglas Wilder of Virginia in 1989; David Patterson of New York who, as Lieutenant Governor, succeeded Elliott Spitzer after he resigned because of a sex scandal, and Patterson will not run for election in 2010; and Deval Patrick of Massachusetts.

If one looks at the seat of corporate power and wealth in our society, those individuals who hold the corporate reins, very little power sharing at the highest levels of corporate America has occurred since the implementation of affirmative action in the 1960s. Studies of class mobility by Federal Reserve economist Bhashkar Mazumder[8] show that the United States affords its citizens less opportunity for intergenerational mobility than many European and some Asian nations (e.g. South Korea). In fact, Mazumder found that 60 percent of a son's life income is determined by his father's level of income.

The landmark study of intergenerational mobility by sociologists Peter Blau and Otis Dudley Duncan in 1967 revealed that the American Dream of upward mobility was possible but not probable for most people. While some upward mobility was achieved, the majority of movement was within social class levels. It was unlikely for sons to jump far above their father's socioeconomic position.[9] A unique longitudinal study of Social Security earnings data for workers in commerce and industry in the United States between 1937 and 2004 demonstrated that men had significantly higher levels of upward mobility than overall workers, and women and blacks had significantly lower levels of mobility than overall workers. Interestingly, women and blacks made larger gains following World War II in part because their wages were far lower than white men. The war and changing attitudes and behavior regarding the participation of women and blacks in the labor force helped to boost their labor force participation and wages. Unfortunately, the researchers recorded a slight decline in black mobility since 1965.[10] Recent analyses of occupational and earnings mobility in the United States confirm the importance of the combination of ascribed characteristics such as gender and color with regional, national, and international political economies.[11]

Contemporary research on sociologist C. W. Mills'[12] legendary Power Elite by social scientists Richard Zweigenhaft and G. William Domhoff revealed that while this coterie of influential people has diversified in recent decades, allowing in women and ethnic minorities, it is still disproportionately dominated by white Christian males. Even more startling was their conclusion that "... the racial, ethnic, and gender diversity celebrated by the power elite and the media actually reinforces the unchanging nature of the class structure and increases the tendency to ignore class inequalities."[13] Zweigenhaft and Domhoff discovered that a large proportion of the newly diverse members of the Power Elite were drawn from the same educational, business, and professional backgrounds as the existing elite. For example, one-third of the women who became corporate directors were from the upper class, and most of the Cuban Americans and Chinese Americans who ascended into the elite were from ruling classes.[14]

For many years, women and people of color complained about their inability to achieve high levels of corporate power. This impermeable "glass ceiling" was built, they contended, by white males to exclude them. In 1991, under the auspices of President George H. W. Bush, the U.S. Department of Labor embarked on a study of the purported "glass ceiling." A 21-member commission was formed, authorized by the Civil Rights Act of 1991. Four years later, during the first administration of President Clinton, the report of the commission, "Good for Business," was released.[15] Among the most revealing findings was that 97 percent of the managers of the Fortune 1000 industrial companies and Fortune 500 companies were white males. Of the Fortune 2000 Industrial and Service companies, only 5 percent were women and all of them were white.

In 1996, black entrepreneur George E. Curry published *The Affirmative Action Debate,*[16] a compendium of thirty years of progress since President Johnson signed affirmative action into law. At the time, white males composed 33 percent of the population, but they constituted 86 percent of the partners in major law firms, 88 percent of the holders of management-level jobs in advertising, 90 percent of the top positions in the media, 90 out of 100 United States Senators, and 95 percent of all senior managers at the rank of vice president or above. Then, in the Fortune 1000 industrial and Fortune 500 service industries, white men held 97 percent of senior management positions while African-Americans held 0.6 percent, Asian Americans 0.3 percent, and Latinos held 0.4 percent.[17]

While progress has been made in the hiring and promotion of women and minorities in the years since the report was released, as of February 2010, there were only nine African-American CEOs in the Fortune 500.[18]

It was hoped that the passage of the Sarbanes-Oxley Act in 2002 would reform corporate governance and bring diversity to the corporate boardrooms of America. Unfortunately, that hasn't happened. A *Wall Street Journal* analysis in 2008 found that only a tenth of the CEOs of largest corporations in the United States were racial and ethnic minorities and their percentage on boards of directors was virtually unchanged since 2000. In fact, the percentage of companies in the Standard and Poor's 500-stock index with no minority directors *increased* from 36 percent to 41 percent between 2000 and 2007. Among those corporations with minority directors, 81 percent had only one in 2007, a 3.7 percent decline from 2003.[19] The publication *Black Enterprise* reported in February 2008 that of the thousands of people who serve on the boards of directors of the nation's 250 largest corporations (and receive an average $100,000 annual fee), only fifteen African-Americans served on three or more. Women don't fare much better with only 13 heading Fortune 500 corporations in 2007 and 25 of the Fortune 1,000. There have been only 43 women CEOs in the Fortune 1,000 in the last 35 years.[20] Ironically, the rationalization for excluding women and minorities from access to power on the nation's corporate boards is the same time-worn excuse that has been used for decades—they lack experience. Isn't it curious that corporations and other sectors of our society such as higher education, which has a paucity of women and people of color in strategically powerful positions, are using risk-aversion as an excuse for excluding women and minorities, when they boast to the world that it was the willingness of capitalists to engage in risk taking that made them great!

Why have white males been reluctant to share power? The obvious reason is greed. In 1997, Ward Connerly launched a campaign to end affirmative action in Florida through a state constitutional amendment. A competing group called FREE (Floridians Respecting Equity and Equality) campaigned for a constitutional amendment to keep it.

Public opinion polling indicated that a large segment of Florida's electorate was not in favor of affirmative action and the chief opposition was coming from building trades. The pro-affirmative action amendment would have required a percentage of state contracts be let to women and minorities if they were qualified. The uproar over this proposal among the building trades was instructive. The white male-dominated industries already received 98 percent of the state building contracts, and they didn't want to relinquish their stranglehold over the industry. One might even conclude that they were fighting for the remaining two percent.

Before the electorate was able to make a decision, Governor Jeb Bush abolished the state's affirmative action program in 1999, and substituted a program called One Florida. The plan called for a greater percentage of state contracts to be given to women and people of color, and provided minority students admission to Florida universities if they were in the top 20 percent of their high school graduating class. Since its enactment more than a decade ago, there are more women and minority vendors in Florida receiving state contracts; and by 2007 there were 50 percent more Latinos entering college, but the percentage of African-American college students declined from 14.4 percent in 1999 to 13.8 percent in 2007.

In the years following Connerly's abortive legislative attempt to abolish affirmative action in Florida, he succeeded doing so in Washington State, Michigan, and Nebraska, which join California, his first triumph, and he continues to mount campaigns in other states. How ironic that a black man is helping the white power structure maintain the status quo.

Our system of public and private education also reflects these trends, with women and minorities holding positions of power in relatively few institutions of higher learning. As of this writing there were four women presidents of Ivy League schools (including Ruth Simmons, who is African-American, at Brown University), but the vast majority of colleges and universities are headed by white men. A similar picture emerges in public schools, where 90 percent of school superintendents are white and 84 percent are male. Two-thirds of the nation's school principals are males and more than eight out of ten of them are white.[21] Clearly, the message being sent to children of color is that whiteness equates with power and they see it on a daily basis.

NOTES

1. Interview on *60 Minutes*, November 9, 1997.

2. A similar case can be made for the treatment of women and other marginalized groups in most societies, e.g. the differently-abled, elderly, religious and sexual minorities. Paula Rothenberg makes the case for considering the similarities in forms of oppression against these marginalized groups in *Race, Class and Gender in the United States,* Eighth edition, N.Y.: Worth Publishers, 2009.

3. For a fuller discussion of white privilege see Peggy McIntosh, "White Privilege: Unpacking the Invisible Knapsack," *Independent School*, Winter, 1990, 49, pp. 31–36; Tim Wise, "Whites Swim in Racial Preference," AlterNet, February 20, 2003 and his DVD "On White Privilege: Racism, White Denial and the Costs of Inequality," available at: http://www:timewise.org; Paula Rothenberg, ed., *White Privilege: Essential Reading on the Other Side of Racism,* Second edition, N.Y.: Worth Publishers, 2005; Allan G. Johnson, *Privilege, Power, and Difference,* Second edition, N.Y.: McGraw-Hill, 2006.

4. For a summary of this case see: Steve Watkins, *The Black O: Racism and Redemption in an American Corporate Empire,* Athens, Georgia: The University of Georgia Press, 1997.

5. Alexandra Kalev, Frank Dobbin, and Erin Kelly, "Best Practices or Best Guesses? Assessing the Efficacy of Corporate Affirmative Action and Diversity Policies," *American Sociological Review,* 71, August, 2006, pp. 589–617.

6. See: *http://www.diversityinc.com/public/department289.cfm.*

7. Kalev, Dobbin, and Kelly, 2006.

8. "Revised Estimates of Intergenerational Income Mobility in the United States," Federal Reserve Board of Chicago, Working Paper 2003-16, and Bhashkar Mazumder, "Sibling Similarities, Differences and Economic Inequality," Federal Reserve Board of Chicago, Working Paper 2004-13. See also Jeff Madrick, "Goodbye, Horatio Alger," *The Nation,* Feb. 5, 2007: 20–24

9. Peter Blau and Otis Dudley Duncan, *The American Occupational Structure,* N.Y.: John Wiley, 1967.

10. Wojciech Kopczuk, Emmanuel Saez, and Jae Song, "Uncovering the American Dream: Inequality and Mobility in Social Security Earnings Data Since 1937," September 15, 2007. Found at: *http://www.columbia.edu/~wk2110/bin/mobility-short .pdf.*

11. Stephen J. McNamee and Robert K. Miller, Jr., *The Meritocracy Myth,* Second edition, Lanham, MD.: Rowman & Littlefield Publishers, 2009.

12. C.Wright Mills, *The Power Elite,* N.Y.: Oxford University Press, 1956.

13. Richard Zweigenhaft and G. William Domhoff, *Diversity in the Power Elite,* Lanham, MD.: Rowman and Littlefield Publishers, 2006, p.229.

14. Ibid., p. 230. See Helene Cooper, "Meet the New Elite, Not Like the Old," *New York Times,* July 26, 2009, Week in Review: 1, 6. Cooper presents information on affirmative action in education that contradicts the column's title. Quoting Nicholas Lehmann, Dean of Columbia University Graduate School of Journalism on why educational affirmative action may have been implemented in the late 1960s: "The cynical version of why they did this is they said 'We can't control this country, it's becoming too diverse, we need to socialize the brighter minorities and make them more like us.'"

15. "Good for Business: Making Full Use of the Nation's Human Capitol," A Fact-Finding Report of the Federal Glass Ceiling Commission, Washington, D.C., 1995.

16. Perseus Books, Cambridge, Mass.

17. See also Doreen Cobbs, "Journey to New Horizons: Thoughts on Racism, Poverty, and Inequality in the American South," Center for the Study of the American South, March 1998: 6–7.

18. Aylwin Lewis of Sears Holding Corporation, Kenneth Chenault at American Express, Ronald Williams of Aetna Inc., Clarence Otis at Darden Restaurants Inc., Rodney O'Neal of Delphi Corporation, Franklin Delano Raines at Revolution LLC, Richard Dean Parson at Citigroup, Stan O'Neal at Merrill Lynch, and on May 22, 2009, Xerox Corporation announced the promotion of Ursula Burns to the position of CEO, thereby making her the first African-American woman to head a Fortune 500 corporation.

19. Phred Dvorak, "Some Things Don't Change," *Wall Street Journal,* January 14, 2008, p. R4.

20. Derek T. Dingle, "Power in the Boardroom," *Black Enterprise,* February, 2008.

21. H. Roy Kaplan, *Failing Grades: The Quest for Equity in America's Schools,* Second edition, Lanham, MD: Rowman & Littlefield Education, pp. 130–132.

Chapter 12

Social Inequality from the World of Work to Society

In some ways...the dream has been downsized in recent years. Whatever the likelihood of attaining the American Dream in the future, however, one thing is certain—it will be more attainable for those closer to the top of the system than the bottom.

—Stephen J. McNamee and Robert K. Miller, Jr.,
The Meritocracy Myth

THE RICH GET RICHER

How effective can diversity programs be in schools and workplaces that are stultifying, regimented, hierarchical, secretive, and competitive? The structure of work in America is predicated on reinforcing power and privilege for the few who occupy the highest rungs on the corporate ladder. The corporate power elite wallow in immense wealth.

Prior to the 2007 economic downturn, CEOs in the nation's largest corporations, nearly all white males, earned 275 times more than the average non-managerial worker—more in one day than a worker earns in a year. From 1989 to 2007 the average CEO pay rose 167.3 percent, while the average workers' pay rose 10 percent.[1] Despite the serious economic downturn in the nation's economy, financiers received $18.4 billion in bonuses in 2008, the sixth largest bonus compensation package on record.[2] Even more disturbing was a report in the *Wall Street Journal* that employees at major 23 major U.S. investment banks, hedge funds, and commodities exchanges would receive 20 percent more in 2009 than they earned in 2007—over $130 billion—in the midst of the nation's most critical economic crisis since the Great Depression.[3] A report revealed that executives at the nation's 29 largest public financial corporations that received federal bailout funds during the 2007–2008 financial crisis received *more* in benefits and perks in 2008 at the height of the crisis than in the previous year ($11 million versus $10.6 million). Covered were items for limousines, chauffeurs, country club fees, and reimbursements for taxes.[4]

These findings were in line with trends observed over the last decade. An analysis by economists Emmanuel Saez of the University of California at Berkeley and Thomas Piketty of the Paris School of Economics showed that the wealthiest 10 percent of our population received 44 percent of pretax income in 2005, an amount that was significantly higher than the 32 percent during the years 1945–1980. A year later Saez reported that the top decile share of pre-tax income earning Americans, those families with market income above $104,700, accounted for nearly half (49.7 percent) of the total income of United States families, the highest level since 1917, surpassing even the stock market bubble year of 1928. Further, families in the top percentile (those having incomes above $382,600) grew their income at a rate of 5.7 percent per year from 1993–2006, or 105 percent over this 13-year period. This accounted for half of the overall economic growth of the nation's families during this time. Between 2002 and 2006 the top percentile of family incomes accounted for three-quarters of the nation's income growth.[5]

The Economic Policy Institute's report, *The State of Working America 2008–2009*, provides evidence of the increased wage and wealth disparity in the United States. Tracing the concentration of income back to 1913, the authors concluded that the top one percent of wage earners now have 23 percent of total income in the country, the highest income inequality level in history with the exception of 1928. The report noted that in the last few years $400 billion of pretax income flowed from the bottom 95 percent of earners to the top 5 percent. This was equal to an average loss of $3,660 per household in the bottom 95 percent.

The redistribution of wealth from the poor to the rich was facilitated by tax cuts implemented during the administration of President George W. Bush. These tax cuts had virtually no impact on low income families in 2008, but lowered the tax liabilities of middle income families by approximately $1,000, and created tax reductions of over $50,000 for families in the top one percent of incomes.[6]

AND PEOPLE OF COLOR GET POORER

In the midst of this affluence, poverty is pervasive among African-Americans and Latinos, especially their children. More than a third (34 percent) of African-American children and 29 percent of Latino children live below the official poverty level in this country. These figures are even more perplexing when we consider that the number of children living in poverty in the United States has been *increasing* since 2000, and now encompasses over 13 million. While this figure is disturbing, it may be an understatement because the method of assessing poverty is outdated. Experts contend that a more realistic figure would be closer to 28 million children (39 percent of all the nation's children).[7]

The plight of black and Latino children becomes more intelligible when we consider that 34 percent of black male workers and 41.8 percent of Latino workers earned poverty-level wages in 2007 compared to 26.4 percent of all workers that year.[8] In 2007, median earnings of black males ($35,652) was less than three-quarters (71 percent) of white males ($50,139), while black females' median earnings of $31,035 was 85 percent that of white females ($36,398).[9] In that year, three times as many African-Americans (24.5 percent) as whites (8.2 percent) were living below the poverty line, and more than a third of African-American children under 18 years of age (34.5 percent) were in this group.[10]

In November 2009 a report published in the *Archives of Pediatric and Adolescent Medicine* revealed how pervasive and debilitating poverty was among children, especially children of color in America. Researchers Mark Rank and Thomas Hirschl analyzed thirty years of data on 4,800 households in the United States and found that nearly half of all children and 90 percent of black children will be on food stamps at some point during their childhood, and the present economic recession is increasing these numbers. Noting that children on food stamps are at risk for food insecurity, malnutrition, and health problems, the authors concluded that the negative impact of poverty on the health of children in this country annually raises direct expenditures on health care by $22 billion.[11]

The PEW Charitable Trusts reported that 45 percent of African-Americans born into solidly middle-class families have spiraled down into the bottom 20 percent of income distribution compared to 16 percent of white children. This phenomenon occurred while the families in the highest income brackets grew richer.[12] Census data show the disastrous effects of the recession as the downward trend continued for low income people. In 2008, 13.2 percent of the United States population had incomes below the poverty level, an increase of 1.1 million people, and median household income dropped 3.6 percent to $50,303.[13]

A report issued by the Institute on Assets and Social Policy in May 2010 confirmed the PEW findings and revealed just how serious the economic divide between white and African American families is in this country. Analyzing the wealth (excluding home equity) of black and white families from 1984 to 2007, the authors of the report concluded that the wealth gap between whites and blacks increased more than four times, from $20,000 to $95,000. Even more disturbing was the finding that middle-income white households experienced greater gains in financial assets than *high income* African Americans ($74,000 versus $18,000 in 2007). Ten percent of African Americans owed at least $3,600 in 2007, nearly double the debt they had in 1984, and a quarter of African American families had *no assets at all*.[14] The authors attributed these disparities to public policies that give economic advantages to whites over blacks, such as tax cuts on investment income and inheritance, tax deductions for home mortgages, and retirement accounts. The heavy reliance of African Americans on high-interest loans and mortgages and other questionable lending practices acts to penalize them in their attempt to make ends meet. Further, the report concluded that job achievement cannot adequately predict family wealth holdings given the huge disparities between blacks and whites in the same income categories.

In contrast to this picture, the top one percent of earners in 2006 had average annual earnings of $576,000. This group experienced growth of 144.4 percent from 1979 to 2006 compared to 15.6 percent for the bottom 90 percent of wage earners in the nation. And those in the upper 0.1 percent experienced annual earnings growth of 324 percent during that time period or 77 times the earnings of the bottom 90 percent.[15]

Among the richest one percent of the population are 18,000 lawyers, 15,000 corporate executives, 33,000 investment bankers, and 2,000 athletes.[16] With the exception of the last group, the ranks of the others are predominantly white. Only one African-American, (Oprah Winfrey, worth $2.3 billion) made the Forbes list of the 400 richest Americans (number 141). A minimum net worth of $1.3 billion is necessary to qualify.[17]

Researchers report that there is little mobility in or out of the wealthy elite in the United States. The probability of remaining in the top percentile has been remarkably stable since 1970.[18] This conclusion is confirmed by the research of social scientists Richard Zweigenhaft and G. William Domhoff on the relative impermeability of the "power elite." There is some opportunity for admission to this rarefied inner sanctum of corporate and social power brokers, but not much.[19]

Income inequality between whites, blacks, and Latinos in the United States was further dramatized in a report issued by the United Nations Development Program which ranked countries around the world. The United States was ranked as the country with the third most unequal distribution of income in the world. The Scandinavian countries, Japan, and the Czech Republic exhibited the least income inequality. As we have seen, the disparity in wealth between whites and people of color is wide and growing.[20]

Through the systematic construction of policies and laws that advantage whites over people of color, whites have accumulated a disproportionate share of the wealth in this country. This situation is ironic given the ethos of this nation that prides itself on fairness, equality, civil rights, and democracy, with noble, awe-inspiring speeches and documents testifying to these principles. Yet we condone behavior that systematically deprives women, people of color, religious and ethnic minorities, the elderly, sexual minorities, and the differently-abled access to the "right to life, liberty, and the pursuit of happiness."

While affirmative action laws and prodding from government agencies, such as the Equal Employment Opportunity Commission, have had a beneficial impact by reducing discrimination in employment, progress has been slow. According to William Rodgers III, former chief economist of the U.S. Department of Labor, disparities in earnings and quality of life between blacks and whites have increased over the last fifty years as the Federal government has decreased funding for social expenditures.[21] Today, African-American men working full time year round earn 71 percent of the average earnings of white men in comparable jobs.

The National Urban League's *The State of Black America 2009* Equality Index, which compares African-Americans to whites in economics, education, health, social justice, and civic engagement stood at 71.1 percent in 2009, down 0.4 percent from the previous year, reflecting the impact of the recession on African-Americans. According to the Urban League's statistics, African-Americans are not quite at three-quarters of the quality of life of average white Americans.[22]

The index is derived from the original version of the U.S. Constitution that counted blacks as three-fifths of a white person. According to this logic, the Equality Index then (1789) was equal to 60 percent. In the ensuing 220 years much progress has been made, yet the Equality Index has remained relatively stagnant for years. Perhaps most significant, the economic component of the index of 57.4 percent was only slightly more than half of the white.

Today, more than three times as many blacks live below 125 percent of the poverty level as whites, and black median household income is only 65 percent that of whites. For the first time in 45 years, a new method of determining the poverty level is being introduced by the Obama administration. This will factor in taxes, medical expenses, and child care in measuring income as well as the value of benefits such as food stamps. The cost of living will be adjusted based on the location of residence. Nevertheless, the traditional measure based on the cost of obtaining a nutritionally sound diet will still be used.

Even though wealthy people felt the sting of the latest recession in 2007-2008, the situation for blacks and Latinos became more desperate. As of January 2010, the white unemployment rate stood at 8.7 percent, while the African-American rate reached 16.5 percent and the unemployment rate for Latinos was 12.6 percent. According to United for a Fair Economy, African-Americans were experiencing the brunt of the recession. Nearly 30 percent of blacks have zero or negative worth compared to 15 percent of whites. Only 18 percent of people of color have retirement accounts compared to 43.4 percent of whites.[23] The disparity in savings and retirement accounts has ominous implications for the future quality of life for millions of people, even if they are not presently distressed.

And for the millions of children living in poverty who have insufficient food, health, and living accommodations, the prospect of successful educational experiences in the nation's schools is grim. Many children living in such deprived conditions are in social, physical, and psychological conditions which severely impede their ability to concentrate, learn, and achieve in school. Educators must be aware of the multiple challenges faced by their students before assuming that they are presenting themselves in a state prepared to absorb the information they want them to learn. It's akin to Abraham Maslow's need hierarchy: people focus on the satisfaction of lower level needs—food, safety, security, love, and affection—before turning to the intellect and self-actualization. If our society continues to avoid its responsibility for providing for the basic needs of its children, we are destined to perpetuate poverty and inequality and relegate millions of innocent children to dismal futures.

NOTES

1. Lawrence Mishel, Jared Bernstein, and Heidi Shierholz, *The State of Working America: 2008–2009,* Washington, D.C.: Economic Policy Institute, 2009, p 9. See a list of the pay of the top 200 CEOs in 2007 and their accumulated wealth in *The New York Times,* April 6, 2008: 10–11.

2. *The St. Petersburg Times,* January 29, 2009, p. 6B.

3. Aaron Lucchetti and Stephen Grocer, "Wall Street on Track to Award Record Pay," *The Wall Street Journal,* at: *http://www.thestreet.com/story/10611097/1/wall-street-firms -dishing-out-record-pay.html.* Retrieved: 10/14/09.

4. "Bailed Out, but Lavishing Perks," *St. Petersburg Times,* October 21, 2009: 1A, 8A.

5. Robert J. Samuelson, "As Rich Get Richer, the Rest of Us Fume," *St. Petersburg Times,* April 20, 2007:A19; Thomas Piketty and Emmanuel Saez, "Income Inequality in the United States, 1913–2002," November 2004 at: *http://elsa.berkeley.edu/~saez/ piketty-saezOUP04US.pdf.* Retrieved 5/22/09. Emmanuel Saez, "Striking it Richer: The Evolution of Top Incomes in the United States. Update using 2006 preliminary estimates University of California, Department of Economics, March 15, 2008 at: *http://elsa.berkeley.edu/~saez/saez-UStopincomes-2006prel.pdf.* Retrieved 5/22/09.

6. Mishel, Bernstein, and Shierholz, loc. cit.

7. Sarah Fass and Nancy K. Cauthen, "Who are America's Poor Children? The Official Story." National Center for Children in Poverty, Columbia University, Mailman School of Public Health. Found at: *http://www.policyarchive.org/bitstream/ handle/10207/11238/text_834.pdf?sequence=1.*

8. Mishel, Bernstein, and Shierholz, op. cit. p .6.

9. *The State of Black America, 2009,* The National Urban League, p. 26.

10. Ibid. p. 26.

11. Mark R. Rank and Thomas A. Hirschl, "Estimating the Risk of Food Stamp Use and Impoverishment During Childhood," *Archives of Pediatric and Adolescent Medicine,* vol. 163, 11, November 2009, pp. 994–999.

12. Julia B. Isaacs, "Economic Mobility of Black and White Families," PEW Charitable Trusts, The Economic Mobility Project, November 13, 2007.

13. "Poverty 2007 and 2008: American Community Surveys," U.S. Bureau of the Census, September 2009.

14. Thomas M. Shapiro, Tatjana Meschede, and Laura Sullivan, "The Racial Wealth Gap Increases Fourfold," Institute on Assets and Social Policy, Research and Policy Brief, The Heller School for Social Policy and Management, Brandeis University, May, 2010.

15. Mishel, Bernstein, and Shierholz, op. cit. p. 8.

16. Steven N. Kaplan and Joshua D. Rauh, "Wall Street and Main Street: What Contributes to the Rise in the Highest Incomes?" CRSP Working Paper No. 615, July 2007, at: *http://www.nber.org/papers/w13270.* Retrieved 5/22/09.

17. "The Richest People in America," Special Report, *Forbes*, Matthew Miller and Duncan Greenberg, September 30, 2009 at: *http://www/forbes.com/2009/09/30/ forbes-400-gates-buffett-wealth-rich-list-09_land.html.*

18. Wojciech Kopczuk, Emmanuel Saez, and Jae Song, "Uncovering the American Dream: Inequality and Mobility in Social Security Earnings Data Since 1937," September 15, 2007 at: *http://www.columbia.edu/~wk2110/bin/mobility-short.pdf.* Retrieved 5/22/09.

19. Richard L. Zweigenhaft and G. William Domhoff, *Diversity in the Power Elite,* New Haven: Yale University Press, 1999.

20. Bruce Einhorn, "Countries with the Biggest Gaps Between Rich and Poor," *Business Week,* October 16, 2009. See: *http://finance.Yahoo.com/banking-budgeting/ article/107980/countries-with-the-biggest-gaps-between-rich-and-poor.*

21. William M. Rodgers, "Understanding the Black-White Earnings Gap," *The American Prospect,* September 22, 2008 at: *http://www.prospect.org/cs/ articles?article=understanding_the_black_white_earnings_gap.*

22. *The State of Black America, 2009,* The National Urban League, 2009.

23. Amaad Rivera, et al., *The Silent Depression: State of the Dream, 2009,* United for a Fair Economy, Boston, 2009, p. iii.

Chapter 13

Racial Disparities in Health and Wellness

And while the law of competition may be sometimes hard for the individual, it is best for the race, because it ensures the survival of the fittest in every department.

—Andrew Carnegie

QUESTIONING THE QUALITY OF CARE

Although blacks were stigmatized as being subhuman during much of this nation's history, that did not prevent white southern medical schools from using black cadavers to instruct their students on human anatomy. The irony of this practice was not lost on W. Montague Cobb, professor of anatomy at Howard University and editor of the *Journal of the National Medical Association*, when he noted that physical equality of the races was restricted only to corpses.[1] Despite overwhelming evidence of the common origins and physiological similarities among different ethnic groups, extensive evidence points to glaring differences in morbidity and mortality rates attributable to social, psychological, and cultural factors.

Margaret Chan, the Director-General of the World Health Organization, tried to call the attention of the world to the tragedy associated with health disparities when she proclaimed in 2008, "Health inequity really is a matter of life and death." Since the landmark 1985 study, *Report of the Secretary's Task Force on Black and Minority Health,* (commonly referred to as the Heckler Report after then-Secretary of Health and Human Services Margaret

Heckler), public health professionals have increasingly been writing and speaking on this topic. Government at the local, state, and national levels, along with private organizations such as the Kaiser Foundation, Robert Wood Johnson Foundation, and Commonwealth Fund, have funded studies and projects to inform the public and improve the quality of health care that minorities receive—to little avail.

The health status of people of color in the United States was again scrutinized as the nation considered reorganizing its health care system in 2009–2010. The Agency for Healthcare Research and Quality within the U.S. Department of Health and Human Services, is responsible for producing an annual *National Healthcare Quality Report* and a *National Healthcare Disparities Report.* Other notable organizations that compile data on this issue are the Centers for Disease Control and Prevention, the Joint Commission on the Accreditation of Healthcare Organizations, and the National Quality Forum.

A recent summary of racial disparities in health care, "Changing Outcomes—Achieving Health Equity," published by the Office of Minority Health revealed,[2] once again, that African-Americans are particularly disadvantaged in health outcomes. Studies confirm significant differences between blacks and whites ranging from five years less for life expectancy (73.2 for blacks versus 78.3 for whites) to more than twice the infant mortality (9.1 for blacks versus 3.7 infant deaths per 1,000 live births for whites) and more than three times the rate of maternal mortality (31.7 for blacks versus 9.6 per 100,000 live births for whites). Twice as many black Americans than white Americans do not have health insurance (19.9 percent versus 11.6 percent), but the rate of uninsured Latinos dwarfs even that: 41.5 percent.[3]

Latino health is actually superior to whites and blacks in life expectancy: 83.7 years for females and 77.2 years for males versus 80.1 for white females and 74.7 for white males compared to 75.1 years for black females and 68.4 years for black males. However, they suffer from higher rates of asthma, HIV/AIDS and STDs, obesity, diabetes, and Pulmonary Obstructive Disease than blacks and whites.[4] Like whites and blacks, the two leading causes of death are heart disease and cancer, but the third most prominent cause of death among Latinos are accidents.

Studies consistently demonstrate that African-Americans have higher infant mortality rates than the white population. In 2005, African-American infant mortality (the number of babies who die within the first year of life) was 2.3 times higher than whites. And black babies are three times more likely than white babies to be born with very low birthweight, while Puerto Rican babies are twice as likely as white babies to be born that way.[5] Black women also suffer from the ravages of inequitable health care, having a maternal mortality rate, measured in deaths per 100,000 births, almost four times higher than white women (34.8 versus 9.1)[6]

In 2006, African-Americans had 2.1 times the rate of diabetes mellitus and Hispanics 1.4 times the rate of whites. Black men had 2.3 times the rate of prostate cancer than white men, and Hispanics had 1.5 times the rate for chronic liver disease and cirrhosis than whites. The rate for HIV among African-Americans was nearly nine times higher than whites, and the HIV rate for Latinos was 2.1 times higher than the white rate.[7]

A report in the *American Journal of Public Health,* estimated that an excess of nearly 900,000 African-American deaths occurred between 1991 and 2000 that were attributable to racial disparities in health care.[8] Studies have found that blacks receive different treatment for cardiovascular problems than whites, such as fewer bypass surgeries, and after having a heart attack, they are less likely to be transferred to hospitals performing such procedures than whites.[9]

A disturbing finding was reported in *The Journal of Pain* that a survey of 190 pharmacies in Michigan revealed that pharmacies in black areas were much less likely to carry sufficient supplies of opioid painkillers than white neighborhoods ... even when income levels were similar. The researchers concluded that people living in predominantly minority areas experienced significant barriers to accessing pain medication, a finding consistent with other studies that indicate doctors are less likely to prescribe opioid painkillers to minorities than to whites.[10]

Similar conclusions were drawn by the National Alliance for Hispanic Health, which found 55 percent of Latinos in emergency rooms for broken bones (mostly elderly patients) received no pain medication compared to 26 percent of non-Hispanic whites. As with African-Americans, Latinos reported differences in access to post-operative treatment, heart disease medication, and treatment for HIV/AIDS.[11]

Social scientist Arline Geronimus at the University of Michigan, posited a theory of "weathering," which seeks to explain health disparities between people of color and whites. She contends that racism per se is a key stressor in the lives of people of color contributing to higher rates of hypertension, stroke, heart disease, and accelerated aging as they struggle with prejudice and discrimination. This takes a toll on their physical and mental health.[12]

Anthropologist Clarence Gravlee's research supports the finding that societal pressure exerts a negative impact on the health of people of color. After reviewing health disparities literature, he concluded that society and man-made environmental stressors interact with biology to produce and perpetuate

observed differences in health that may be carried forward into future generations, a phenomenon he referred to as *embodiment*.[13]

In September 2009, the Washington-based Joint Center for Political and
Economic Studies released a report on the economic impact that health
inequalities have on the U.S. economy. The researchers found that more
than 30 percent of direct medical costs faced by African-Americans, Latinos,
and Asian Americans were excess costs related to health inequities, total-
ing over $230 billion from 2003 through 2006. Adding indirect costs such
as shorter life spans, lost wages and productivity, absenteeism, and lost tax
revenue pushed the economic loss for the four-year period to a staggering
$1.24 trillion. The report noted that African-Americans bore the brunt of the
negative impact from the effects of health inequalities—nearly three-fifths
($135.9 billion) in direct excess medical costs, with Latinos accounting for
$82 billion in direct excess medical expenses.[14]

The gap in the amount, type, quality, and outcomes of health care between
people of color and the white population is so profound and perplexing that
the United States government established the Office of Minority Health in
1985 within the Department of Health and Human Services. In 2005 the mission of the organization was broadened, but despite the accumulation of evidence linking health disparities to adverse outcomes for millions of minorities
in the United States, its funding remained stagnant during the presidency of
George W. Bush. Now the office is proposing a National Plan for Action to
remediate the problem.[15]

A landmark analysis of racial and ethnic health disparities, *Unequal Treatment: Confronting Racial and Ethnic Disparities in Healthcare*, conducted for
Congress by the Institute of Medicine of the National Academy of Sciences
concluded that "Racial and ethnic minorities tend to receive a lower quality
of healthcare than non-minorities, even when access-related factors, such as
patients' insurance status and income, are controlled. The sources of these
disparities are complex, are rooted in historic and contemporary inequities,
and involve many participants at several levels, including health systems,
their administrative and bureaucratic processes, utilization managers, health
care professionals, and patients." The report further noted, "Consistent with
this charge, the study committee found evidence that stereotyping, biases, and
uncertainty on the part of healthcare providers can all contribute to unequal
treatment."[16]

On its homepage the Office of Minority Health displays the theme:
"Minority Health Determines the Health of the Nation," which makes the
words widely attributed to Dr. Martin Luther King, Jr. more prescient: "Of
all the forms of inequality, injustice in health care is the most shocking and
the most inhumane."

THE PRESIDENT AND THE POLITICS OF
HEALTH CARE REFORM

President Obama's campaign to reform the United States' health care system which began in the summer of 2009 unleashed a torrent of criticism against him. In town hall meetings around the country, angry crowds heckled elected officials and jostled participants. Some protestors were enraged as they demonstrated their displeasure with the plan to increase coverage for the uninsured and provide a public option to compete with private health insurance.

Some of this hostility was the expression of the fear of change and "the other." Many anti-change protestors were elderly whites, prodded to attend by right-wing talk show hosts, and incited by patently false assertions about elements of the plan, such as the statement that "Death Panels" would be used by the government in end-of-life decisions, promulgated by former Republican Vice Presidential candidate, Sarah Palin.

Were some of these anti-health care outbursts actually racist missiles directed at Obama? Some of his African-American supporters, like Georgia Congressman David Scott, whose district office sign was defaced with a swastika, believed they were. Congressman Scott also received racist faxes addressing him as a nigger, and picturing the President as the Joker from Batman. Another fax castigated him as a racist because he belongs to the Congressional Black Caucus and "whites are denied membership in it."

When President Obama addressed a joint session of Congress to discuss the health care crisis on September 9, 2009, he was met with derision and called a liar by Congressman Joe Wilson, a Republican from South Carolina. His incivility was followed by a reluctant apology at the behest of his party. But Wilson remained defiant and used the incident to raise over $2,000,000 within a week after his intemperate outburst.

Sadly, the comment that provoked Wilson was the president's contention that no funds would be spent on health care for the 12 million illegal (mostly Latino) immigrants in the United States. Wilson and his supporters did not believe the president; contending instead that illegal immigrants, their children and families, do not deserve compassion and care. Unfortunately, the president, in an attempt to garner votes for his health care reform, reflected these sentiments, no doubt further straining relationships between the African-American and Latino communities. The irony is that a visiting American would be treated very differently in Mexico's system of government subsidized health care.

The day before the historic House of Representatives vote to reform health care in America, protestors in Washington, D.C. again unleashed their vitriol against the president and democrats, spitting on African-American

Congressman Emmanuel Cleaver (D-Missouri) and calling Congressmen Andre Carson (D-Indiana) and John Lewis (D-Georgia) niggers. Lewis is revered as a civil rights activist who was severely beaten by white thugs in May 1961 as he engaged in a freedom ride to desegregate public transportation in the south.

Is the cause for this and similar outpourings of disaffection with the first black president the result of deep philosophical disagreements, a general lowering of the level of civil discourse in a nation that was on the brink of economic disaster (which the Obama Administration averted), or lack of respect for a man of color whom they resent occupying the highest office of a nation founded by and for white men?

Tim Wise, an anti-racist author, developed a persuasive case that Obama's color was a critical factor in evoking negative, even hostile reactions from whites against health care reform. Citing psychological studies, Wise demonstrates that people who are racially biased were more likely to oppose the President's proposals than people who manifested low amounts of racial prejudice.[17]

Another national furor occurred over his speech to students on Tuesday, September 8, 2009. Billed as a presidential boost for incoming school children, it was an eloquent appeal to students to work hard, achieve, and contribute to the country. Prior to the speech there was widespread dissension among conservatives who contended the president would try to indoctrinate students into his socialistic orientation ... what they feared would be another instance of Big Government attempting to take over an American institution.

The leader of the Republican Party in Florida at that time (he was fired and indicted for misusing funds in the fall of 2010), Jim Greer, said he would not allow his children to listen to the speech. Angry parents around the nation concurred with the statement released by the Republican Party of Florida that school children "will be forced to watch the president justify his plans for government-run health care, banks, and automobile companies, increasing taxes on those who create jobs, racking up more debt than any other president."

Upon seeing a copy of the president's text, Greer and other critics relented, but thousands of students across the nation were denied the opportunity to hear the first man of color in the nation's highest office extol the virtue of hard work and ask for their commitment to education. Two previous presidents, Ronald Reagan and George H. W. Bush, addressed students and did not evoke such a negative backlash.

On Saturday, September 12, 2009 thousands of "Tea Party" protestors marched in Washington, D.C. demanding an end to Obama's Big Government intrusion into their lives. Once again the crowd was virtually all white and brandished signs with the same code words, slogans, and depictions of Obama as a communist, socialist, and fascist, variously shown as the Joker, Lenin, and Adolph Hitler.

Obviously, there is more here than tax protesting. Whether racist sentiments have intruded into the growing debate over the role of government in the lives of Americans, surely common sense has not. No government, with the exception of a handful of Middle Eastern oil-rich countries, can exist without taxation. The Preamble to the Constitution of the United States charges the government with the responsibility for promoting the general welfare of *all* the citizens of this country.

Taxes are the primary way of generating revenue for government at all levels—local, state, and national. The government uses the revenue to provide services ranging from police and fire protection to education and hospitalization. From scholarships to immunizations, the government provides services that most people take for granted but fail to recognize are made possible through taxes, agreed upon by the commonweal and their elected representatives, and implemented by their fellow citizens in a collaborative endeavor.

Take for example our system of compulsory education. Children and their parents do not pay directly for their schooling; it is financed through taxes. So, too, are the land grant state universities which collect only a fraction of the cost to run their institutions from tuition. The salaries of teachers, professors, student supplies, technology, building construction and maintenance, even the lunches students eat, are subsidized through taxes. The roads and bridges we travel over and the various modes of transportation we take are regulated and subsidized through taxes that help government perform responsibilities integral to the maintenance of society.

These arrangements are all forms of socialism or mixed capitalism. We do not reside in a purely capitalist society, but the tenor of the comments unleashed by opponents of Big Government reflect ignorance of the economic reality of these mechanisms. What is perplexing about their denunciations, which purportedly rail against Big Government, is the blatant greed and insensitivity, if not outright racist implications of their motives. Every social trend has its time and this may be the one for incivility derived from selfish, egoistic, shibboleths about government intrusion into citizens' lives. But most white folks already have health care insurance and don't want any changes in it. Nor do they want to share resources with the less fortunate. How ironic it is to watch elderly protestors demonstrating against government subsidies for the poor and socialized medicine when they receive Social Security and Medicare.

The unspoken sentiment amidst all the signs and slogans is the underlying fear of a demographic revolution that is changing society, altering the balance of power in their lives. They fear being swallowed up in a sea of color, enveloped by the daunting needs of the new immigrants and the nation's poor who finally have a person in the highest office of the land that resembles the feared horde on the outside looking in. They don't want to share the little they have with "the other;" they want to be left alone to continue their profligate materialism. The rising expectations and aspirations of a growing number of Americans threaten their way of life. More importantly, it questions their perception of what the nation is becoming, so they march, scream, and wish for something that can no longer be.

Could it be that these outpourings of discontent are masking a more deeply divisive distrust not of the government as they contend, but of a black man whom they did not vote for, do not feel is competent, and does not deserve their support? Watching these gatherings is like watching symbolic lynchings where public servants and the President are ridiculed and castigated by white mobs bereft of sanity and decency. Among people with the facts, such perspectives have as much credibility as the position of the "Birthers" who contend that Obama's presidency is illegitimate. Despite evidence to the contrary, they want to believe he was not born in the United States. Bigotry provides fertile ground for conspiracy theories and is inimical to the truth. We should remember the words of Voltaire: "Anyone who has the power to make you believe absurdities has the power to make you commit injustices."

NOTES

1. David B. Smith, *Health Care Divided: Race and Healing a Nation,* Ann Arbor: University of Michigan Press, 1999, p. 25.

2. The National Plan for Action to End Health Disparities, Office of Minority Health, U.S. Department of Health and Human Services, 2010 at: *http://minorityhealth .hhs.gov/npa/templates/browse.aspx?lvl=;&v;OD=31.*

3. Gallup Poll, July 22, 2009.

4. Carolina Reyes, Adloph P. Falcon, Leticia Van de Putte, and Richard Levy, National Alliance for Hispanic Health, Genes, Culture and Medicines: Bridging Gaps in Treatment for Hispanic Americans, Washington, D.C., February 2004.

5. "Changing Outcomes—Achieving Health Equity," p. 41.

6. "Changing Outcomes—Achieving Health Equity," 2010, p. 39. Also see Amnesty International's 2010 sobering report on racial disparities in maternal deaths in the United States, *Deadly Delivery: The Maternal Health Care Crisis in the USA* at *www.amnestyusa.org/deadlydelivery.*

7. "Changing Outcomes—Achieving Health Equity," 2010, p. 37, Exhibit 2-4.

8. Steven H. Woolf, et al., "The Health Impact of Resolving Racial Disparities: An Analysis of US Mortality Data," *American Journal of Public Health,* vol. 94, no.12, December 2004, pp. 2078–2081.

9. Ioana Popescu, "Differences in Mortality and Use of Revascularization in Black and White Patients with Acute MI Admitted to Hospitals with and Without Revascularization Services," *Journal of the American Medical Association,* vol. 297, no. 22, June 13, 2007, pp. 2489–2495.

10. Carmen R. Green, S. Khady Ndao-Brumblay, Brady West, and Tamika Washington, "Differences in Prescription Opioid Analgesic Availability: Comparing Minority and White Pharmacies Across Michigan," *The Journal of Pain,* vol. 6, no. 10, October 2005, pp. 689–699.

11. Reyes, Falcon, Van Putte, and Levy, loc. cit.

12. For a summary of her ideas see: Ryan Blitstein, "Weathering, the Storm," *Miller-McCune,* vol. 2, no. 4 , July-August 2009, pp. 48–57. Also: A.T. Geronimus, J. Bound, T.A.Waidmann, C.G. Colen, and D. Steffick, "Inequality in Life Expectancy, Functional Status, and Active Life Expectancy Across Selected Black and White Population in the United States," *Demography,* vol. 38, no. 2, 2001, pp. 227–251. See the discussion of the effects of racism on the health of African Americans in Tim Wise's *Color-Blind.* San Francisco: City Lights Books, 2010, pp. 112–126.

13. Clarence C. Gravlee, "How Race Becomes Biology: Embodiment of Social Inequality," *American Journal of Physical Anthropology,* 2009, vol. 139:47–57.

14. Thomas A. LaVeist, Darrell J. Gaskin and Patrick Richard, "The Economic Burden of Health Inequalities in the United States," Joint Center for Political and Economic Studies, Washington, D.C.: September, 2009.

15. Available at: *http://minorityhealth.hhs.gov/npa/templates/browse.aspx?lvl=lID=31.*

16. Washington, D.C.: National Academies Press, 2003, p.1. For a review of the issues surrounding health disparities see: Richard Wilkinson and Michael Marmot, eds. *Social Determinants of Health: The Solid Facts,* Denmark: The World Health Organization, second edition, 2003.

17. Wise, op. cit., pp. 144–146.

Chapter 14

Crime and Punishment

...if it is right for America to draft us, and teach us how to be violent in defense of her, then it is right for you and me to do whatever is necessary to defend our own people right here in this country.

—Malcolm X

DISPARATE SENTENCING

The United States has the highest number of people incarcerated of any country in the world. In 2008, 2.4 million people, or about one in every 133 residents were locked up in local, state, and national facilities. But the scales of justice are not balanced for people of color in America. The Social Justice component of the Equality Index of the National Urban League exhibited the greatest gain in 2008 as a result of reductions in the length of jail sentencing for blacks. Still, evidence confirms racial disparities in sentencing and incarceration.

At the end of 2008, the incarceration rate for white men in state or federal prison sentenced to a year or more was 487 per 100,000. For black men it was 3,161 per 100,000, and 1,200 per 100,000 for Hispanic men. The incarceration rate for white women was 50 per 100,000; 149 per 100,000 for black women, and 75 for Hispanic women. African-Americans accounted for 38 percent of all inmates, Latinos 20 percent and whites 34 percent.[1]

Disparities in incarceration rates for drug offenses reveal the breadth of the impact of racism: at the end of 2005, there were 253,300 state prison inmates serving time for drug offenses, and of these 113,500 (45 percent) were black, 51,100 (20 percent) were Hispanic, and 72,300 (29 percent) were white.[2] Sadly, there are more African-American college-age youth in prison, on probation, or on parole than are enrolled in college.[3]

RACIAL PROFILING

The influence of racism cannot be overlooked as a cause of these dispari-ties, and blacks and Latinos know it all too well. The profiling of people of color, especially black and Latino males, by law enforcement, has been widely documented, even admitted as the New Jersey Superintendent of the State Police acknowledged in 2000 (and he was then fired by Governor Christine Todd Whitman). Stories of police harassment of minorities by white and black officers are rampant, and so are reports on the topic by organizations like the American Civil Liberties Union and the United Nations.

It is common knowledge among black families that their children, espe-cially boys, may encounter police for no other reason than "DWB" (driving while black). Pamphlets instructing black parents on how to educate their children to react to unprovoked and unwarranted police stops have been circulated in urban areas. These caution teenagers against overreacting in police encounters, using appropriate deferential behavior, and techniques for de-escalating tension in such situations.[4]

Apparently, Harvard Professor Henry Louis Gates Jr. didn't read them before he was accosted by a Cambridge, Massachusetts policeman while breaking into his own home because he was locked out. Like other notable negative encounters with law enforcement, this event triggered a proliferation of news stories around the nation in late July 2009. Even President Obama was drawn into the maelstrom when he referred to the police action as "stu-pid" during a press conference. He later backtracked and invited the arresting officer and Professor Gates to the White House for a beer.

The incident fueled the debate about the extent of racism and racial profiling—something many whites would rather not address. After all, hav-ing a black man in the White House ostensibly demonstrates the enormous progress that people of color have made. Periodic racial perturbations like this muck up the idyllic image of the United States as a progressive society. Sociologist Eduardo Bonilla-Silva refers to white denials of contemporary racism as "color-blind racism," not as overt as its Jim Crow predecessor, but insidious and pernicious because it is embodied in an ideological belief system that rationalizes and justifies discrimination. Sociologists Leslie Picca and Joe Feagin contend that there is a generic meaning system in this country that systematically frames whites' views about people of color depicting them in negative stereotypical images.[5]

Of course, the arrest of Professor Gates was an ill-conceived act on the part of the police. So, too, was the merciless beating of Rodney King by Los Angeles police officers in March 1991. As was the murder of the African immigrant Amadou Diallo by four New York City policemen, who riddled his body with 41 bullets after mistakenly thinking he was reaching for a gun on a dark February night in 1999. The shooting death of Sean Bell in New York City, just hours before his scheduled wedding on November 25, 2006, was another notorious case of police contretemps, as was the disparate treatment of six African-American teenagers in Jena, Louisiana in 2007 who were threatened by the State Attorney "I can take away your lives with a stroke of my pen."

These are only a few of the more outrageous incidents of racism perpetrated by law enforcement on people of color. Each time monstrous offenses like these occur it brings forth a torrent of condemnation and a concomitant protestation that it was an aberration. Certainly, such cases are not the norm, but that should not inure us to the daily insults and intimidation endured by people of color. Common affronts range from DWB, to being followed when shopping, or having to produce multiple IDs when a suspicious clerk requests proof that you are really who you purport to be. They do not include the black and brown teens beaten and killed by police during high speed chases, drug busts, and community interventions for minor purported offensives such as traffic stops.

But how could such behavior be any different when our society is built on a foundation of racial stereotypes that perpetuate the image of dark-skinned people as dangerous, untrustworthy, and violent? In virtually all of these sensational cases the police were exonerated.[6] Research indicates that students of color complain bitterly about unfairness and inconsistency in the disciplinary decisions of teachers and administrators.[7] One wonders about how impartial the system of discipline is in our nation's schools.

The outcome of such cases is easy to predict given the social milieu in which they occur. If people of color are depicted as dangerous thugs and police officers are dispatched into "high crime areas" to apprehend suspected deviants, law enforcement personnel become the emotional instruments of racism, acting on prevailing stereotypes about the area and persons who they are sent to apprehend.

It makes no difference about the color of the law enforcement personnel—black and brown police are not immune to internalizing the stereotypes about their own ethnic groups. Nor are they any less likely than their white counterparts to experience fear and trepidation upon encountering "suspicious" people of color in "dangerous areas." They, too, feel the tension and rapid heart beat of the chase and, they, too, know that their lives are in jeopardy because they live in a society and work in an occupation that has taught them to be wary of people of color and to protect themselves—which may mean to shoot first.

The treatment of Professor Gates after his irate response testifies to the corrosive effect of racial profiling in this country. Here was a black man who supposedly had made it—a Harvard scholar with considerable popularity among the intelligentsia, even, to some extent the masses, through his television series on black history and genealogy. Here was a black man screaming out "I am not a nigger!" to a white male cop whose actions indicated otherwise. The pique that President Obama displayed at his press conference revealed the same frustration and disgust, the same attempt to affirm his accomplishments and status in the face of what he knew to be the lingering disease of racism that infects social relationships in our society. Obama, too, had experienced the same kind of demeaning racist behavior as he revealed in his book, *The Audacity of Hope.*[8]

John Hope Franklin, recently deceased Professor Emeritus of History at Duke University, author of the acclaimed book *From Slavery to Freedom,*[9] Presidential Medal of Freedom recipient, and chairman of President Bill Clinton's task force on race relations, *One America*, used to spend time as a Visiting Professor at Eckerd College in St. Petersburg, Florida. It was said that he was conspicuously followed while shopping in a local department store for no other reason than his color.[10]

It's difficult for whites to comprehend the extent and impact such daily insults have on people of color. In his book, *The Rage of a Privileged Class*, Ellis Cose[11] presented interviews with talented African-Americans who, to outward appearances were very successful. Nevertheless, they bemoaned their inability to reach the pinnacle of their organizations and receive the acceptance and recognition they deserved. Nearly two decades later, Cose acknowledged that the situation of African-Americans has improved, but the success of a few black entrepreneurs and politicians like President Obama does not signify the beginning of a post-racial America—much work must still be done before equality is achieved.[12] E. Franklin Frazier's classic *Black Bourgeoisie* and Manning Marable's characterization of this situation as "symbolic racial representation" with "black faces in high places," also address the issue of tokenism among upwardly mobile African-Americans.[13]

Most people of color have endured the insults that stem from racism. They have their own horror stories. In discussing the Gates case on the *Larry King Show*, retired general and former Head of the Joint Chiefs of Staff, later Secretary of State, Colin Powell, recalled how he met a visiting dignitary at

Dulles International Airport in his capacity as National Security Advisor to the President. The surprised official was dumbfounded that a black man held such a position in our government.

Being black is more than a little inconvenient; it can cost you your dignity and even your life. Sociologist Brian Withrow's analysis of studies of racial profiling demonstrates that while most racial profiling is about drug trafficking, statistics consistently reveal that minorities are *no* more likely than whites to possess drugs. Fully three-quarters of criminal activities are perpetrated by whites, and while blacks are twice as likely as whites to have their cars stopped and searched, police are twice as likely to find evidence of illegal activity in cars driven by whites.[14]

After analyzing hundreds of studies, Withrow concluded that there are serious methodological and definitional problems surrounding the issue of racial profiling, but it was apparent that black and Hispanic drivers are disproportionately stopped more often than whites; they are searched more often than whites during traffic and pedestrian stops; and such searches are less likely to yield contraband. Not coincidentally, stops of minorities are more likely to result in more formal or punitive sanctions.[15]

The most shocking and despicable application of racial profiling and other forms of discrimination occur when they are institutionalized in our social system. The cumulative effects of individual acts of discrimination and hate pale in comparison to the systemic policies and procedures that stigmatize, dehumanize, and disadvantage large numbers of people. In the case of New Jersey, for example, over 91,000 pages of evidence were produced detailing official state police policy supporting racial profiling for stopping and searching cars of minority drivers.

A report by Amnesty International (AI)[16] concluded that "Racial profiling is a serious human rights problem affecting millions of people in the United States in even the most routine aspects of their daily lives." Amnesty concluded based on a year long study of the phenomenon, that 32 million Americans reported being victims of racial profiling and 87 million Americans, including African-Americans, Native Americans, Asian Americans, Hispanic Americans, Arab Americans, Persian Americans, American Muslims, and many immigrant and visitors, (virtually all non-whites) were at high risk of being subjected to this in the future.[17]

In June 2009, the American Civil Liberties Union released a report condemning the policies of the Bush era, which, they contended, led to a persistence of widespread racial profiling by law enforcement agents against African-Americans, Asians, Latinos, Arabs, and Muslims.[18]

If you don't think race and class count in America, go to any courtroom for a day and observe the traffic—poor whites, blacks, and Latinos paraded in and out like cattle before predominantly white male judges; represented by white middle and upper class lawyers. The comings and goings of these people belie the blindfolded Statue of Justice—the system is neither colorblind nor race neutral—and she's peeking out to make sure it stays that way.

Although evidence exists indicating the utilization of racial profiling by law enforcement around the country, some sociologists and criminologists are reluctant to acknowledge the extent and, more importantly, intent of perpetrators. Sociologist Karen Glover explains this counterintuitive intransigence of law enforcement, government, and some members of society by utilizing critical race theory, a method of analysis that became popular in the 1990s. Glover and other critics of traditional sociological analyses contend that quantitative survey statistical methods used by researchers provide an incomplete picture of the pervasive and insidious nature of racial profiling. From their perspective, such approaches are mired in the dominant white racist world view which denigrates and discounts the perspectives of people of color while bolstering existing social institutions. Instead of statistics, charts, and tables, critical race theorists focus on in-depth qualitative interviews with people who have experienced racial profiling. The results, though not necessarily generalizable, reveal the pathos of racial profiling from the perspective of its victims.[19]

WHAT IS THE VALUE OF A BLACK LIFE?

One indication of the different value placed on the lives of people of color was brought home to me as a child. My father was an attorney and had a number of African-American clients. One of them, Ernie, was a plumber who smoked a pipe. One day Ernie went into the basement of a building that was under construction and lit up. He was immediately engulfed in flames produced by a gas leak. Ernie was burned severely around his face and arms, but survived.

I'll never forget the day my father came home from court after getting the jury verdict on Ernie's case. He was jubilant. I asked him how he did and he replied "We got a $100,000." Then he sighed "If only he was white."

From the inception of our nation, dark-skinned people have been devalued as human beings compared to whites. Although the word slave never appears in the United States Constitution, slavery and African-American slaves are addressed in it. Article 1, Section 2 which dealt with the issue of the number of representatives each state would get, prompted spirited debate. Some delegates wanted equal numbers for each state while others wanted the number of representatives apportioned based on the state's population. The ensuing compromise established a bicameral legislature with two senators from each state and the House of Representatives comprised of members based on states' population.

But the issue was joined when Northern states opposed Southern attempts to count slaves to prevent them from having more political influence. Thanks to the work of James Madison, who later became the fourth president of the United States, a compromise was reached which counted all "those bound to service" as three-fifths of one person.[20]

Nearly half (25 of 55) delegates to the Constitutional Convention were slave owners. This compromise effectively guaranteed the southern states a significant voice in the Congress and helped elect slave-holders as presidents in the early decades of the Republic. Twelve presidents owned slaves: Washington, Jefferson, Madison, Monroe, Jackson, Van Buren, Harrison, Tyler, Polk, Taylor, Johnson, and Grant.

The Constitution effectively established the second class citizenship of African-Americans until the Thirteenth Amendment was passed in 1865, which outlawed slavery and indentured servitude. But the residue of racial inferiority that stained society and the founders of the nation remain to this day, and are reflected in disparate tort settlements between blacks and whites.

In an analysis of disparities in damages between white and black plaintiffs obtained through tort litigation between 1865 and 2007, law professor Jennifer Wiggins concluded that "race and racism have affected the calculation of damages, largely to the detriment of African-American claimants."[21] Many factors contribute to the disparate awards between white and black plaintiffs including the preponderance of white jurors, lawyers, and judges, as well as prevailing racist norms which stereotyped blacks as inferior and unequal to whites. Wiggins contends that the introduction of contingency fee agreements between lawyers and plaintiffs opened up the system by affording a higher rate of compensation to black plaintiffs since white attorneys now had the financial incentive for representing them.

Courts have traditionally relied on race and gender-based tables as guides for establishing damages in tort cases including tangible elements such as lost wages, loss of future earnings, pecuniary loss, and medical expenses. Less objective factors figuring into settlement equations are pain and suffering, mental anguish, and loss of consortium. Reliance on established earnings tables to determine settlements has traditionally worked to the disadvantage of African-Americans because their life expectancy, wages, and lifetime earnings are substantially below whites. As law professor Martha Chamallas found, race and gender-based tables result in significantly lower awards for minority men and women.[22]

Quoting a classic railroad settlement, Wiggins demonstrates that court decisions in the early twentieth century were suffused with racist beliefs "A brakeman is not always a brakeman. A white brakeman is a brakeman; but a negro brakeman is most likely only a negro."[23] Consequently, the deaths of black people were treated differently than those of whites with lower compensatory scales that are still reflected in contemporary settlements.

An analysis of appellate wrongful death and survival cases in Louisiana from 1900 to 1950 revealed damage amounts to surviving black family members were less than half the amount awarded to surviving white family members. The average award for black family members per case was $3,559 compared to $8,245 for to surviving white family members.[24]

In the ensuing years, the pattern of disparate awards persisted, despite changes in the judicial system that have enabled African-American representation on juries and the bench. A classic study of tort remedies in over 9,000 cases from Cook County, Illinois, concluded that "race seemed to have a pervasive influence on the outcomes of civil jury trials." The researchers found that successful black plaintiffs received only three-fourths of the awards of white plaintiffs.[25]

CAPITAL PUNISHMENT AND COLOR

While differentials in economic awards are unfair by standards of decency, disparities in sentencing carry racial bias to a higher and more malevolent level. Knowledge of the prejudice that leads juries and judges to sentence nonwhites, especially African-Americans, to harsher prison sentences than whites, was used to establish a moratorium in the death penalty in the United States. A 5–4 United States Supreme Court decision (*Furman v. Georgia* 408 U.S. 153, 1972) held that the death penalty was a violation of the Eighth Amendment, constituting cruel and unusual punishment because juries imposed capital punishment arbitrarily. Three justices (Douglas, Stewart, and White) also held that the Fourteenth Amendment guaranteeing due process was violated by death penalties because of racial bias against blacks.

From 1930, when statistics began to be collected systematically, to 1967, 3,859 people were executed in the United States. Over half (54 percent) of them were black. Sixty percent of the executions were in the South. Twelve percent (455) men were executed for the crime of rape and 90 percent of them were black. In 1977 the United States Supreme Court ruled that the death penalty in the case of rape was unconstitutional (*Coker v. Georgia*, 433 U.S. 584) because the sentence was disproportionately used against African-Americans.

In 1997 the American Bar Association's (ABA) House of Delegates passed a resolution calling for a halt in executions until the nation's courts could ensure that such cases are "administered fairly and impartially, in accordance with due process," and with minimum risk of executing innocent people. The ABA also noted its desire to eliminate racial discrimination in capital sentencing.[26]

Between 1967 and 1972, 600 death row inmates had their sentences lifted, but the backlog of criminals awaiting execution for capital offenses climbed and pressure was exerted on the Court to reinstate capital punishment. In 1976 the United States Supreme Court modified its position on capital punishment, ruling that a two-stage trial for defendants in capital cases no longer violated the Eighth Amendment consideration of cruel and unusual punishment (*Gregg v. Georgia* 428 U.S. 153). Other states followed with similar modifications and executions were reintroduced. As of 2009, only 15 states and the District of Columbia do not allow capital punishment.[27]

The pattern of racial disparities in executions in the United States has continued. There were 50 executions in 2008—30 whites, 14 blacks, 2 Latinos and 4 Asians. A report by the United States Department of Justice in 2000 found significant racial and geographical disparities. Between 1995 and 2000, in 75 percent of cases where federal prosecutors sought the death penalty, the defendant was a minority group member and over half were black.[28]

In 2003 an Amnesty International Report revealed how black lives are still devalued in the criminal justice system in the United States. Looking at the 845 people executed since the resumption of capital punishment in 1977, Amnesty researchers found killers of white people were six times more likely to be put to death—80 percent of the murderers of whites were executed compared to 13 percent of people who killed blacks.[29] The American Civil Liberties Union reported in 2007 that from 1976 through 2003, 33 of the 55 people sentenced to death in federal courts were of color. U.S. Attorneys General were more likely to seek the death penalty in cases involving white victims, and death sentences were reduced in plea bargains for white defendants twice as often as for defendants of color.[30]

Such findings are even more shocking since the introduction of DNA research to establish defendants' guilt or innocence. From 1973 until 2009, 135 people on death row have been exonerated including 68 African-Americans, 53 whites and 12 Latinos.[31]

HOW RACE MATTERS

The process of demonizing and disparaging shades of skin, facial characteristics, and hair texture is often done unconsciously. It is the accepted norm, or so it is assumed by whites, who have made their features the standard against which non-Europeans are compared. When one group makes the rules and writes history in a way that reinforces their self-image at the expense of others, the effects can be devastating.

These facts illustrate the persistence of color as a determining and defining factor in how we relate to one another. W. E. B. Du Bois' comment about race being the defining issue of the twentieth century was prescient and prophetic. It looms as a central issue of the twenty-first century as well.[32] Despite the growing chorus among social scientists that class is a more important determinant of social status and discrimination than race, every day in myriad ways, we see, as philosopher and social critic Cornell West notes, "race matters."[33]

Race matters in the way we see the world. The prism of race colors our perceptions of one another and our decisions and judgments. Every law enforcement officer (and each one of us) sees society through the lens of learning we have been exposed to. All our prior experiences influence how we perceive social reality. Rightly or wrongly, our cognition is a function of who we are.

It is absurd to presume that law enforcement officers are capable of dissociating themselves from their prior learning and occupational experiences. Of course they profile people—that is the very foundation from which deductive reasoning and criminal investigations emanate. To the extent that they are successful at minimizing the derogatory effects of selective perception from their experiences, they are able to pursue their work in a more objective, impartial manner. But they, as everyone else, are products of our society and subject to the situational stressors which may produce biased, discriminatory, even horrendous outcomes.

This fact of human behavior highlights the hypocrisy of the U.S. Senate confirmation hearings of Judge Sonia Sotomayor in July 2009. A Puerto Rican woman who graduated from Princeton University and Yale Law School, appointed to the U.S. Appeals Court by President Bill Clinton in 1997, she was nominated by President Barack Obama to succeed Justice David Suter, who retired from the U.S. Supreme Court. When she was sworn into office on August 8, 2009 she became only the third female in history to serve on the Court and the first Hispanic.

Since she had an outstanding educational and judicial record, the white male conservatives had little evidence they could use to block her confirmation. They seized on statements she had made about judicial decision making, which, they contended, impugned her ability to be impartial. Comments she made at the 2001 Judge Mario G. Olmos Law and Cultural Diversity Lecture at the University of California, Berkeley caught their attention. She was demonstrating the importance of having people from diverse backgrounds on the bench and noted that "I would hope that a wise Latina woman with the richness of her experiences would more often than not reach a better conclusion than a white male who hasn't lived that life."

Charges of bias and subjectivity were leveled at her by white male Senators. However, Judge Sotomayor was only being candid in her observation that judges, like all humans, are products of their environment and experiences. Indeed, one of the arguments used to defend affirmative action has been the infusion of diverse perspectives into educational institutions and workplaces, making them more representative and inclusive. While she acknowledged that "the ethnicity of a judge may and will make a difference in our judging," she also pointed out that she questioned her "opinions, sympathies, and prejudice" in her quest for impartiality.[34]

Judge Sotomayor rightly noted that "to judge is an exercise of power," and that lies at the heart of the white male conservative reaction to her statements. In the final analysis, what they feared was her attempt at impartiality—the prospect that she might bring a different perspective to the bench—one that could challenge the entrenched power of white males in America. The relentless barrage unleashed because of her candid comments were twisted into sanctimonious disingenuous remarks by men who had fashioned policies of exclusion for decades and feared an erosion of their power. They, as she, knew all too well the meaning of Justice Oliver Wendell Holmes Jr.'s comment "A mind once stretched by a new idea never regains its original dimension," and they wanted to maintain their white privileged hegemony in the face of this threat.[35]

As Judge Sotomayor moved through several days of questioning by Senators, she managed to placate most of her adversaries by backtracking, recanting, and modifying her position. Since 1790, 111 people have served on the United States Supreme Court. Only two African-Americans and four women have been among them. Is it safe to assume that the 106 white males were unbiased because they represented the dominant color of society?

Rest assured, Justice Sotomayor will not be able to erase the images and experiences that brought her to the position she occupies any more or less than her white male predecessors. That is precisely why she was nominated by President Obama—to bring a different perspective to the highest court in the land.

Political scientist Andrew Hacker[36] analyzed research on these and other disparities and confirmed the 1968 Kerner Commission's[37] conclusions about the cause of racial unrest in the nation: America was two nations, one black and the other white, separate, distinct, and unequal. A recent analysis details the lingering effects of racism in our institutions and reveals that four decades later a more appropriate observation of our society would be that we are really four nations, one black, one brown, one yellow and one white, still separate, distinct, and unequal.[38] As educators, we must contemplate the significance of this discussion on the way we teach and how we view students of color in our classrooms.

NOTES

1. "Prisoners in 2008," Bulletin, U.S. Department of Justice, Bureau of Justice Statistics, December 2009, NCJ 228417.

2. William J. Sabol and Heather Couture, "Prison Inmates at Midyear, 2007," Bureau of Justice Statistics, U. S. Department of Justice, Washington, D.C., 2008, p. 21. On July 28, 2010 the U.S. House of Representatives passed legislation narrowing the sentence disparities between crack and powder cocaine convictions. The former drug is preponderantly used by blacks and the latter by whites, and sentences for possession and use of crack have been considerably harsher than those for powder cocaine. The Senate previously passed similar legislation and President Obama indicated he would sign the final bill.

3. See Michelle Alexander, *The New Jim Crow: Mass Incarceration in the Age of Colorblindness,* N.Y., The New Press, 2009, for an analysis of the phenomenon of high incarceration rates among African-American males and its relationship to drug laws in the U.S.

4. To gauge a sense of black concern see Beverly Daniel Tatum's discussion of this in *Why are All the Black Kids Sitting Together in the Cafeteria?* N.Y.: Basic Books, 1997.

5. Eduardo Bonilla-Silva, *Racism Without Racists,* Third edition, Lanham, MD: Rowman & Littlefield Publishers, Inc., 2010; Leslie Houts Picca and Joe R. Feagin, *Two-Faced Racism: Whites in the Backstage and Frontstage,* N.Y.: Routledge, 2007.

6. The trial and acquittal of three Los Angeles policemen for beating Rodney King, and the deadlocked jury on the fourth led to riots in Los Angeles in April, 1992 where 50 people were killed. A subsequent federal trial of the four officers eventuated in the conviction of two of them in April 1993. They were sentenced to 30 months for violating Mr. King's constitutional rights because of the excessive use of force. Police officers were exonerated in the Diallo and Bell cases.

7. H. Roy Kaplan, *Failing Grades: The Quest for Equity in America's Schools,* Second edition, Lanham, MD: Rowman & Littlefield Education, 2007.

8. Barack Obama, *The Audacity of Hope,* N.Y.: Barnes and Noble, 2006.

9. N.Y.: Random House, 2009.

10. Franklin's autobiography, *Mirror to America* (N.Y.: Farrar, Straus, and Giroux, 2005) is replete with similar affronts and indignities he experienced and endured. Elie Wiesel, another Visiting Professor at Eckerd College, Nobel Peace Laureate, Medal of Freedom recipient, and Holocaust survivor, was heckled by anti-Semitic white supremacists during a speech he gave in the Tampa area.

11. N.Y. Harper Perennial, 1994.

12. Ellis Cose, *Newsweek Magazine*, January 24, 2009.

13. E. Franklin Frazier, *Black Bourgeoisie*, Glencoe, Ill.: Free Press, 1957; Manning Marable, *The Great Wells of Democracy: The Meaning of Race in American Life*, Cambridge, Mass.: Basic Civitas Books, 2002.

14. Brian Withrow, *Racial Profiling from Rhetoric to Reason*, Upper Saddle River, N.J.: Pearson Education, Inc., 2006, p. 24.

15. Ibid. pp. 39–76.

16. "Threat and Humiliation: Racial Profiling, National Security, and Human Rights in the United States," N.Y.: Amnesty International USA, October 2004.

17. See also the American Civil Liberties Union for their "Campaign Against Racial Profiling." at: *http://www.aclu.org/racial-justice/racial-profiling*.

18. See: *http://www.aclu.org/intlhumanrights/racial/justice/40069prs20090630. html*.

19. Karen S. Glover, *Racial Profiling: Research, Racism and Resistance*, Lanham, Md.: Rowman & Littlefield Publisher, Inc., 2009. For collections of writings on race from the "critical" perspective see: Kimberle Crenshaw, Neil Gotanda, Gary Peller and Kendall Thomas (eds.), *Critical Race Theory: The Key Writings that Formed the Movement*, N.Y.: The New Press, 1995; Richard Delgado and Jean Stefancic (eds.), *Critical Race Theory: The Cutting Edge*, Second edition, Philadelphia: Temple University Press, 2000; Philomena Essed and David Theo Goldberg (eds.), *Race Critical Theories: Text and Context*, Malden, Massachusetts: Blackwell Publishers, 2002.

20. "Representatives and direct taxes shall be apportioned among the several states which may be included within this union, according to their respective numbers, which shall be determined by adding the whole number of persons, including those bound to service for a term of years, and excluding Indians not taxed, three-fifths of all other persons."

21. Jennifer B. Wiggins, "Damages in Tort Litigation: Thoughts on Race and Remedies, 1865–2007, *The Review of Litigation*, vol. 27, 2008, p. 39.

22. Martha Chamallas, "Civil Rights in Ordinary Tort Cases: Race, Gender, and the Calculation of Economic Loss," Ohio State University Moritz College of Law Working Paper Series, #16, 2005 at: *http://law.bepress.com/osulwps/moritzlaw/art16*.

23. Wiggins, op. cit., p. 48.

24. Wiggins, loc. cit., p. 57.

25. Audrey Chin and Mark A. Peterson, *Deep Pockets, Empty Pockets: Who Wins in Cook County Jury Trials*, Santa Monica, Cal: Institute for Civil Justice, Rand Corporation, 1985.

26. For information on the American Bar Association's Death Penalty Moratorium Project go to: *http://www.abanet.org/moratorium/*.

27. Sources: PBS Frontline at: *http://www.pbs.org/wgbh/pages/frontline/angel/ timeline.html*. "History of the Death Penalty and Recent Developments," University of Alaska Justice Center at: *http://www.justice.uaa.alaska.edu/death/history.html*.

28. Raymond Bonner and Marc Lacey, "Pervasive Disparities Found in Federal Death Penalty," *New York Times*, September 12, 2000, p. A 18.

29. "Death Penalty and Racism," Fight the Death Penalty in USA at: *http://www. fdp.dk/uk/racism.php.*

30. "The Persistent Problem of Racial Disparities in the Federal Death Penalty," American Civil Liberties Union Capital Punishment Project, at: *http:www//aclu.org/ pdfs/capital/racial_disparities_federal_deathpen.pdf.*

31. Death Penalty Information Center at: *http://www.deathpenaltyinfor.org/ innocence-list-those-freed-death-row.*

32. W. E. B. Du Bubois, *The Souls of Black Folk*, N.Y.: New American Library, 1903.

33. Cornell West, *Race Matters,* N.Y.: Vintage Books, 1993.

34. For more on her perspective see: Charlie Savage, "A Judge's View of Judging Is on the Record," *New York Times,* May 14, 2009: A21.

35. Compare the business as usual Supreme Court decision of *Citizens United v. Federal Elections Commission* rendered on January 21, 2010 which lifted corporate spending on election campaigns, effectively permitting the white-dominated corporate establishment to bankroll candidates who favor and perpetuate *their* perspectives. For a review of the decision see: Adam Liptak, "Justices, 5-4, Reject Corporate Spending Limit," *New York Times,* January 22, 2010, p. A1.

36. Andrew Hacker, *Two Nations,* N.Y.: Scribner, 2003, First edition, 1992.

37. The National Advisory Commission on Civil Disorders.

38. Matthew Desmond and Mustafa Emirbayer, *Racial Domination, Racial Progress,* N.Y.: McGraw-Hill, 2010.

Chapter 15

How the Military Shaped Blacks' Progress

I don't care about the color of your skin, just kill as many sons of bitches wearing green as you can.

—General George S. Patton

BLACK MILITARY EXPERIENCES

While attitudes are one way of assessing the status of race relations in the United States, they are an imperfect barometer of the situation. People may disguise their true feelings and, while personally liking or disliking someone, they may behave differently based on the situation they're in. As we have seen, there is a wealth of behavioral data that reveals the ongoing effects of racism in the United States.

One of the most blatant and pernicious forms of discrimination in our society is in housing, and this is inextricably linked to blacks' participation in the military. There is a long tradition of housing segregation in the United States dating back before the Civil War, and public policies of every presidential administration perpetuated this despite blacks' outstanding service to their country, which they hoped would bring freedom and a better life.

When President Lincoln signed the Emancipation Proclamation on January 1, 1863, he freed only those slaves in Confederate breakaway states, not loyal Border States or those in Confederate regions under Union control. Lincoln assumed that the move would cripple the South's already beleaguered economy and lead to rebellion among slaves and their enlistment in the Union Army. In fact, 180,000 blacks fought in segregated units for the Union during the Civil War, although racist attitudes and policies prevented them from participating fully. Many were relegated to support services, but a number of all-black "Colored" units served as assault troops and distinguished themselves in battle. For example, the vaunted Massachusetts 54th Volunteer Infantry assaulted Fort Wagner on Morris Island, South Carolina near Charleston, and included Lewis and Charles Douglass, sons of the famous ex-slave and orator, Frederick Douglass. The film *Glory* was based on their heroics.

A day before, on July 17, the First Kansas Colored Infantry Regiment fought in what is now Oklahoma and routed a Confederate force. Their white commander, General James Blunt exclaimed "I never saw such fighting as was done by the Negro regiment … The question that negroes will fight is settled, besides they make better troops in every respect than any I have ever had under my command."[1]

But their valor was largely ignored. Following emancipation and the passage of the Thirteenth Amendment, blacks had no where to go, so many stayed on, became sharecroppers, and were tyrannized by the KKK and Jim Crow segregation laws. The 40 acres and a mule that had been promised freed slaves by General Sherman in Special Field Orders, No. 15 were in effect for one year, from 1865 to 1866 and limited to blacks who settled on islands "from Charleston, south, the abandoned rice fields along the rivers for thirty miles back from the sea, and the country bordering the St. Johns river, Florida."[2]

Blacks who served in World War I were also misled and disappointed. Although 400,000 were drafted or enlisted, only 10 percent fought in combat units which were, as in previous conflicts, segregated, and most of these were in France. Although 127 Medals of Honor were awarded to U.S. servicemen, none were given to blacks. Sergeant Henry Johnson, a black serviceman, was, however, the first American to receive the French Croix de Guerre. In 1991, President George H. W. Bush, awarded the Congressional Medal of Honor posthumously to Corporal Freddie Stowers for leading an assault against a German-held position in France.

MIGRATION, SEGREGATION, AND THE PERSISTENCE OF DISCRIMINATION

Although the goal of "making the world safe for democracy" in President Wilson's words sounded noble, the life experience of African-Americans and black soldiers did not ring true to the ideal. But the mass migration of blacks out of the South in search of work, housing, and a better life began in earnest. What awaited them in the North was segregation and discrimination—perhaps more subtle at times, but nevertheless pernicious and demeaning.

Writing about black migration into Detroit, Thompson[3] notes that the number of African-Americans living outside the South went from 800,000 to 9.7 million between 1910 and 1966, with 5.5 million migrating after 1940. African-American migration following World War II is referred to as the third wave of black migration from the South, preceded by the first wave between 1840 and 1890 and the second wave from 1916 to 1930.[4] A contemporary fourth wave has been bringing African-Americans back to the South with the prospect of jobs and lower living costs.

Although African-Americans moved into northern cities in search of a better life, every big northern city had (and still has) its equivalent of housing apartheid—an inner core inhabited by the most recent wave of immigrants and blacks. Rigid territorial boundaries demarcated one ethnic group's territory from another, such as New York City's Little Italy (Italian), Hell's Kitchen (Irish), Harlem (African-American), Spanish Harlem (Latino), the Bronx (Jewish), Astoria (Greek), and Washington Heights (Dominicans). Living conditions in these places were substandard with tenements, slums, poverty, and crime.

White immigrants suffered and toiled under these conditions too, but their color was their ticket out. They and their descendants could learn the language, change their names, and leave, while darker-skinned inhabitants were denied that opportunity and many remain there to this day.

The great economic boom produced by World War II liberated enslaved people all around the world. From occupied Europe with its death camps, to China and Africa, people emerged from under the Axis boot and began rebuilding democratic societies, often basing their constitutions on principles enunciated in the U.S. Declaration of Independence and Constitution. But though they fought bravely for these ideals abroad, freedom, economic success, even democracy eluded African-Americans at home.

In fact, over one million African-Americans served in the military in World War II—in segregated units. And once again, many of them were relegated to support roles because of commanders' racist beliefs that they were lazy, unruly, and incapable of mastering rudimentary military tactics and skills. Yet, without the considerable help of African-American troops, the Alcan (Alaskan Highway) could not have been built in 1942—in just eight months by the all black 364th regiment after they were transferred from Camp Van Dorn near Centreville, Mississippi following racial disturbances between the black soldiers and the white Jim Crow town.

The Lido Road between India and China, built predominantly by African-American soldiers, provided indispensable supplies to our allies in the war against the Japanese. The all-black Tuskegee Airmen in the 99th Pursuit Squadron and the 332 Fighter Group, exhibited exceptional flying skill and valor, and put the lie to white supremacists' contentions that blacks weren't smart enough to fly. They never lost a bomber they escorted, and again proved African-Americans' ability and desire to be included in the promise of America.[5]

Yet, the U.S. military was still segregated during World War II. Some of the most important contributions to social science research were the outcome of experiments conducted by social scientists[6] to determine whether it was prudent and possible to integrate the United States' Armed Services. Based upon their findings, and building pressure to extend minimal liberties to black soldiers who fought and sacrificed for American ideals on foreign soil without enjoying the same rights at home, President Harry S. Truman signed Executive Order 9981 on July 26, 1948, desegregating the U.S. military.[7]

While today's military is thought to offer minorities access to upward mobility, African-Americans are still underrepresented in the highest ranks. Although blacks make up nearly 17 percent of the military, they only account for 9 percent of officers. Only 5.6 percent of the 923 general officers and admirals were black, including only one of 38 four-star generals or admirals serving as of May 2008. Just ten African-American men have ever attained four-star rank, five in the Army, four in the air force, and one in the Navy.[8]

The "Armed Forces Equal Opportunity Survey" issued in 1999 found major differences in the perceptions of black and white personnel in regard to race relations. Both groups thought race relations were better in the service than in the nation as a whole, and opportunities in the military were better than five years previously. But more whites felt this way than blacks, and blacks were significantly more likely than whites to report a negative military experience such as punishment, poor evaluation, or disadvantageous assignment. Blacks were the most likely group to state that the military paid too little attention to racial/ethnic discrimination and harassment (62 percent versus 17 percent for whites).[9]

While 432 Congressional Medals of Honor were awarded to servicemen and women in World War II, no African-Americans received that award; that is, not until 1997, when President Bill Clinton awarded seven African-Americans (six posthumously) this honor.

Racism also denied such recognition to the 18,000 gallant Japanese-Americans of the segregated 442 Combat Infantry Brigade who were drafted or volunteered for duty while over 110,000 family and friends were interned in "relocation camps" in desolate parts of the southwest. This unit received 18,000 individual citations, eight Presidential unit citations, and lost 700 men while receiving 9,500 purple hearts. Yet, this most decorated unit in the nation's military history did not receive a single Medal of Honor.

PUBLIC POLICY, RACISM, AND HOUSING

As a gesture of gratitude to the 16.1 million people who served in the U.S. military during World War II, Congress passed the Servicemen's Readjustment Act of 1944, better known as the G.I. Bill of Rights. It contained provisions to assist returning veterans in pursuing higher education and obtaining affordable housing through federally subsidized loans and mortgages. But the benefits were unevenly apportioned and blacks did not receive nearly as much as whites.[10]

Southern white democrats created a formidable block in the United States Congress. Following World War II they were able to omit African-Americans from progressive legislation, notably Social Security coverage for farm workers and domestic servants, as well as laws covering them for minimum wages and working hours. Anti-discrimination provisions in laws were also omitted from social programs such as school lunches, hospital construction grants, and community health services. "... at the very moment when a wide array of public policies was providing most white Americans with valuable tools to advance their social welfare—insure their old age, get good jobs, acquire economic security, build assets, and gain middle-class status—most black Americans were left behind or left out."[11]

This process was facilitated by writing racially oriented provisions into laws. For example, over 60 percent of the black labor force, including 75 percent of those employed in the South in the 1930s, were excluded from unions, minimum wages, regulated working hours, and Social Security. Placing the administration of these laws in the hands of racist local officials further ensured the perpetuation of Jim Crow society. Powerful Southern democrats lobbied effectively to prevent federal policies from changing the balance of power in their region.[12]

Many of the discriminatory real estate practices that still affect minorities emanate from that G.I. Bill. Although it gave millions of soldiers the opportunity to enter higher education and purchase housing with minimum down payments in Veterans Administration-backed mortgages at around four percent, these avenues to upward mobility were disproportionately reserved for white veterans. In education, most white-dominated schools, especially in the South, would not admit blacks, and private schools had rigid quotas that limited the enrollment of blacks, Jews, and other minorities.

By 1946, only a fifth of the 100,000 blacks who had applied for educational benefits had registered for college. Historically black colleges and universities did, however, experience a dramatic increase in enrollment. Between 1940 and 1950 enrollment in these schools increased from 1.08 percent to 3.6 percent of the total United States college and graduate enrollment.[13]

In real estate, federal agencies "endorsed the use of race-restrictive covenants until 1950, and explicitly refused to underwrite loans that would introduce 'incompatible' racial groups into White residential enclaves."[14] Furthermore, the private sector mimicked these policies. According to the National Commission on Fair Housing, "By the 1920s, deeds in nearly every new housing development in the North prevented the use or ownership of homes by anyone other than 'the Caucasian race.'"[15] Although the U.S. Supreme Court held them unenforceable in 1948, the practice continued.

From 1930 through 1960, the National Association of Real Estate Board's ethical guidelines stipulated that a realtor "should never be instrumental in introducing to a neighborhood a character or property or occupancy, members of any race or nationality, or any individual whose presence will be clearly detrimental to property values in a neighborhood."[16]

While the federal government established a public housing program to improve the quality of life of low income people in the 1930s, most of the affordable housing was in segregated public housing projects. In fact, public housing projects were segregated by law in the South, and elsewhere around the nation they adjoined segregated neighborhoods or were constructed in undesirable areas.[17]

The stench of racism penetrated into public housing policy in other ways. In an effort to democratize housing, New Deal programs were developed, but these primarily benefited whites. They also fostered the development of predominantly white suburbs as blacks and other minorities were confined to the central cities. To influence lending policies the Federal Housing Authority prepared "'neighborhood security maps' that were based largely on the racial, ethnic, and economic status of residents."[18]

During this time, the American Institute of Real Estate Appraisers implemented a ranking system based on the racial composition of the community. English, Germans, Scotch, Irish, and Scandinavians ranked on top and blacks and Mexicans at the bottom.[19] The magnanimous and "benevolent" policies of FDR's "New Deal" actually prevented blacks from obtaining quality housing. FDR's Administration's Underwriting Manual described the "risks posed by the commingling of 'inharmonious racial groups,'" and it maintained "that properties shall continue to be occupied by the same social and racial classes." Further, it "instructed appraisers to predict 'the probability of the location being invaded by ... incompatible racial and social groups.'"[20]

The impact of such policies on African-American home ownership was catastrophic. The FHA's Underwriting Manual that was distributed to lenders between 1930 and 1960, prevented African-Americans from owning homes. During the thirty years when the Federal Housing Administration was helping whites secure homes and build the American Dream, fewer than one percent of all mortgages were issued to blacks.[21]

Sociologist Dalton Conley maintains that this policy not only prevented African-Americans from increasing their wealth and social status by becoming suburban homeowners, it accelerated the decline of real estate values in central cities because willing sellers could not find buyers.[22]

Similar discriminatory policies by the United States Department of Agriculture (USDA) led to the demise of most of the black farmers in the United States. On April 14, 1999 Federal District Court Judge Paul L. Friedman approved a settlement agreement and a consent decree resolving a class action discrimination suit (*Pigford v. Glickman*, No. 97-1978) by black farmers who had contended for decades that they were being denied USDA farm loans and forced to wait longer than white loan applicants.

A 1994 investigation commissioned by the USDA confirmed the complaints of black farmers. It was found that the largest USDA loans went to corporations and white male farmers. Loans received by black male farmers averaged $4,000 less than white farmers, and 97 percent of disaster payments went to white farmers.

Although the class action suit proceeded and the government agreed to the Consent Decree, it underestimated the number of claimants. As of June 15, 2009, the Office of the Monitor appointed to oversee the case certified that there were 22,719 eligible members in the class and 15,630 (69 percent) had been approved. At that time the awards totaled $763,950,000 in cash ($50,000 per claimant), and $1,512,000 in non-credit awards ($3,000 per claimant), $190,987,500 for which claimants are entitled as IRS payments, and total debt relief of $38,082,668.

On February 18, 2010 the Obama Administration announced a $1.25 billion settlement to bring closure to the case. Congress must still pass the measure. Most claimants were entitled to a cash settlement of $50,000 plus loan forgiveness and offsets for tax liability. Another group of claimants pursued a higher award based on evidence of discrimination and damages they produced.[23]

KEEPING NEIGHBORHOODS WHITE

Although relatively few African-Americans live in predominantly white residential areas, whites fear black intrusion. White racism precipitated the practice of "blockbusting" by unscrupulous realtors who, relying on stereotypical fears of white homeowners, would move black families into white areas to produce panic selling and purchase homes at fire-sale prices. Although illegal today, the National Commission on Fair Housing found widespread "racial steering" where realtors routinely guide whites to more affluent areas and blacks and other minorities to less desirable places. A study by the United States Department of Housing and Urban Development (HUD) in 2000 that utilized testers in metropolitan areas found very high levels of discrimination and steering against blacks, Latinos, Asians, and Native Americans looking for homes.[24]

This practice persists irrespective of income level. Racial segregation among African-Americans and Latinos with incomes above $60,000 is nearly as great as that among lower economic groups and these disparities increased more substantially during the 1990s.[25] This translates into a pattern of residential segregation wherein whites in metropolitan areas of the United States live in neighborhoods that are 80 percent white and just seven percent black, and blacks live in neighborhoods that are only 33 percent white and 51 percent black.[26]

A report by the U.S. Census painted a more optimistic assessment of residential discrimination based on an analysis of segregation in housing patterns. It noted that declines in segregation among blacks were most prominent among all the ethnic groups they observed between 1980 and 2000, but "segregation was still higher for African-Americans than for other groups across all measures," and the most segregated large metropolitan areas of the United States were in the Northeast-Midwest "Rust Belt."[27]

Nevertheless, the United Nations Committee on the Elimination of Racial Discrimination (CERD) concluded in January 2008, that housing segregation in the United States was still widespread. "Racial segregation is an insidious and persistent fact of American life. Discrimination on the basis of race, while on the decline according to some estimates, continues to pervade nearly every aspect of the housing market in the United States." Further, the report faults the United States government as well as state and local governments for "failure to fulfill its obligations related to housing under the International Convention on the Elimination of All Forms of Racial Discrimination," by pursuing policies and practices that "perpetuate segregation and concentrate poverty in communities of color...."[28]

The report singled out budget cuts and policies at the federal level that have restricted affordable housing choices and mobility for people of color, and the increase in racial steering of prospective clients by realtors. For example, the construction of public housing in racially segregated communities perpetuates racial segregation. Today, 69 percent of public housing residents are people of color and over a quarter of the residents of public housing projects live below the poverty level. Only eight percent of households in public housing have incomes over $20,000.[29]

Predatory lending practices affecting non-whites were found to persist, and the report noted that people of color were 30 percent more likely to receive a higher rate subprime loan than similarly situated white borrowers.[30] Such practices keep African-Americans at the lowest rate of homeownership of any ethnic group in the U.S., 47.5 percent versus 74.9 percent for whites and 48.9 percent for Latinos in 2008.

THE SUBPRIME CATASTROPHE AND RACIST REAL ESTATE PRACTICES

Amassing wealth and passing it down to one's descendants is often done through owning property, but federal policies that influenced the GI Bill of Rights and federal home loan initiatives during the 1930 and 1940s fostered discrimination against blacks. The confinement of blacks to less desirable and inexpensive property by redlining (denying loans and mortgages to blacks in the inner city) deprived them of living in better areas and realizing appreciation of their property. The median home value for blacks in 2000 was $80,600 compared to $123,400 for whites. The median equity in black homes in 2002 was $40,000 compared to $79,200 for whites.[31] The public advocacy group, United for a Fair Economy, estimated that African-Americans lost $71 billion to $93 billion in home value wealth from the effects of subprime loans between 1998 and 2006 *prior to the recession of 2006-2008*.[32]

The fact that whites' median wealth is ten times that of blacks ($109,100 versus $10,000 in 2009) reflects the effects of such policies, as well as provisions in Social Security that excluded domestic servants and farm workers from benefits. The recent downturn in the U.S. housing market has been particularly onerous on black and Latino Americans. A report issued by the now-defunct Association of Community Organizations for Reform Now (ACORN) in 2007 revealed widespread abuse of minorities by lenders.

African-American and Latino home purchasers were 2.7 and 2.3 times more likely than white borrowers to be issued high cost home loans. The report also noted that for refinance loans African-American and Latino borrowers were 1.8 and 1.4 times respectively more likely than white borrowers to be issued high cost loans. These disparities existed even among homeowners *of the same income level*. Upper income African-Americans were 3.3 times more likely than upper income whites to receive a high-cost loan when purchasing a home, and upper income Latinos were 3 times more likely to receive a high-interest loan than their white counterparts.[33]

The ACORN study also looked into questionable subprime mortgage lending practices. It reported that minorities were disproportionately represented among subprime mortgage borrowers and they were paying higher rates for adjustable rate mortgages (ARMS) which, they correctly predicted, would explode creating an enormous number of foreclosures that would adversely affect blacks and Latinos. ACORN estimated that over $1 trillion in ARMS were expected to reset over the next three years affecting over 2 million existing loans that could be foreclosed. The irony of this situation was that between one-third and one half of the subprime loan borrowers could have qualified for standard fixed rate loans and lower cost mortgages.[34]

A PEW Hispanic Center report on trends in homeownership among Latinos and blacks found a decrease in housing purchases among these groups in recent years, with evidence that costlier subprime mortgages were being disproportionately sold to them. In 2007, 27.6 percent of Hispanics and 33.5 percent of blacks purchased subprime mortgages compared to 10.5 percent of white customers. Subprime mortgages had a 3 point higher annual percentage rate for blacks and 2.5 point higher rate for Latinos than the typical 30 year fixed-rate conventional mortgage.[35]

The *New York Times* reported alleged racist policies by former Wells Fargo Bank loan officers who participated in predatory subprime mortgage transactions with minority clients. They admitted switching customers qualified for traditional mortgages to more expensive subprime loans. One former loan officer at the bank said blacks were referred to as "mud people" and subprime lending as "ghetto loans."[36] The *Times'* own analysis of mortgage lending in New York City revealed that black households with annual income over $68,000 were nearly five times more often found to hold high interest subprime mortgages than whites with comparable or even lower income, and mortgage defaults for blacks and Latinos were three times higher in mostly minority census tracts compared to white ones. Minority customers were targeted for risky subprime mortgages. A third of the subprime mortgages given in 2007 went to borrowers with credit scores that would have qualified them for cheaper conventional loans.[37]

In March 2009, the NAACP filed lawsuits in Washington, D.C. and California against two of the nation's largest lending institutions: Wells Fargo and HSBC. The lawsuits alleged "systematic, institutionalized racism in subprime home mortgage lending." The NAACP alleged that African-American homeowners were being issued higher loan rates than white borrowers and studies revealed this practice was pervasive. "It is time for these lenders to be held accountable," said Benjamin Todd Jealous, President of the NAACP. "Predatory lending policies and practices are legally actionable, morally reprehensible, and fiscally irresponsible," said Austin Tighe, lead counsel for the NAACP.[38]

The NAACP had similar pending litigation against other mortgage companies including Accredited Home Lenders, Inc., Ameriquest Mortgage Co., Bear Sterns Residential Mortgage Corp., First Tennessee Bank d/b/a First Horizon National Corp., Fremont Investment and Loan, GMAC Mortgage Group, LLC, GMAC ResCap, Long Beach Mortgage, and Sun-Trust Mortgage.

"Lenders named in the suits, on average, made high-cost sub-prime loans to higher qualified African-Americans 54 percent of the time, compared to 23 percent of the time for Caucasians," according to Angela Ciccolo, Interim General Counsel for the NAACP. Although the defendants denied wrong-doing (Wells Fargo termed the suit "unfounded and reckless"), earlier in the year a federal court denied a motion by defendants to dismiss a similar case, finding that the NAACP had standing to bring the lawsuit and it had adequately stated its claims for the suit to proceed. In fact, one lender entered into a preliminary settlement with the NAACP and a number of others were engaged in similar discussions.[39]

As the number of home foreclosures in the United States soared to over four and a half percent of all home mortgages in 2009, largely as a result of subprime mortgages in default, the federal government sought to provide some relief to home buyers whose American Dream had become a nightmare. But programs aimed at modifying troubled mortgages were having little impact with relatively few mortgages being restructured. A report by The National Consumer Law Center explained that little progress had been made because loan servicers, those individuals and organizations who, for the most part collect monthly mortgage payments and fees, receive more profit from foreclosed loans than from modifying them. The present mortgage lending system thereby incentivizes and perpetuates greed and social inequality.[40]

Bank of America became an accessory to the mortgage debacle when it purchased Countrywide Financial Corporation in July 2008. Three senior Countrywide executives were charged with civil fraud and insider trading in 2009, including Angelo Mozilo, former CEO of the company. On June 7, 2010, Bank of America agreed to pay $108 million to settle federal charges that Countrywide collected exorbitant fees for services such as property inspections and landscaping from borrowers who were behind in their mortgages. Federal Trade Commission chairman, Jon Leibowitz, character-ized Countrywide's actions as "callous conduct, which took advantage of consumers already at the end of their financial rope." He noted that Coun-trywide profited at both ends of the subprime mortgage transactions by making risky loans to homeowners during the boom years and again when the loans failed.[41]

FEDERAL INTERVENTION

It is evident that racial inequality in housing was precipitated through policies that were implemented by the federal government during the 1930s. Together with racist lending policies and restrictive covenants that forbade the sale of homes to blacks, Jews, and other ethnic minorities, African-Americans and other people of color were relegated to the inner cities and toiled in the same types of support services they had undertaken in the military—cooking, cleaning, day labor, child care, and caring for the sick and elderly. Though these endeavors were essential for the existence of society, they were inadequately compensated, further perpetuating social inequality in the nation's cities.

Despite federal efforts to democratize society, discrimination continued. It was not until 1968 that the Federal Fair Housing Act, (Title VIII of the Civil Rights Act) was passed prohibiting discrimination in housing and housing-related transactions based on race, color, religion, and national origin. This legislation was amended and extended in 1984 and 1988. Complimentary legislation, the Home Mortgage Disclosure Act, was passed in 1975 and amended in 1989, and the Community Reinvestment Act of 1977 sought to attenuate discrimination in housing and equalize opportunities for blacks and other minorities.

Housing disparities and discrimination in the United States are widespread even in the face of attempts to eliminate them. Although there are 108 state and local agencies as well as the federal government involved in efforts to ensure equality of access to housing, the federal Department of Housing and Urban Development received 10,150 complaints alleging unfair practices in 2007, a 25 percent increase since 2003 and 75 percent increase over the last 10 years. HUD studies consistently reveal African-Americans, Hispanics/ Latinos, Asians, and Native Americans receive unfavorable treatment 20 percent of the time they seek to purchase or rent a home.[42]

While experts generally agree that some progress in reducing discrimination in housing has occurred since the passage of this legislation, it is not clear whether the laws are responsible for advances or other factors such as changing residential patterns and norms produced these changes.[43] As our country becomes increasingly more ethnically diverse, much work remains to be done.

Indeed, a report by the Civil Rights Project at UCLA demonstrates how residential segregation has created school districts throughout the United States that are more segregated today than before the momentous Supreme Court decision of Brown vs. Board of Education in 1954. The report noted that two in five black and Latino students attend "intensely segregated" schools and 60 percent of the students come from families living near or below the poverty line.[44]

In the more than four decades since the passage of the Fair Housing Act some progress has been made in reducing residential segregation, but the Report of the National Commission on Fair Housing and Equality Opportunity concluded that "Despite all of the evidence that deeply entrenched discrimination and segregation continue, and the evidence that large parts of our communities are at risk, there has been no national government leadership, and no national message, about the importance of these issues."[45]

After conducting hearings in Chicago, Houston, Los Angeles, Boston, and Atlanta, the Commission stated that "… discrimination continues to be endemic, intertwined into the very fabric of our lives." And "despite strong legislation, past and ongoing discriminatory practices in the nation's housing and lending markets continue to produce extreme levels of residential segregation that result in significant disparities between minority and non-minority households, access to good jobs, quality education, homeownership attainment, and asset accumulation. This fact has led many to question whether the federal government is doing all it can to combat housing discrimination. Worse, some fear that rather than combating segregation, HUD and other federal agencies are promoting it through the administration of their housing, lending, and tax programs."[46]

The United Nations (CERD) report was especially critical of HUD, noting that 2 million complaints of racial discrimination in housing occur annually, fully 40 percent of HUD's volume, but HUD has been largely unresponsive to them with less than half of one percent of fair housing violations resulting in formal complaints processed by that organization. In the few cases it decides to pursue, HUD takes an average of 470 days to close them. Only 3.3 percent of all cases filed with HUD between 1989 and 2003 resulted in a reasonable cause of determination for investigating discrimination being issued.

The consequences of housing discrimination are reflected in our nation's schools, not just in the obvious resegregation which reflects disparities in color, but in the racial and class antagonisms among and between students, teachers, and administrators as they grapple with the latent and manifest legacies of ideologies that influence the ways they perceive and interact with one another.

NOTES

1. History of African-Americans in the Civil War, National Park Service, *http://cwar.nps.gov/civilwar/africanamericans.htm.*

2. "Forty Acres and a Mule: Slavery is Over," PBS, see: *http://www.pbs.org/wgbh/amex/reconstruction/40acres/ps_so15.html.* Retrieved 2/5/09.

3. Heather Thompson, *Whose Detroit: Politics, Labor and Race in a Modern City,* Ithaca: Cornell University Press, 2004.

4. See Eric Arnesen, *Black Protest and the Great Migration: A Brief History with Documents,* Boston: Bedford/St. Martins, 2003.

5. For more on this topic see: Bernard C. Nalty, *Strength for the Fight: A History of Black Americans in the Military,* N.Y.: The Free Press, 1986.

6. See Samuel Stouffer et. al. *The American Soldier,* 4 vols. Princeton, N.J.: Princeton University Press, 1949.

7. See Carol Anderson, *Eyes Off the Prize,* N.Y. Cambridge University Press, 2003 for a discussion of the political machinations that led President Truman to issue that order, which, in effect was an attempt to attract the black votes he needed to win the election.

8. "Blacks Still Rare in Top U.S. Military Ranks," *USA Today,* July 23, 2008.

9. Jacquelyn Scarville, et al., "Armed Forces Equal Opportunity Survey," Defense Manpower Data Center, Survey and Program Evaluation Division, Department of Defense, Arlington, VA, 1999.

10. For an extended discussion of this point see: Ira Katznelson, *When Affirmative Action Was White,* N.Y.: W.W. Norton Company, 2005.

11. Ibid., pp. 22–23.

12. Ibid., pp. 22–23. This book offers a comprehensive analysis of the deceitful machinations at the local and federal level that provided the foundation for the perpetuation of second class status for black Americans.

13. "African-Americans and the GI Bill" Encyclopedia at: *http://en.allexperts .com/e/a/af/african_americans_and_the_g.i._bill.htm.* In July 2008 the U.S. Congress passed a new GI Bill which went into effect in August 2009. It provides more generous educational benefits to service members who served on active duty for ninety or more days since September 10, 2001. For a summary of these benefits go to: *http://www.gibill.va.gov/.*

14. "The Future of Fair Housing," Report of the National Commission on Fair Housing and Equal Opportunity, December 2008, p. 8

15. Ibid., p. 7.

16. Ibid., p. 8.

17. Ibid., p. 8.

18. Ibid., p. 8. See the description of how President Franklin Roosevelt's Home Owners Loan Corporation legitimized racism by prioritizing homogeneous communities of "American business and professional men" in David Kushner's *Levittown,* N.Y.: Walker and Co., 2009; and Beryl Satter's *Family Properties: Race, Real Estate, and the Exploitation of Black Urban America,* N.Y.: Metropolitan, 2009, for an insightful personal account of how federal housing policies created hardship and financial distress among African-Americans in the Chicago area.

19. Ibid., p. 8.

20. Cited in "Residential Segregation and Housing Discrimination in the United States: Violations of the International Convention on the Elimination of All Forms of Racial Discrimination," A Report of the U.N. Commission on the Elimination of

Racial Discrimination, (CERD Report), The Poverty and Race Research and Action Council and The National Fair Housing Alliance, Washington, D.C., January 2008, p. 4. For a further discussion of these policies see: Christopher Bonastia, *Knocking on the Door: The Federal Government's Attempt to Desegregate the Suburbs,* Princeton, N.J.: Princeton University Press, 2006.

21. D. L. Kirp, J. P. Dwyer and L. A. Rosenthal, *Our Town: Race, Housing, and the Soul of Suburbia,* New Brunswick, N.J.: Rutgers University Press, 1995, p. 7.

22. Dalton Conley, *Being Black, Living in the Red: Race, Wealth, and Social Policy in America,* Berkeley: University of California Press, 1999, p. 37.

23. For background on this case see: "The Pigford Case: USDA Settlement of a Discrimination Suit by Black Farmers," Congressional Research Service Report for Congress, Order Code RS20430, December 6, 2005; "National Statistics Regarding *Pigford v. Vilsack* Track A Implementation as of June 15, 2009," Office of the Monitor, *Pigford v. Vilsack* (D.D.C.) Brewington v. Vilsack (D.D.C.). For further information on the Pigford case see: Timothy C. Pigford, et al., Plaintiffs, v. Dan Glickman, Secretary, The United States Department of Agriculture, Defendant, Civil Action No. 97-1978 (PLF), U.S. District Court for the District of Columbia, and a review of the case in Tadlock Cowan and Jody Feder, "The Pigford Case: USDA Settlement of a Discrimination Suit by Black Farmers," Congressional Research Service Report for Congress, 7-5700, at: *http://digital.library.unt.edu/ark:/67531/ metacrs9671/.* An earlier attempt at a settlement revealed that the federal government miscalculated when a flood of similar class action suits were filed by other minority groups of farmers. They viewed the consent decree as a way of obtaining redress for their grievances, too. Native American (*Keepseagle v. Johanns*), Latino (*Garcia v. Vilsack*) and women (*Love v. Vilsack*) farmers all sought to bring class action suits alleging similar types of discrimination. The Native American and Latino cases are still in litigation and affect thousands of claimants. The women farmers' case was dismissed.

24. The Future of Fair Housing, op. cit., p. 10.

25. John Logan, "Separate and Unequal: The Neighborhood Gap for Blacks and Hispanics in Metropolitan America," Lewis Mumford Center for Comparative Urban and Regional Research, 2002.

26. CERD Report, op. cit., p. 2.

27. John Iceland, Daniel H. Weinberg, and Erika Steinmetz, U.S. Census Bureau, Series CENSR-3, "Racial and Ethnic Residential Segregation in the United States: 1980–2000," U.S. Government Printing Office, Washington, D.C., 2002: 4, 72.

28. CERD Report, op. cit., p. i.

29. CERD Report, op. cit., p.6.

30. Ibid., p. 16.

31. The State of Black America, 2009: 27.

32. Barbara Ehrenreich and Dedrick Muhammad, "The Recession's Racial Divide," *The New York Times,* September 13, 2009, Sunday Opinion:17.

33. ACORN, "Foreclosure Exposure: A Study of Racial Disparities in Home Mortgage Lending in 172 American Cities," September 5, 2007. New Orleans, LA: 1–2.

34. Ibid., p. 2.

35. Rakesh Kochhar, Ana Gonzalez-Barrera and Daniel Dockterman, "Through Boom and Bust: Minorities, Immigrants and Homeownership," PEW Hispanic Center, May 12, 2009. See: *http://pewresearch.org/pubs/1220/home-ownership-trends-blacks-hispanics.* Retrieved on 6/10/09.

36. Michael Powell, "Suit Accuses Wells Fargo of Steering Blacks to Subprime Mortgages in Baltimore," *New York Times,* June 7, 2009: A16.

37. Michael Powell and Janet Roberts, "Minorities Affected Most as New York Foreclosures Rise," *New York Times,* May 16, 2009.

38. Found at*: http://www.naacp.org/news/press/2009-03-13/index.htm.*

39. Found at: *http://www.naacp.org/news/press/2009-03-13/index.htm.* In April, 2010 the NAACP reached a settlement with Wells Fargo. It agreed to drop its racial discrimination lawsuit in exchange for having the right to review the bank's lending practices and recommend ways to "improve credit availability to African American and diverse businesses and consumers." See: Bob Tedeschi, "Bias Accord as Harbinger," *The New York Times,* April 21, 2010, found at: *http://www.nytimes.com/2010/04/25/realestate/25mort.html?pagewa*

40. Diane E. Thompson, "Why Servicers Foreclose When They Should Modify and Other Puzzles of Servicer Behavior," National Consumer Law Center, Inc., Boston, Mass., October 2009.

41. Alan Zibel, "Bank of America to Pay Borrowers $108 Million," *The Washington Post,* June 7, 2010 at: *http://www.washingtonpost.com/wp-dyn/content/article/2010/06/07/AR2010060701971.html.*

42. "Enforcement of the Fair Housing Act of 1968," written statement of Kim Kendrick, Assistant Secretary of Fair Housing and Equal Opportunity, U.S. Department of Housing and Urban Development, Hearings before the Subcommittee on the Constitution, Civil Rights, and Liberties, Committee on the Judiciary United States House of Representatives, June 12, 2008.

43. William Collins, "Fair Housing Laws." EH.Net Encyclopedia, Robert Whaples (ed.), February 10, 2008.

44. "The Integration Report," UCLA Civil Rights Project, Issue 18, April 18, 2009 at: *http://theintegrationreport.wordpress.com/2009/04/.*

45. The Future of Fair Housing, op. cit., Executive Summary, p. vii.

46. Ibid., p. vi.

Chapter 16

The Myth of the Meritocracy

No greater injury can be done to any youth than to let him feel that because
he belongs to this or that race he will be advanced in life regardless of his
own merits or efforts.

—Booker T. Washington

MAKING IT IN AMERICA

What is the cumulative effect of overt and covert racism? Aside from the
obvious negative impact of discrimination on the social, economic, and
psychological well-being of victimized groups and individuals, there are profound societal implications. These range from quantifiable indices of adverse
effects of racial discrimination on physical health and educational and economic development on a societal level to social and psychological insults that
result in crime, violence, deviant behavior, and poverty.

There is a growing body of literature indicating that people who are victims
of racism have poorer mental and physical health than non-victims.[1] As we
have seen, discrimination in housing, employment, education, and health
care wreak untold misery on the victims. Yet, a society that is supposedly
predicated on merit, equality, and equal opportunities must maintain a façade
of denial when it confronts victims of prejudice, discrimination, and racism.
This denial often takes the form of "blaming the victim"[2] for their life situation rather than analyzing the systemic bias in societal institutions.

Proponents of the meritocracy position contend that society is open to
all—the great American Dream is equally accessible to anyone with the

intelligence, creativity, enthusiasm, and fortitude willing to work hard, sacrifice and take risks. The fabled rags to riches characters popularized by Horatio Alger in the mid-nineteenth century, which extolled the virtue of hard work and individual initiative, kindled a wanderlust in exuberant teens who yearned for fame and fortune. This attitude persists today.

The annual national survey of college freshmen conducted by UCLA and a poll by the Pew Research Center of 18–25 year olds both reported that more than three-fourths of respondents prioritized getting rich as a life ambition. This figure was up over 30 percent compared to the 1966 cohort.[3]

CORPORATE WELFARE

The hypocritical side of the meritocracy argument was highlighted during the economic debacle of 2008. The United States government felt compelled to bail out insurance giant American International Group (A.I.G.) with over $180 billion of taxpayer money. The public was outraged to learn that large bonuses were paid to the very executives whose work shattered the world's economy. Over 100 workers each received a million dollars and seven received $3 million a piece as bonuses for their work with complex financial instruments such as bundled mortgage loans, derivatives, and credit-default swaps. One writer in the *New York Times* believed that they deserved the money because these "brainiacs" were among the most astute minds in the field.[4]

One of the most demonstrative examples of the double standard which undergirds the wealthy at the expense of the middle class and poor occurred during the waning days of the Bush Administration in the fall of 2008. With the economy teetering on the brink of collapse, Secretary of the Treasury Henry Paulson, formerly the Chairman and Chief Executive Officer of the investment firm, Goldman Sachs, presented Congress with a three page "plan" for bailing out financial institutions.

Congressman Barney Frank, Chairman of the House Financial Services Committee, balked at Paulson's proviso that there should be no discussion of the terms of the Bush administration's plan. After initially rejecting Paulson's plan in September 2008, Congress passed the Emergency Economic Stabilization Act of 2008 in October. This legislation provided $700 billion in a Troubled Asset Relief Fund (TARP) for a wide range of initiatives includ-ing the purchase of questionable mortgages and loans from troubled financial institutions including insurance giant AIG, and 21 banks that each received at least $1 billion. Among the recipients were Bank of America (which was pressured by the Bush administration into buying ailing brokerage house Merrill Lynch), Citigroup, and JPMorgan Chase.

Within one month Congress and the Bush administration engineered the most significant economic realignment of the nation's financial institutions since the Great Depression. Designed to stabilize the country's failing lending institutions and provide funds for loans to stimulate durable goods purchases like automobiles and mortgages for homes, the infusion of the first $350 billion was ingested by the recipients without a trace and failed to relax the tight credit markets that were impeding the nation's economic recovery.

An Associated Press analysis attempted to track the distribution and utilization of the first $350 billion TARP funds in January 2009. Their efforts were met with resistance by the banking institutions that received the funds. AP contacted 21 banks that each received at least $1 billion, and none of them provided specific answers about how the money was used. Worse still, some banks acknowledged that they didn't know where the money was going. It was evident that some of the money was used to pay exorbitant salaries, expense accounts, and bonuses to executives in some of the firms. It is likely that, given the prevailing climate of greed and distrust among these institutions, they were reluctant to divulge any information that could assist the government and competitors in assessing the extent of their liabilities (toxic assets).[5]

The irony of this corporate welfare is all the more repugnant in the face of opposition to President Barack Obama's health care initiative. The reforms to our health care system that were passed on March 21, 2010, and, because of technicalities raised by Republicans, again on March 25, 2010, are designed to improve a system which annually costs over $2 trillion. Yet, the United States' population ranks 37th in the world in the health status (longevity, mortality, etc.). The new legislation is designed to provide health care to over 30 million Americans with no insurance and improve the care of an additional 50 million people who are underinsured, including 12 million children. These are the poor whites, ethnic minorities, middle-, and working-class residents of a nation built on false promises of an American Dream that has turned into a nightmare. It is an ideology of hope and faith in an economic system skewed in favor of the wealthy few to the detriment of increasingly impoverished masses.

SUCCESS AND THE MYTH OF MERIT

Strident opposition to health care reform as seen in trenchant unruly demonstrations, threats, name-calling, and racial epithets hurled at black legislators is the kind of illogical thinking that supports prevailing capitalist mythology about meritocracy and rationalizes whites' superior position over people of color. It is assumed that whites occupy most of the positions of power and influence because they deserve them. It has always been that way. It is the natural order of society—whites on top and people of color on the bottom. If society is a meritocracy, with a level playing field, the industrious will rise to the top as Englishman Herbert Spencer and William Graham Sumner (his American sociological counterpart at Yale) observed. Whites' positions of preeminence not only proved their case but obfuscated the reality of racism and discrimination.[6]

It was this type of mythology along with the promise of liberty and freedom that brought 22 million immigrants to Ellis Island between 1892 and 1924. Most of them quickly learned that our streets were not paved with gold as they struggled to eke out a subsistence living in sweatshops and factories while trying to survive in crowded disease-ridden tenements. They were brainwashed into believing that the true path to success was, like the biblical intonation "by the sweat of thy brow," but inheriting money was far easier for the children of the elite.

These immigrants became victims of discrimination and racism as they landed on the shores of a country that needed their cheap labor but stigmatized them because of their cultural differences. From the Irish to the Italians, the Swedes to the Eastern European Jews, Russians, Slavs, and Poles, each group of immigrants was greeted by mixed messages. They, like Chinese laborers on the West Coast, learned that the words of Emma Lazarus inscribed on the Statue of Liberty were more idealistic than the reality they faced: "Give me your tired, your poor, your huddled masses yearning to breathe free, the wretched refuse of your teeming shore, Send these, the homeless, tempest-tossed to me, I lift my lamp beside the golden door!" (1883)

The playing field was not level. Some people, wealthy patricians, for the most part white Anglo-Saxon Protestants, made and enforced the rules in a game of life for which new immigrants had been unprepared and blacks systematically excluded. That many immigrants and people of color managed to survive and even thrive testifies to their indomitable spirit, fortitude, and industriousness. Such traits were championed by one of the greatest robber barons in the history of this nation, Andrew Carnegie, a man who made a fortune off the toil and travail of American workers while he extolled the virtue of being reared "in the bracing school of poverty."[7]

While the lives of European immigrants were far from idyllic, they had one important feature in common with the majority of the indigenous population—they were light skinned. This fact facilitated their entrance and ultimate acceptance into mainstream American society. Despite different languages, customs, and traditions, they could assimilate far easier than people of color, who had been here for hundreds of years prior to their arrival.

LIVING THE MYTH: A SELF-FULFILLING PROPHESY

Although the lot of the lower class working man and his family was far from the stuff dreams were made of, they quickly learned how to protect what they had by upholding existing norms and laws that denied equal access to upward mobility to people of color. Living arrangements were modified into restrictive covenants. Red lining and racial steering were introduced and white Anglos, and later, white ethnics, moved further out from the central cities which became de facto apartheid living quarters for blacks and Latinos. When barriers to housing and entertainment persisted, upwardly mobile ethnics like Jews established their own resorts and subdivisions. But these, too, remained beyond the pale of most people of color who struggled trying to run uphill on the supposedly level playing field.

In the world of work, white ethnics found opportunities for advancement in the blue collar factories whose manufacturing led the way through much of the twentieth century industrialization. Here, too, people of color were often excluded or relegated to lesser paying entry-level positions by unions dominated by white ethnics barring them from admission.

This pattern of exclusion and repression began with slavery and was based on theological and ideological myths that depicted people of color as inferior subhumans. It was transformed into a cruel self-fulfilling prophesy by whites. In their fallacious reasoning, based on the popular mythology of a meritocracy that rewards individual initiative, whites stereotyped non-whites as lazy, indolent, violent, and misfits. This typology emanated from whites' belief in the level playing field, yet they enforced norms and created institutions that prevented full participation of non-whites in a social system rigged against them.

Even more insidious was white ideology which held that non-whites are intellectually inferior. By every measure of academic accomplishment, non-whites (except Asians) perform at lower levels than whites. The public school system is replete with examples of non-white failure from graduation rates (the percent of students graduating in four years—20–30 percent lower than whites), to the achievement gap (the difference in standardized test scores between whites and non-whites which stands at 30–40 points below whites and Asians in reading, math, and science). The percentage of black and Latino students, especially males, graduating high school and attending college is small and in the case of blacks has been declining.

The high unemployment rate of blacks and Latinos (nearly double that of whites for decades) coupled with their clustering in low paying, menial jobs, lends credence to whites' perceptions of non-whites as only being suited to servile positions in the labor force. The adage "Last hired, first fired" is defended in a mindset steeped in the natural superiority of whites over people of color. Why should whites believe otherwise? They created the system of domination and exploitation. They benefit from perpetuating it, and they justify it by concocting fables like the level playing field and their natural superiority.

If non-whites are "prone" to social pathologies like crime, poverty, and other forms of deviant behavior, the whites' world view is confirmed. The system is seen as functioning normally; the aberration is the behavior of non-whites. In a meritocracy, one gets what one earns. Our children are taught this carefully from their earliest days of cognition in the home, through the media, and especially in school.

White people, even people of color, buy into the prevailing meritocracy mythology believing like so many Social Darwinists that in life, you get what you deserve. If whites control the vast majority of the seats of power in society, CEOs, senators and congressmen, Supreme Court justices and other jurists, governors, scientists, and military leaders, that is because they deserve it, for under the myth of meritocracy they earned it. It matters not that one to two percent of the population controls a majority of wealth in the nation and hereditarily transfer this wealth to their progeny; or that a significant proportion of congressmen and senators are the sons, daughters, and widows of their fathers and husbands, or that a small cadre of corporate elite control all but a handful of the corporations that dominate our (and the world's) economy.[8]

DREAMING OF A BETTER LIFE

What is important is to keep the myth of the American Dream alive. To maintain the masses' belief in the virtue of hard work and its rewards, despite the economic meltdown of 2008–2009 wrought by these same corporate geniuses who, in many cases, managed to secure their own golden parachutes and bonuses using taxpayers' dollars to bail them out.

In what may be the quote of the century, former chairman of the Federal Reserve, Alan Greenspan, attributed his failure to prevent an economic disaster in the United States' economy to "A flaw in the model that I perceived is the critical functioning structure that defines how the world works .... I made a mistake in presuming that the self-interests of organizations, specifically banks and others, were such that they were best capable of protecting their own shareholders and their equity in firms."[9]

Many white aspiring millionaires and retirees learned that even they were betrayed by a system consumed with greed. What is worse: to tantalize with the promise of wealth and comfort through the myth of meritocracy, or to drown the American Dream in the acid of prejudice, discrimination, and racism? It is the perfect trap—deprive blacks, Latinos, and other people of color opportunities in education and jobs, then stereotype them for being uneducated, naïve, stupid, and poor. Blame the victims for their deficiencies instead of society (systemic racism, de facto segregation, and discrimination), and create a self-fulfilling prophesy that justifies the perpetuation of social inequality and the ideological system underpinning it.

If minorities can't succeed it's because of their innate deficiencies— biological and psychological weaknesses that leave them unfit and unable to compete with whites. These myths and stereotypes arose to ensure white hegemony and supremacy. They depict nonwhites as subhuman animals only capable of menial work, bereft of ethics and morality (ape-like, inhuman) and incapable of being civilized and assimilated into white society.

In a society suffused with material values, where whites dominate, it is understandable why they are opposed to programs designed to ameliorate social problems and level the playing field. Nurtured on the myth of meritocracy, they deny the playing field is slanted in their direction. Deeply imbedded in their psyches are the memories, thoughts, and values depicting nonwhites as inferior and untrustworthy and, most saliently, as potential competitors for increasingly scarce resources. Therefore they are not only undeserving of government assistance, they must be prevented from any programs that might give them a semblance of an advantage, a glimmer of hope to level the field and obtain the promise of a better life.[10]

THE PERSISTENCE OF WHITE PRIVILEGED THOUGHT

Despite whites' vociferous denial of the existence of white privilege, it is ubiquitous. When Attorney General Eric Holder noted on February 18, 2009, "Though this nation has proudly thought of itself as an ethnic melting pot, in things racial we have always been and continue to be, in too many ways, essentially a nation of cowards," he was echoing the call for interracial dialogue, the same call of President Clinton's commission on race relations "One America in the 21st Century" a decade before.[11] The very fact that his comments created a backlash testifies to the insidious white supremacist ideology that obfuscates the landscape of social reality.

While feigned outcries of indignant whites attempted to misrepresent Holder's remarks, truth belies their disingenuous protestations of denial. Hasn't the time for naivety passed? What prevents some whites from recognizing the injustice and inequality at home that they are so quick to criticize abroad? Why do whites fear the people they enslaved, stole land from, and committed genocide against? Is it because they feel the guilt of centuries, or the erosion of their white privilege that has heretofore insulated them against the competition from upwardly aspiring non-whites who are becoming more vocal and visible as their numbers increase?[12]

Maybe the act of acknowledging complicity to a system that depended on the enslavement of human beings has left a residue of guilt. In its magnanimity, the United States Senate unanimously passed a resolution apologizing for slavery on June 18, 2009, with the stipulation that it would not entitle descendants of slaves to reparations. Perhaps, acquiescing to the charge of racism and its implications of inequality is too much for whites who have been brainwashed into believing that this is "The land of the free and the home of the brave," where "All men are created equal," "With liberty and justice for all."

These noble words were written by aging aristocratic white men who sought to establish a social order that preserved slavery and denied the very rights they demanded while ignoring women and relegating blacks to three-fifths of a person. Our educational system has done a wonderful job of inculcating such democratic myths and symbols in our children without the critical reasoning to analyze their meaning and impact on our society.

Many of us can recite the Pledge of Allegiance, Preamble to the Constitution, and Gettysburg Address because we memorized these "sacred" words as children. But we have a child-like understanding of them because there was no attempt to teach what these words and principles meant or put them into historical perspective. We simply mouthed them in a ritualistic manner for the encomiums of teachers and parents. As such, these revolutionary concepts, which possess the power to challenge the status quo and form the basis of a critique that could help undermine the stultifying layers of entrenched inequality in our society, are little more than trite phrases. Their ring is as hollow as the callous purveyors of a false consciousness which denies the persistence of racism and social inequality in a social system bereft of critical analysis.

Shouts of "traitor" are hurled at people who attempt to break the veneer of defensiveness that masks relationships between people of color and whites. Ensconced in their comfortable white privileged society, they recoil when confronted with the possibility that their idyllic island of materialism might be predicated on the perpetuation of inequality and injustice. Such thoughts are not only troubling to "patriotic" Americans, they are heretical. They are incapable of deconstructing and critiquing the "American Way" in their unquestioning adolescent stupor reinforced through a moribund educational system. An educational system where less than half of the children of color graduate from high school and only 70 percent of whites do. A system that ranks our children 26 in the world in math and science, where half of the new teachers leave in the first five years. A system that is more segregated today than before the Brown decision.

Whites have never been particularly interested in dialogue about race relations because they are in a state of denial about the existence of privileges and advantages they have by virtue of their color. They do not have to grapple with the negative stereotypes about loose morals, laziness, inferior intellects, and primitive subhuman phenotypes. They do not have to contend with prejudice and discriminatory actions designed to stigmatize, deprive, and perpetuate second class citizenship. They do not have to contemplate whether the actions of others in their community, school, workplace, and even houses of worship are influenced by value judgments formed on the basis of the color of their skin. They do not have to overcome the burden of negativity that demeans and degrades one's psyche. And they do not have to assume that everyone who looks different from them may be their enemy or at least, not an ally in their struggle for equality.

Perhaps one of the most pernicious legacies of racism is its ability to contaminate human relationships by perpetuating a climate of disingenuousness. One has only to hear or experience racism (or other forms of discrimination) for it to make an indelible mark on one's psyche. This plants the seed of doubt about the intentions of others. Experiencing any of life's myriad disappointments may be interpreted as the result of discriminatory actions because the scar of race has left its permanency. Rather than looking within for the reason one was fired, not hired or promoted, denied a raise, or laid off, one conjures up the demons of prejudice, discrimination, and race.

Just as whites are quick to blame the victim, so, too, are people of color prone to blame race for failure. But people of color have over 300 years of discrimination and disappointments to draw from as justification for their attribution, while whites have only an ideology of stereotypes and privilege that justifies their own social status.

NOTES

1. Yin Paradies, "A Systematic Review of Empirical Research on Self-Reported Racism and Health," *International Journal of Epidemiology*, vol. 35, no. 4, April, 2006, pp. 888–901. See also Tim Wise's interesting review of this phenomenon in *Color-Blind*. San Francisco: City Lights, 2010.

2. William Ryan, *Blaming the Victim*, N.Y.: Knoph Doubleday, 1976.

3. Associated Press, "Material Generation: Wealth is Top Priority," *St. Petersburg Times*, 1/23/07: 7A.

4. See "The Case for Paying Out Bonuses at A.I.G.," Andrew Ross Sorkin, *New York Times,* March 17, 2009: B1.

5. For an analysis and critique of attempt to track TARP funds see: William Patalon III, "U.S. Banks Refuse to Detail How They're Spending Federal Bailout Money," at: *http://moneymorning.com/2009/01/06/us-banks-federal-bailout/.*

6. Herbert Spencer, *Social Statics,* London: John Chapman, 1851, and William Graham Sumner, *What Social Classes Owe to Each Other,* N.Y.: Harper and Brothers, 1883.

7. Andrew Carnegie, *The Gospel of Wealth,* "The Advantages of Poverty," N.Y.: The Century Co., 1901.

8. The most comprehensive analysis of the structure and politics of the U.S. Senate was done by political scientist Donald R. Matthews, *U.S. Senators and Their World,* Westport, CT.: Greenwood Press, 1980.

9. "Greenspan Admits 'Flaw' to Congress, Predicts More Economic Problems;" see *http://www.pbs.org/newshour/bb/business/july-dec08/crisishearing_10-23.html.* Retrieved 2/23/09.

10. For a comprehensive analysis of the fallacy of the American Dream and the myth of meritocracy see Stephen J. McNamee and Robert K. Miller, Jr., *The Meritocracy Myth,* Second edition, Lanham, MD: Rowman & Littlefield Publishers, Inc., 2009.

11. *One America in the 21st Century: The Report of President Bill Clinton's Initiative on Race,* New Haven: Yale University Press, 2008.

12. Eduardo Bonilla-Silva does an admirable job of attempting to understand this dynamic in his book *Racism Without Racists,* Third edition, Lanham, MD: Rowman & Littlefield Publishers, Inc., 2010. Joe R. Feagin's book *Systemic Racism,* New York: Taylor and Francis, 2006, links the persistence of racism in the United States to an entrenched economic system of domination and exploitation similar to the thesis of this book.

Chapter 17

More than Talk

Why Dialogue is Not Enough

There is no true word that is not at the same time praxis. Thus, to speak a true word is to transform the world.

—Paulo Freire, *Pedagogy of the Oppressed*

TALKING ABOUT RACE

In the months leading up to the 2008 presidential election in the United States, Michele Norris and Steve Inskeep of National Public Radio held a series of conversations about race and presidential politics in the homes of prospective voters in York, Pennsylvania. The participants included diverse people from different ethnic, political, and socioeconomic backgrounds. The discussions ranged over a variety of issues, but the most revealing comments were those that focused on the participants' perceptions of Barack Obama's suitability for president.

Their words were revealing, not just for the political differences exhibited between Democrats and Republicans on how to repair our damaged economy and the myriad other problems plaguing the country. In their candid, off-the-cuff remarks, listeners were able to apprehend the gulf that separates whites and blacks in this society. From naïve, even innocently spoken words with no intended insults, to blatant racial stereotypes, the conversations demonstrated how far apart blacks and whites are in understanding and acknowledging the causes of poverty and the extent of discrimination and racism in the United States:

Inskeep (white): Do black people make too much of discrimination?
  Charlotte Bergdoll (white female): ... just expect that it's gonna happen. Very often it's because they're Hispanic or African-American.

Inskeep: Do you think America is ready to elect a black president?

Don Geddes (white male): The media. They don't say anything bad about him. It's never reported.

Calvin Weary (black male): Every time we attain another high level it's like white Americans feel we've torn something from them.

Some white participants believed Obama was unpatriotic and incompetent:

Leah Morland (white female): I feel if we put Obama in the White House there will be chaos.

By providing these forums, National Public Radio (NPR) gave listeners insight into the enormous work that needs to be done to create common ground for dialogue between people of color and whites. A dialogue from which understanding and empathy can emanate so we can begin to move forward together to solve the problems that challenge the viability of this society. Even more disconcerting were the comments some listeners posted to NPR criticizing them for airing such purportedly divisive, unrepresentative views:

I heard the piece that aired on Friday, October 24 (2008), and felt that it may have the result of fanning the flames of racial fear and hatred rather than bring-ing us together or giving us a deeper understanding across racial lines. I hope you do less of that kind of reporting in the future and more reporting that cre-ates an understanding that we're all in this together. That whether we're black, white, Hispanic, Asian, or something else, that we all want to be safe, fulfilled, educated, and employed and that we want to care for our children and have hope for their futures.[1]

We have no way of knowing if these comments are any more or less repre-sentative of the population of this nation than the words of the participants in the dialogue, but each in their own way reflects themes that permeate our thoughts and discussions about race relations in this nation. Having conducted hundreds of dialogues on race relations, I am able to discern a strain of white denial, bordering on naïveté, that is invariably invoked to conceal shame, guilt, or complicity in the palpable disparities in the quality of life between whites and people of color in this society. Protestations are made that most whites are in favor of equality and treat blacks fairly, but facial expressions belie their pronouncements about equity and reveal their disbelief of stories of injustice recounted by people of color in the discussion.

The search for common ground in race relations dialogues has been called for by scholars, community organizers, and politicians for decades. Long before President Bill Clinton's Initiative on Race, *One America in the 21st*

Century, published in September 1998,[2] and candidate Obama's impassioned speech in Philadelphia that called for understanding and reconciliation between whites and blacks, tens of thousands of Americans were gathering in homes and public places under the auspices of organizations like the Study Circles Resource Center[3], Kettering Foundation National Issues Forums,[4] the National Conference of Christians and Jews[5], and the National Coalition for Dialogue and Deliberation[6] to dialogue about race relations and find common ground.

These initiatives have helped to keep the issue of race relations in the public consciousness as hundreds of communities engaged in conversations about prejudice, discrimination, and racism. It would be absurd to denigrate the work of organizations and volunteers who have sought to improve communication between people of color and whites and other ethnic groups, but it is difficult to quantify the impact such programs have had in light of the overt manifestations of racism in our institutions and society. There are so many dimensions of racism in America and myriad manifestations that may (or may not) be racist, that it is virtually impossible to determine whether such dialogues have made progress toward realizing the American dream of justice and equality for all.

Nevertheless, it is undoubtedly true that engaging in dialogue about the issue of race relations has a salubrious effect on participants and communities. It helps to identify areas in need of remediation by affording participants an opportunity to learn about the concerns and grievances of others. It educates participants by helping them to understand the structure, function, and limitations of services available for addressing community needs. It opens lines of communication among participants who might not ordinarily meet and discuss such issues outside of the dialogue. Dialogues also help to defuse tension and conflict within a group and community by allowing participants to channel their concerns and anger into socially acceptable civil activities.

All of these can be positive outcomes of racial dialogue, but dialogue, while necessary for the establishment of rules governing civil society, is not sufficient in and of itself in moving participants from what is essentially still a race- and class-based social system to a more cooperative egalitarian society.[7]

A NOTE ON DIALOGUES IN SCHOOL

While much of the preceding discussion is relevant to students and schools, there are some facts and circumstances that should be considered before launching a dialogic program in your school. First, it is essential to create on-going discussions among students and teachers to provide opportunities to share interests and concerns about challenges and relationships. Parents should also be included in these discussions, creating what I have referred to as "Talking Schools."

Elsewhere[8] I demonstrate how to construct dialogues in schools. The process is not easy because, as with society in general, many people are reluctant to candidly share their views. This is especially true of adolescents who may appear to lack the maturity to engage in such activities, but it can be accomplished by training students to facilitate the discussions, and the results can be very satisfactory.

School teachers and administrators may also find such enterprises daunting in the face of enormous pressures exerted on them to focus on standardized test preparation. Time is at a premium, and activities deemed extraneous are frequently abandoned. One strategy I use to persuade teachers and administrators about the efficacy of engaging in campus dialogues is to highlight the value of such activities for reducing tension and conflict among students as well as staff. Schools are no different than other kinds of workplaces— students, teachers, and administrators go to work carrying social and cultural baggage that can impede effective communication. Having dialogues affords them opportunities to learn about the human side of the education process and establish lines of communication for sharing information and developing insight about their peers and colleagues.

Following the Columbine High School tragedy I was requested to develop a series of dialogues at a large upper middle class predominantly white Blue Ribbon high school. The principal called me in within days of the disaster. The demographics of his school mirrored those of Columbine and it was clear that he was anxious about the similarities. My staff and I trained 150 students as facilitators. Each Thursday they were charged with engaging students in a 40-minute discussion on their choice of subjects in an extended home room period.

I remember when he introduced the project to his faculty: "You will do this and you will not interfere with the student facilitators. They can talk about anything they want. You'll be like a fly on the wall and won't tell me anything about what they say unless it's about abuse or neglect. I'll be in the halls during this time watching to see how things go."

The project lasted for a semester. Some of the student facilitators were ineffective and some of the teachers assumed traditional positions of authority, running the discussions. Overall, however, the project was deemed successful by students and staff, and it helped to calm the campus in a volatile time. As part of our involvement at this school, the principal asked me to meet periodically with 15 teachers at a time for a day to discuss diversity issues. He provided lunch and mandated that all of his teachers attend one of the workshops.

Some of the teachers seemed disinterested, like the middle-aged man who sat reading a catalogue about construction tools as I spoke. After an hour he pushed the catalogue aside, looked at me, and said this was one of the most interesting and important workshops he had ever attended.

Another time a young male teacher interrupted me after a couple of hours and defiantly proclaimed: "What does any of this have to do with my students? I teach college chemistry and all of my students are going to college."

I replied "What makes you think that your class is the only one they have? That they don't have five other equally demanding classes? Or that they don't have dating or sexual issues on their minds. Or problems with their parents? Or issues with alcohol or drugs?"

He sat back and listened intently for the rest of the workshop. Six months later he asked me for a job.

WHY DIALOGUE ALONE CAN'T WORK

There are pros and cons to dialogue, and it is not the panacea for racial harmony some proponents contend. To understand why dialogue alone is incapable of creating qualitative social change in our society, we must examine the social and psychological reasons people participate in it and the design of the dialogic experience. The professed goal of dialogue is open, candid, honest conversation to inform, even improve, race relations and, hopefully, change peoples' lives. But this promise will remain unfulfilled as long as our social system is based on and accentuates materialism and scarcity. With double digit unemployment and depressed property values, cutbacks in social services, reluctance to lend by financial institutions, millions of home foreclosures, and rising deficits and taxes, it is naïve to assume that the privileged white society will entertain, much less, actively engage in, activities that they perceive will advantage non-whites and disadvantage themselves.

In effect, when white people are asked to participate in race relations dialogues, they are affirming their privileged status in a racist society—an assumption that is not widely acknowledged by the white population. Whites persist in their belief of the meritocracy and Social Darwinist perspectives about the inferiority of the poor and people of color. People who attend race relations dialogues are therefore already predisposed to accepting the validity of these negative propositions. What ensues is a litany of testimonials from people of color about insults and injustices perpetrated against them by insensitive, racist whites in positions of power and authority, while likeminded white participants nod in agreement and acknowledge their brothers' and sisters' pain.

The recognition and acknowledgement of social injustice can be cleansing and instructive, but there must be a diversity of ideas and participants present to learn and appreciate the information being revealed. A crucial condition for the attainment of meaningful dialogue is the creation and maintenance of a safe environment for the dialogue to occur. This is a precondition for candid discussion, which, if met, will facilitate a frank exchange of ideas.

If people of color are willing to make disclosures about their lives, two other necessary conditions must be met: First, there must be a diverse group of participants who represent a range of philosophies and ideas. Second, there must be an inclination or willingness to listen and attempt to comprehend the import of the experiences being discussed. While skilled facilitators are often utilized to maintain decorum and lend structure to the dialogic process, they cannot alter the mindset of individuals who are averse to accepting the validity of the information being imparted by aggrieved people of color. Indeed, what may occur in this exchange of attitudes and values is a hardening of conservative philosophy among skeptical whites who were lured into the process.

Too often, the dialogue becomes a forum for angry people who, having been prevented from obtaining satisfaction for real or presumed offenses against them, attempt to turn the activity into a personal diatribe against elected officials and power centers in their community. Even seasoned facilitators find themselves in the precarious position of having to assuage the anger and emotion of the accuser while trying to mollify other participants so they don't leave or withdraw from future sessions. The frequency of such encounters at dialogues on race relations testifies to the enduring emotional scars that racism has left on people in our society.

Although personal storytelling is often a desired technique for beginning the dialogic process, it can lead to deterioration in the quality and satisfaction of the group dynamics and derail the process because skeptical whites, living under their own financial, health, and social burdens, may not empathize with people who they perceive as bearing the responsibility for their own misfortunes. Whites may recoil at the insinuation that their democratic country is not living up to its ideals. They reject the possibility that they, by virtue of history and advantages of white privilege, may be implicated in activities that impoverish and perpetuate inequality. The American infatuation with the underdog ostensibly testifies to their concern for the less advantaged. Challenging this assumption of noblesse oblige is tantamount to criticizing the Declaration of Independence and Constitution, calling George Washington and Thomas Jefferson slave owners.

Whites vehemently deny complicity in the perpetuation of racism and poverty. When a hint of shared responsibility for the vestiges of slavery and racism is apprehended, they invoke standard defense mechanisms to protect their self-concept from being excoriated by the taint of racism and social inequality in our glorious meritocracy. Refusing to acknowledge the veracity of the "others" stories avoids confronting the fallacy of the American Dream and allows them to wallow in the nightmare of materialism that cripples and engulfs us all.

In such situations, skeptical whites often choose to reject challenges to their materialistically packaged world. First recoiling from the encounter, they then absent themselves from future discussion, denying themselves and other participants an opportunity to hear their stories, and forfeiting the opportunity of altering states of consciousness about society.

Another unfortunate event that may occur during the dialogue is blaming all white people for the state of race relations, poverty, and other social injustices. The typical white reaction to the insinuation that they share responsibility for such conditions is disbelief and repulsion, followed by demurrers and even denunciation. If the dialogue group is fortunate enough to have skeptical whites attending, participants should be sensitive to their sensibilities and not drive them away. Recognizing that whites have the power in society, they should be cultivated so they can become allies. This recognition of power relationships does not mean that aggrieved parties should refrain from candid comments, but they should be cautious, not accusatory, and understand that not everyone in the group has attained the same level of awareness about the distribution of power and privilege in society.

The preceding discussion assumes that there will be some skeptical whites in attendance at the dialogue, but the reality is that, as with other voluntary forms of behavior meant to inform and educate, some of the people most in need of the experience will not attend. It is unlikely that people with different political and social ideologies will be present at ostensibly impartial dialogues on race relations, because they are unwilling to risk bearing their core values in front of friends and strangers. They are being asked to question the logic of the very foundation upon which their social and political world rests, and to subject their pseudo existence to a critique which could challenge their reality and threaten their sense of reason and self. Combine this with the fear of misspeaking or being labeled naïve, ignorant, or even racist for words or sentiments widely endorsed but unspoken in public, why would they subject themselves to public opprobrium? If well-intended skeptical whites are in attendance, why would they risk being ganged up on by people of color who might have an anti-white agenda? And why would working class whites participate in a discussion with people of color about discrimination when they believe they and their children have been victimized by affirmative action programs that unfairly advantage people of color? For that matter, why would people of color choose to continue to spill their guts to whites about their misfortunes and victimization in the face of persistent racism and white refusals to redress their grievances?

A NOTE ON DIALOGUES IN SCHOOL

While much of the preceding discussion is relevant to students and dialogues in schools, there are some facts and circumstances that should be considered before launching a dialogic program in your school. It is essential to create ongoing discussions among students and teachers to provide opportunities to share interests and concerns about challenges and relationships.

ANOTHER WAY

Dialoging about race relations and racism is like walking in a verbal mine field—at any moment a comment may evoke an emotion which threatens the viability of the group. Attorney General Eric Holder was accurate in his depiction of this country as "a nation of cowards" when it comes to talking about race relations:

> Though race-related issues continue to occupy a significant portion of our political discussion, and though there remain many unresolved racial issues in this nation, we, average Americans, simply do not talk enough with each other about things racial. This is truly sad. Given all that we as a nation went through during the civil rights struggle, it is hard for me to accept that the result of those efforts was to create an America that is more prosperous, more positively race-conscious, and yet is voluntarily socially segregated.[9]

Here are a few of the responses his comments elicited on the Free Republic blog immediately after he spoke:

"We wants yo' wimmins an chilluns."

"We are rapidly degenerating into South Africa or Zimbabwe."

"Eric, white people are not allowed to openly discuss 'things racial.'"

"Holder is a racist and not fit to serve in his office."

"Yeah ... right. Let's see, the black attorney general in a black president's cabinet says we're a racist nation."

"The problem is, it seems we will never STOP talking about it. What will satisfy them, just what? I want to know. So we can get this over with. Do they want slavery for whites for 200 years? Say so, if that's what they want. I, for one, am tired of this. I never owned any slaves, I never treated anyone unfairly because of their race, I never got a job, as far as I know, that should have gone to someone of another race. I'm just REALLY tired of this."

"Oh, I think Mr. Holder is likely to get quite a bit of 'dialogue' on race, but it won't be the sort he's used to, with one side making accusations and the other apologies. That's the sort cowards have been indulging in for the last half century and as one of them, Mr. Holder ought to know."

"We have a black president. He is attorney general and he's still bitching. This proves you can never, ever satisfy a liberal."

"I don't want to hear this BS, especially from a corrupt race-baiting partisan like Holder."

"Slavery for whites is what they want and they will not stop until they get it. They are full of HATE."

"Holder any time any place you choose your personal weapon—no lawyers, no FBI, no cops. We will see who the coward is."

"I agree. We are cowards. We refuse and are scared to call people like Holder—Race Baiting Racists—because if we do 14 percent of this country's citizens will file lawsuits!"

"Yes, I am cowardly. If I speak the truth on racial matters, I get fired."

"We are cowards for allowing blacks to guilt trip us into treating them differently (better). There is a separate, lower standard for them at nearly every school and large business."

"Hey UP YOURS! I am sick and tired of listening to you people crying about race. I am tired of being accused for being a white race."[10]

There were 35 other memorable remarks on this blog reflecting similar sentiments. The question is, how representative are these comments of the white population? Or more pertinently, what are the probabilities of such people participating in civic dialogue about racism? How likely would they engage in a discussion of reparations to blacks for injustices to their ancestors and the lingering effects of slavery? Would whites be willing to conduct an American counterpart to the South African Truth and Reconciliation panels orchestrated by Bishop Desmond Tutu?

ANOTHER WAY TO SALVAGING SOCIETY

The answer to these questions for the average white American is obvious. If we are to create a climate of acceptance and improve race relations in this country we must engage in something less threatening and more tangible than talk—something that can entice whites to participate because they apprehend the outcome as beneficial to themselves and society. We must tap into the reservoir of noblesse oblige, the call to aid the underdog and the disadvantaged that every religious and ethical system admonishes us to answer.

Although talk may seem to be a necessary precondition to action, and dialogue itself can be a positive component for creating social change—facilitators are fond of noting that the dialogic process is often more important than the product—many participants in dialogue groups leave after a few sessions because they want more tangible forms of action. While some interracial and interfaith dialogue groups have existed for years meeting in one another's homes, dining out, and attending cultural and civic events, many more succumb to inertia and become extinguished from lack of enthusiasm and substantive accomplishments.

The method for resolving this dilemma is contained in the work of renowned social psychologist Gordon Allport, who, more than half a century ago, analyzed the concept of prejudice and posited the salubrious effects emanating from different ethnic groups interacting.[11] Shared positive social interactions where participants work toward a common goal, such as building and remodeling homes (e.g. Habitat for Humanity), caring for the sick and elderly, constructing play areas, cleaning public roads and facilities—all superimpose larger societal needs over individual agendas.

As Allport surmised, the strategy is to bring diverse people together in an activity that reinforces mutual respect. When people work together in an activity that benefits everyone in the community in which they live, individual concerns about color and creed can be transcended in the pursuit of an attainable goal to enhance the commonweal. This is not to deny the resistance and intransigence of some people who, as in the Civil Rights Era from 1950–1970, refused to acknowledge the humanity and worth of people of color. But the legal and political milieu of this country is quite different today. Laws and policies have tempered even the most ardent bigots' overt actions (though they are less constrained to profane race relations through the anonymity of the Internet).

It is conceivable that invoking the principle of Allport's "Contact and Acquaintance" premise, skeptical and reluctant whites, who knowingly or unknowingly bask in the aura of white privilege, can be enlisted in community service projects for the greater good of society. As Allport noted:

> To be maximally effective, contact and acquaintance programs should lead to a sense of equality in social status, should occur in ordinary purposeful pursuits, avoid artificiality, and if possible enjoy the sanction of the community in which they occur. The deeper and more genuine the association, the greater its effect. While it may help somewhat to place members of different ethnic groups side

by side on a job, the gain is greater if these members regard themselves as part of a team.[12]

Although widely engaged in already, community service should become a core value of the American social fabric—one participated in by more people of all ages, especially children and youth. As with adults, positive cross-cultural interaction among children and youth help prevent the formation of pernicious racial stereotypes and can reduce tension and conflict in the nation's schools. Every student from elementary school through college should be required to complete fifty hours of community service as a prerequisite for graduation. The activity should be a group endeavor with people from diverse backgrounds participating and contributing. We can no longer afford the maintenance of racist, sexist, classist, homophobic, and ableist barriers segregating our society into a convoluted quilt based on white privilege, money, and a stereotypical value system that spurns diversity in favor of conformity to white ableist values.

CLARIFYING OUR VALUES

One of the obstacles to bringing such a plan to fruition will be identifying competent and ideologically committed facilitators and sponsors for participating students. In a time of reduced resources we will have to prioritize our goals.[13] Is a more equitable, peaceful, and livable society less important than teaching that emphasizes standardized test scores reflecting the discontinuities derived from social inequalities? We need to make better people not better students. Resources and energy directed into collaborative community service work are investments in the necessary social engagement that must occur if we, as a society, are going to transcend all the culturally oppressive baggage that taints human relationships under the guise of capitalist freedom and competition.

"Freedom from what and for what?" as psychoanalyst Erich Fromm asked more than half a century ago.[14] In order to be free one must have a grasp of and commitment to values and activities that are not only self-fulfilling, but which help to enrich other human lives and the commonweal, for what is man without society, and what is society without collaborative citizens engaged in the creation of mutually satisfying and communally productive endeavors?

Herbert Marcuse, another German Jew who sought refuge in the United States as the Holocaust loomed over Europe, characterized the United States as a society enveloped in "democratic unfreedom." This is a form of existence which places things above people and instrumentalizes human relationships where everyone engages in the pursuit of the satisfaction of "false needs."[15] As long as our society glorifies materialism and consumption, the impetus for perpetuating racism and other forms of discrimination such as classism and sexism will continue. This is because members of the dominating group benefit by reinforcing behavior that disadvantages minorities while elevating and protecting their own social status. The increasing competition for power, prestige, and resources is viewed as a zero-sum game, where white males cling to their advantages and reject the insinuation that they benefit from the color of their skin and their gender. We are not a free society until all men and women have the knowledge of their potentialities and equal opportunity to exercise their right to develop their talents in the manner guaranteed by our Constitution.

The lack of social awareness and concern for the welfare of others evinced by some segments of our society is reflected in societal institutions that are still overwhelmingly structured to maintain white hegemony over education, employment, and politics. That is why it is necessary for adults as well as students to become involved in community service activities and break down the barriers that have for so long separated and divided us. Working for the common good kindles a spirit of camaraderie, and the attainment of shared goals creates good will among participants when they see the joint fruits of their labor. A recognition of the relative importance and contribution of each participant toward achieving a common objective helps to defuse prejudice and racism as Allport predicted.

Voluminous research supports Allport's hypothesis, and indicates how relatively brief interracial interactions can have lasting beneficial effects on participants and society. Proof of the efficacy of interacting with people from different backgrounds comes from a review of 515 studies with 714 samples from 38 countries. In over half a century with over 200,000 participants, psychologists Thomas Pettigrew and Linda Tropp found that intergroup contact reduces prejudice and creates positive effects *beyond* the specific activity to the entire out group. Although prejudiced people avoid intergroup contact, participation in intergroup activities reduced their prejudice toward sexual and religious minorities and people of color.[16]

The husband and wife team of psychologists, Art and Elaine Aron, at the University of New York at Stony Brook have demonstrated the beneficial effects of cross racial encounters by creating situations where people from diverse backgrounds work together to solve problems or engage in mutually beneficial activities. They report that lasting new friendships are formed that transcend racial and class interests after only a few hours of interaction.[17] Clearly, promoting interaction among diverse individuals is beneficial for participants and society, but two crucial impediments remain before we can reach an accommodation among diverse groups, and both are daunting. Though research supports the beneficial effects emanating from cooperative activities and community service, rampant social inequality continues to produce disparities in the crucial areas of education, employment, wealth, health, and criminal justice. These disparities have been and continue to be produced through the institutionalization of systems that reinforce negative stereotypical values and behavior denigrating and disparaging the poor, people of color, religious and ethnic minorities, and women.

Competition can indeed bring out the best in people, but there comes a time when it is dysfunctional for individuals and society. By every indicator we have presented herein, it is obvious that competition for basic human needs on a stilted playing field leads to frustration, anxiety, poverty, racism, and despair. People should not have to compete for food, housing, health care, and education. Most western societies reached this conclusion decades ago and provide considerably more assistance for these for all members of their societies than we do in the United States. As long as people in our country have to struggle for the attainment of basic human needs, pitting one individual and group against another, the flame of prejudice and hate will burn.

This is not to say that racism and prejudice have been extinguished in countries that have adopted more humanistic approaches to providing for the welfare of their inhabitants. In fact, there has been an increase in the number of hate crimes directed against immigrants throughout Europe, Great Britain, and Russia. But reducing some of the more basic and contentious sources of friction through government assistance in the provision of basic social services has no doubt helped to diminish the sources and intensity of social strife.

IMMIGRATION: RUINATION OR SALVATION?

Another major cause of social unrest is just as perplexing: the monumental increase in the transference of ideas through telecommunication, particularly television, radio, and the Internet, and the movement of large numbers of people from diverse backgrounds across national boundaries because of the pressure of population growth facilitated by rapid and mass transportation. Each year over one-sixth of the world's population travels outside of their nation. This trend was expedited by a decrease in the price of air fares which fell by three-fifths between 1970 and 2000. Even more people travel within their own countries. According to the United Nations, the rate of internal migration is six times higher than those who immigrate to other countries— 740 million people annually. Still, 214 million people (3.1 percent) of the world's population moved internationally in 2009.[18]

Over a third of international migration is from developing to developed countries, but half of them move within the region they come from and 40 percent move to a neighboring country. Sixty percent of international migrants move to a country having the same major religion as them, and 40 percent chose to live in a nation with the dominant language the same as theirs. At the present time, intra-Asian migration accounts for 20 percent of all international migration and exceeds the total number of immigrants that Europe receives from all other regions.

People migrate in search of better lives. Three-quarters of international immigrants move to countries with higher standards of living than their own, and United Nations data indicate that the poorest migrants averaged a 15-fold increase in income (about $15,000 per year) while doubling their educational enrollment rate and experiencing a 16-fold reduction in infant mortality (from 112 to 7 deaths per 1,000 live births). Nearly half of all international migrants are women and nearly all temporary migrants leave their home in search of work.

In the Unites States, 30 percent of migrants (4 percent of the population) are irregular work-related persons, while the European Union estimate runs between 6 and 15 percent of the migrant population or one percent of the total population. While migrants have higher income earning capacities than non-migrants and are more likely than non-migrants to have completed secondary school, they are still spurned by many people in their adopted countries because of cultural differences such as language, dress, religion, food, living arrangements, and child rearing practices.

In recent years there has been an unremitting chorus in opposition to immigration in the West, but the proportion of population composed of immigrants was considerably higher at times in the past than the present. At the end of the nineteenth century, 14 percent of the Irish, 10 percent of the Norwegians, 7 percent of the Swedes, and 7 percent of the residents in the United Kingdom entered the United States. Today, the proportion of immigrants from developing countries to developed countries is less than 3 percent of the total population of these countries.

Demographic trends may portend an ominous future unless serious concerted programs are implemented to prevent growing jingoism, anti-immigrant domestic and foreign policies, and flourishing xenophobia and paranoia. From 1960 to 2010 the number of migrants to developed countries increased from 5 to 12 percent. Furthermore, it is predicted that two billion people (40 percent of the world's urban population) will be living in slums by 2030.

One look at the dependency rate, the number of people who are not working age (elderly and children), is even more sobering. Currently, in the developed countries of North America, the European Union, Republic of Korea,

Australia, and New Zealand, 49 people are not working age out of 100. In developing countries there are 53 people not of working age out of every 100 and three-fourths of them are children. Because the population of developed countries is aging, the next forty years will find 71 people out of every 100 who are not working age in the developed countries compared to 55 in developing nations. If immigration was stopped completely, the ratio would rise to 78 per 100 in the developed nations!

If immigration laws were less restrictive, there might be a flood of people from the less developed countries to the developed countries once the current economic recession is reversed. In the present hostile immigration climate the prospect of less restrictive immigration policy may seem counterintuitive, but the low birth rate and aging of the population in developed nations will produce a severe labor shortage within 40 years. While the world's population will grow by one-third to 9.3 billion by 2050, population growth, barring increases from immigration, in developed regions will remain stagnant or decline. This will occur at the same time that the United States is projected to need 40 million new workers. Yet, in the next 15 years, new entrants to the labor force in developing countries will exceed the total number of working age people currently living in developed countries.

It is obvious how increased demand can be met with supply in this situation. What is a cause of consternation is the growing opposition to immigrants in the United States and other developed nations based on a variety of racist myths and associated paranoid depictions that stigmatize immigrants and their culture. Increasing migration and immigration has also been met with growing opposition by organized nativist hate groups. Fueled by the World Wide Web with thousands of hate web sites, scare tactics, xenophobia, and paranoia may become the fuse to ignite a world-wide conflagration of whites versus people of color coming from developing nations in search of better lives.

The United States has, from its beginning, been an immigrant society. Our nation has always drawn on the talent from other nations to enrich our scientific, cultural, and industrial base. Will we allow the xenophobes and fear-mongers to dictate the terms of this debate, backing into an uncertain precarious future, or will we engage in deliberations predicated on reasoned alternatives and assumptions that can guide us into an era of hope and fulfillment?

NOTES

1. Maura Van Heuit, posted October 26, 2008, at: *http://www.npr.org/templates/story/story.php?storyId=96038616*. Retrieved: 1/28/10.

2. See the companion *One America Dialogue Guide,* Washington, D.C., United States Government Printing Office, March 1998.

3. Now called Everyday-Democracy at: *http://everyday-democracy.org.*

4. See: *http://www.kettering.org/about_the_foundation.*

5. Now morphed into a loose National Federation for Just Communities at: *http://www.federationforjustcommunities.org/.*

6. See: *http://www.thataway.org/.*

7. H. Roy Kaplan, *Failing Grades: The Quest for Equity in America's Schools,* Second edition, Lanham, MD: Rowman & Littlefield Education, 2007, pp. 218–224.

8. Ibid.

9. Speech delivered by Attorney General Eric Holder on February 18, 2009, U.S. Department of Justice to honor Black History Month.

10. For comments on Eric Holder and similar sentiments go to: *http://www.freerepublic.com/tag/news-forum/index.*

11. Gordon W. Allport, *The Nature of Prejudice,* Reading, Mass.: Addison-Wesley Publishing Co., 1979, originally published in 1954.

12. Ibid., p. 489.

13. See the list of organizations and activities to assist with service learning projects at: *http://www.studentsinservicetoamerica.org/tools_resources/national.html.*

14. Erich Fromm, *Escape From Freedom,* N.Y.: Henry Holt and Company, 1941.

15. Herbert Marcuse, *One Dimensional Man,* London: Routledge and Kegan Paul, 1964.

16. Thomas F. Pettigrew and Linda R. Tropp, "A Meta-Analytic Test of Intergroup Contact Theory," *Journal of Personality and Social Psychology,* vol. 90, no. 5, 2006: 751–783. See also: Linda R. Tropp, "The Role of Trust in Intergroup Contact: Its Significance and Implications for Improving Relations Between Groups," in U. Wagner, L. R. Tropp, G. Finchilescu and C. Tredoux (eds.), *Improving Intergroup Relations: Building on the Legacy of Thomas Pettigrew,* Malden, Mass. Blackwell, 2008: 91–106.

17. Benedict Carey, "Tolerance Over Race Can Spread, Studies Find," *New York Times,* November 7, 2009: A16, A20. Levin and Nolan make a similar case for participatory problem solving and community service and introduce the important element of good leadership as a means of avoiding intergroup conflict and uniting people in shared communal goals. See: Jack Levin and Jim Nolan, *The Violence of Hate,* Third edition, Boston: Allyn and Bacon, 2011, chapter 5.

18. This discussion draws on information contained in the United Nations report "Overcoming Barriers: Human Mobility and Development," Human Development Report, 2009, chapter 2, United Nations Development Programme. N.Y.: Palgrave Mcmillan, 2009.

Postscript

For those white readers who doubt the veracity of my position and the validity of the title of this book, I have a little challenge. If you want to know whether racism exists in the United States, ask a person of color that question. Then ask him or her to give you a specific instance when they were the victim of racism. You might also ask how often they've been victimized and/or insulted because of the color of their skin. Of course, you might conclude that it was their biased, distorted perception of normal actions—events and activities which they misinterpreted, exaggerated, and blew out of proportion.

Many whites labor under the misapprehension that people of color are too sensitive about race relations and carry a chip on their shoulders. This assumption allows whites to dismiss allegations of racial profiling and the myriad other instances of "everyday racism" as exaggerations of normal friction between people from different backgrounds. It is also a convenient way of denying the existence of white racist behavior and the need for engaging in interracial dialogue. Such attitudes infuriate people of color because they are put in the position of being labeled as overly sensitive or delusional, further widening the gap in communications between and among groups in our society.

It's difficult for some white people to empathize with people of color when they have not had to endure the kind of outrageous situations outlined by one of my students:

I grew up in South Carolina. I can recall at 11 years old, my brother and I were run down by white supremacists as we rode our bikes on the "wrong part of the road." My grandmother had lived on a long stretch of road that became a dirt road at around two miles. As we played hide and seek, we wandered down the road and found ourselves in front of the house we never passed unless on the school bus. We never took that route to church or grocery shopping. It was forbidden. As we stood there, curiosity set in as we observed the flags, graffiti, pick-up trucks, and beer cans. It was definitely not the household I had grown up in.

Then I hear a voice I will never forget. "Hey nigger, what are you doing?" I remember my brother grabbed my hand as we ran to our bikes to ride away. A pick-up truck tore off behind us. My heart was racing. I cried in fear as we rode away but the truck came faster. My brother had been much older and stronger than I was and was ahead of me. I sped off into the woods dragging my bike as far in as I could. I crouched down in the woods as I watched a man get out of the truck and search for me. I cried silently in fear. He laughed loudly when he spotted me and got into his truck and left. I hid there for an hour praying he wouldn't return, hoping that he hadn't gone after my brother. That night, as I hid in the woods down the dark dirt road, I prayed and wondered how I could be so disliked because of the color of my skin. Didn't it matter that I was an honor roll student, or that I was good at basketball? Why didn't it matter that I sang in the church choir every Sunday, or that I helped my grandmother peel field peas when her hands ached? Why didn't they care? What did I do to make someone hate me so? That night was the beginning of an uphill battle with HATE that I have endured most of my life.

—Tiffany Talley, Graduate Student
(This happened in 1999.)

Before you assume that such incidents are isolated, consider that nearly every person of color in this country believes, according to Amnesty International, they have or will be racially profiled. Does some kind of mass paranoia afflict racial and ethnic groups here, or is it conceivable that their reality is quite different from yours, their life chances and experiences circumscribed because of myths, prejudice, and discrimination—a pattern embedded in the fabric of our institutions from the inception of this society? Could it be that your perception is the one in need of a reality check?

In any event, people act on their beliefs about reality. Perception is reality. If you believe something is true then it is truth for you. Perhaps that is why it is so difficult to create meaningful dialogue about racism—we are talking past one another. We must improve our empathetic listening ability. And most of all, we must try to understand someone when they are speaking. Below is a list of actions you can implement to improve interactions with people of color if you care to—or you can continue pretending that the meritocracy rewards those who are deserving and hope for a return of the "good old days."

REDUCING RACISM IN EVERYDAY LIFE

Many of the behaviors that women and people of color find offensive are the result of white males being used to behaving in what they consider the usual or normal way. They operate from a frame of reference that places them at the focal point of discussions without considering that other people, those traditionally defined as less powerful and important, should be afforded equal opportunities to initiate discussion, reflect on issues raised, withhold their judgment, or criticize established trends of thought or traditional ways of doing something.

It is not only the prerogative of white males to assume the mantle of being the initiator or arbiter of the conversation; women and people of color must be viewed as equal partners whose perspectives are valued. They should be allowed to complete their thoughts without being cut-off or having their sentences finished by males who, in their exuberance, monopolize the conversation and make it appear others don't deserve equal time to elucidate their perspectives.

Similarly, offering assistance may seem like a chivalrous act from a white middle-class male vantage point, but it may be perceived as condescending and overbearing by women and people of color because it might convey the notion that they lack the necessary skills and ability to handle the situation themselves. Then too, such offers reinforce power disparities by enhancing the self-esteem and ego of the purported beneficent benefactor at the expense of the weak or inept recipient. Good intentions may not be perceived as such in the light of historical denigration and oppression.

Dark-skinned people can vividly recount instances when they were followed or trailed by department store personnel who were assigned to keep tabs on potential shoplifters, as if the color of one's skin is an indicator of their moral integrity. Just as humiliating is the reluctance of clerks to touch the hands of people of color during transactions, as if black skin could rub off on white clerks. Do teachers unconsciously engage in similar behavior which might evoke insubordination or inhibit the participation of children of color?

Another source of tension between whites and people of color is the propensity of some whites to be too familiar with blacks. Many African-Americans are fond of maintaining formal titles signifying their accomplishments, such as doctor, lawyer, teacher, professor. What may seem as unnecessary formality by whites, who have already achieved recognition through implicit higher status afforded by white privilege, can be a reaction to historical depersonalization when blacks were ridiculed and discredited by using their first name regardless of age and accomplishments. Do not use an African-American's first name unless she/he indicates you should do so. Never address a black male as boy. Some teachers do, even innocently, and permanently risk losing the child's interest and enthusiasm.

These cautions may strike whites as being indicative of hypersensitivity by people of color. They fail to consider the historical and cultural influences that have created conditions that cause people of color to react negatively, even hostilely, to what whites assume are innocent or naive comments. Taken in the context of centuries of enforced status distinctions between dominant whites and submissive blacks, one can better comprehend what some whites might perceive as artificial, disingenuous, or superficial formality. This dynamic also highlights the types of difficulties encountered in interracial dialogues where whites may be reluctant to engage in discussions for fear of antagonizing "sensitive" blacks, and blacks appear to have "a chip on their shoulder." Whites, Latinos, and blacks must learn more about each others' idiosyncratic speech, customs, and culture if successful interactions are to be the norm rather than the exception.

Whites should also be aware that not only the tone of their speech but the terms they use can be off-putting to people of color. For example, the term minorities means less than and unequal to. Since whites account for less than a sixth of the world's population, they are the minority on this planet. Perhaps they should contemplate how it feels to be referred to as that, and consider that this will happen "in their own country" (as if they didn't steal it from people of color at the outset) in a few decades. Whites should also be careful how they use the terms foreigner and alien, neither of which represent the history and tradition of a pluralist nation founded by immigrants from around the world and dependent on them to sustain our labor force and economy. We pull in the welcome mat at risk of driving away the very people who have and will continue to make this nation vibrant.

Every person is unique and deserves to be respected, not stereotyped. They like to be appreciated for who they are, not lumped into categories like minorities, aliens, immigrants, even people of color. When possible try to use someone's name and never (as many teachers have done in my presence) say "I don't see color." This is a desperate attempt to demonstrate that the speaker is not racist. But the pronouncement is offensive because one of the first characteristics you notice about someone is their color. To say you don't see it is like denying their existence. It is disrespectful and painfully naïve.

As our society becomes more diverse the way we refer to one another changes. Terms like Hispanic, oriental, colored, and Negro are dated and offensive. Hispanic is a census term referring to people with Spanish surnames. Latino/Latina are more frequently used. Oriental is no longer used.

Asian is the acceptable term. And Negro and colored have been replaced by black or African-American. If in doubt, ask the person how they would like to be referred to. I did that once with a sixth grade African-American girl and she responded "Why don't you try my name."

It is understandable that some awkwardness exists between groups of people who have traditionally had little interaction with one another. This paucity of communication is further complicated by the continuing evolution of society and our vocabulary. We are not only becoming more culturally and ethnically diverse, our lexicon of terms and usage is undergoing changes as relationships, social status, and the level of awareness and personal consciousness intrudes into references about ourselves and "the other." As these changes occur, it is imperative that we be aware of changes in terminology, avoid obsequiousness, remain respectful of one another, and practice listening and understanding. Reasonable people will appreciate your attempt to improve communication and they will not recoil from dialogue if you are perceived as genuine in your approach. Our ways of referring to one another are evolving, and we all make mistakes from time to time.

If you have offended someone you can apologize and move on. If they choose not to accept your apology, then seek out someone else who is more flexible and understanding. But don't lapse into the stereotype that all members of that group are angry and hostile. Don't assume that all members of an ethnic group think or act alike, just as whites can't be stereotyped by their thoughts and actions. It's insulting to insinuate that blacks and Latinos should have one spokesperson to represent their views. Do whites have someone who speaks for all of them? Even more infuriating is the oft-repeated lament of whites for the late Rev. Dr. Martin Luther King, Jr. "who was the greatest spokesman you folks ever had. We need someone like that now," as if the good works of the many talented African-Americans and Latinos who serve this country in the public and private sector didn't exist.

One of the most perplexing idiosyncratic characteristics of racism is the preoccupation of whites with the physiological features of people of color. From their Eurocentric tradition, imbued and fortified with myths and stereotypes about the natural superiority of light-skinned people over dark-skinned people, normal, average-looking people are presumed to be fair-skinned with aquiline facial features and fine, pliable hair. We have seen how such facile beliefs originated and eventuated in the destruction of millions of people. Though some writers have concluded that social class is a more significant determinant of life chances than skin color, our analysis indicates it is safe to conclude that one's complexion is inextricably intertwined with social class and in some instances one's color alone affects perceptions, interactions, and outcomes in life.

Whiteness continues to stand as a metaphor for goodness, wholesomeness, and acceptability in our society. The closer one's appearance approximates the idealized stylized stereotype of the Aryan Anglo-Saxon, the greater the probability that one will be accepted, hired, passed, promoted, and liked. Despite the growing numbers of people of color and other ethnic groups in the United States, non-whites and other minorities are still viewed as outsiders, "the other," at times ridiculed, ostracized, exoticized, criminalized, and dehumanized.

It is whites' ignorance or denial of basic biological facts about our common origin and genetic similarities that perpetuates prejudice, discrimination, and racism. The path to enlightenment awaits those who wish to transcend the hate, discord, frustration, and defeatism that obscure the promise upon which this country was founded "with liberty and justice for all." One has only to begin the journey that will lead to a better life, but like a child, you have to take that first step.

Reference Section

Adorno, Theodore E. Frenkel-Brunswik, D.J. Levisnon, & R.N. Sanford, The Authoritarian Personality, N.Y.: Harper & Row, 1950.

Alexander, Michelle, *The New Jim Crow: Mass Incarceration in the Age of Colorblindness,* N.Y., The New Press, 2009.

Allport, Gordon W., *The Nature of Prejudice.* Reading, Mass.: Addison-Wesley Publishing Co., 1979.

Altman, Daniel, "Shattering Stereotypes about Immigrant Workers," *New York Times,* June 3, 2007.

Anderson, Carol, *Eyes Off the Prize: The United Nations and the African-American Struggle for Human Rights, 1944-1955,* N.Y.: Cambridge University Press, 2003.

Anderson, Terry H., *The Pursuit of Fairness: A History of Affirmative Action,* N.Y.: Oxford University Press, 2004.

Arnesen, Eric, *Black Protest and the Great Migration: A Brief History with Documents,* Boston: Bedford/St. Martins, 2003.

Arouet, Francois Marie (Voltaire), *Essai sur les moeurs et l'esprit des nations, 1756,* Ann Arbor: University of Michigan, 2009.

Banks, Ingrid, *Hair Matters: Beauty, Power, and Black Women's Consciousness,* N.Y.: New York University Press, 2000.

Banks, James A., and Banks, Cherry A. McGee, *Multicultural Education: Issues and Perspectives,* Sixth edition, Hoboken, N.J.: John Wiley and Sons, 2007.

Barnes, Annie S., *Everyday Racism,* Naperville, Ill.: Sourcebooks, Inc., 2000.

Basler, Roy P. (ed.), *The Collected Works of Abraham Lincoln,* vol. 3, "Fourth Debate with Stephen A. Douglas at Charleston, Illinois," September 18, 1858.

Bauer, Mary, *Under Siege: Life for Low-Income Latinos in the South,* Southern Poverty Law Center, Montgomery, Alabama, 2009.

Bazelon, Emily, "The New Kind of Integration," *New York Times Magazine,* July 20, 2008.

Bergmann, Barbara, "The Continuing Need for Affirmative Action," *Quarterly Review of Economics and Finance,* 39, 1999.

Bertrand, Marianne, and Mullainathan, Sendhil, "Are Emily and Greg More Employable than Lakisha and Jamal? A Field Experiment on Labor Market Discrimination," MIT Department of Economics Working Paper No. 03-22, May 27, 2003.

Blau, Francine D.; Ferber, Marianne A.; and Winkler, Anne E.; *The Economics of Women, Men and Work*, Englewood Cliffs: Prentice-Hall, 2002.

Blau, Peter, and Duncan, Otis Dudley, *The American Occupational Structure*, N.Y.: John Wiley, 1967.

Blauner, Bob, "Talking Past Each Other: Black and White Languages of Race," *The American Prospect*, 10, 1992.

Blitstein, Ryan, "Weathering, the Storm," *Miller-McCune*, vol. 2, no. 4 , July-August 2009.

Bobo, Lawrence, "Race, Interests, and Beliefs about Affirmative Action: Unanswered Questions and New Directions," *American Behavioral Scientist*, 41, 1998.

Boger, John Charles, and Orfield, Gary, (eds.) *School Resegregation: Must the South Turn Back?* Chapel Hill: University of North Carolina Press, 2005.

Bonastia, Christopher, *Knocking on the Door: The Federal Government's Attempt to Desegregate the Suburbs*, Princeton, N.J.: Princeton University Press, 2006.

Bonilla-Silva, Eduardo, *Racism Without Racists:Color-Blind Racism and Social Inequality in Contemporary America*, Third edition, Lanham, MD: Rowman and Littlefield Publishers, Inc., 2010.

Bonner, Raymond, and Lacey, Marc, "Pervasive Disparities Found in Federal Death Penalty," *New York Times,* September 12, 2000.

Bowser, Benjamin P., and Hunt, Raymond G. (eds.), *Impacts of Racism on White Americans*, Second edition, Thousand Oaks, Cal., Sage Publications, 1996.

Carey, Benedict, "Tolerance Over Race Can Spread, Studies Find," *New York Times,* November 7, 2009.

Carlyle, Thomas, "Occasional Discourse on the Negro Question," *Fraser's Magazine for Town and Country*, 40, February 1849.

Carnegie, Andrew, *The Gospel of Wealth,* "The Advantages of Poverty," N.Y.: The Century Co., 1901.

Carroll, Thomas G., and Foster, Elizabeth, "Learning Teams: Creating What's Next?" National Commission on Teaching and America's Future, Washington, D.C., April 2008.

Cavalli-Sforza, Luca L.; Menozzi, Paolo; and Piazza, Alberto; *The History and Geography of Human Genes*, Princeton: Princeton University Press, 1994.

Chin, Audrey, and Peterson, Mark A., *Deep Pockets, Empty Pockets: Who Wins in Cook County Jury Trials,* Santa Monica, Cal: Institute for Civil Justice, Rand Corporation, 1985.

Clark, Kenneth B., and Clark, Mamie P., "Emotional Factors in Racial Identification and Preference in Negro Children," *Journal of Negro Education*, vol. 19, no. 3, Summer 1950.

Clark, Kenneth B., *Prejudice and Your Child*, Second edition, Boston, Beacon Press, 1963.

Cobbs, Doreen, "Journey to New Horizons: Thoughts on Racism, Poverty, and Inequality in the American South," Center for the Study of the American South, March 1998.

Cohen, Jon, and Agiesta, Jennifer, "3 in 10 Americans Admit to Race Bias," *Washington Post,* Sunday, June 22, 2008.

Combe, George, *A System of Phrenology,* Boston: B.B. Mussey and Co., 1851.

Conley, Dalton, *Being Black, Living in the Red: Race, Wealth, and Social Policy in America,* Berkeley: University of California Press, 1999.

Cooper, Helene, "Meet the New Elite, Not Like the Old," *New York Times,* July 26, 2009.

Cooper, P.M., "Does Race Matter? A Comparison of Effective Black and White Teachers of African American Students," in J.J. Irvine (ed.), *In Search of Wholeness: African American Teachers and Their Culturally Specific Classroom Practice.* N.Y.: Palgrave, 2002.

Cose, Ellis, *The Rage of a Privileged Class,* N.Y.: HarperCollins, 1993.

Crenshaw, Kimberle; Gotanda, Neil; Peller, Gary; and Thomas, Kendall (eds.); *Critical Race Theory: The Key Writings that Formed the Movement,* N.Y.: The New Press, 1995.

Daniels, Jessie, *Cyber Racism: White Supremacy Online and the New Attack on Civil Rights,* Lanham, MD: Rowman and Littlefield, 2009.

Darwin, Charles, *The Descent of Man and Selection in Relation to Sex,* N.Y.: D. Appleton and Co., 1871.

Darwin, Charles, *On the Origin of Species by Means of Natural Selection, or the Preservation of Favoured Races in the Struggle for Life.* London: Murray, 1859.

Delgado, Richard, and Stefancic, Jean (eds.), *Critical Race Theory: The Cutting Edge,* Second edition, Philadelphia: Temple University Press, 2000.

Demmert, W.G., and Towner, J.C., "A Review of the Research Literature on the Influences of Culturally Based Education on the Academic Performance of Native American Students," Final Paper, Portland, Oregon: Northwest Regional Educational Laboratory, 2003.

Desmond, Adrian and Moore, James, *Darwin's Sacred Cause: How a Hatred of Slavery Shaped Darwin's Views on Human Evolution,* Boston: Houghton Mifflin Harcourt, 2009.

Desmond, Matthew, and Emirbayer, Mustafa, *Racial Domination, Racial Progress,* N.Y.: McGraw-Hill, 2010.

Devlin, Bernie; Fienberg, Stephen E.; Resnick, Daniel P.; and Roeder, Kathryn (eds.); *Intelligence, Genes and Success: Scientists Respond to The Bell Curve,* N.Y.: Springer, 1997.

Diamond, Jared, *Guns, Germs, and Steel: The Fates of Human Societies,* N.Y.: W.W. Norton, 1999.

Dingle, Derek T., "Power in the Boardroom," *Black Enterprise,* February, 2008.

Dinkes, R.; Cataldi; E.F.; and Lin-Kelly, W.; *Indicators of School Crime and Safety:* 2007, NCES 2008-021/NCJ 219553. National Center for Education Statistics,

U.S. Department of Education, and Bureau of Justice Statistics, Office of Justice Programs, U.S. Department of Justice, Washington, D.C., 2007.

Doherty, R.W., "Five Standards and Student Achievement," *NABE Journal of Research and Practice*, 1, 2003.

Donovan, M. Suzanne, and Cross, Christopher, *Minority Students in Special and Gifted Education*, Washington, D.C.: National Academy Press, 2002.

Duberman, Martin B., *Paul Robeson*, N.Y.: Alfred Knoph, 1988.

Du Bois, W. E. B., *Autobiography of W. E. B. Du Bois: A Soliloquy on Viewing My Life From the Last Decade of Its First Century*, N.Y.: International Publishers, 1968.

Du Bois, W. E. B., *The Souls of Black* Folk, N.Y.: New American Library, 1903.

Dvorak, Phred, "Some Things Don't Change," *Wall Street Journal*, January 14, 2008.

Ehrenreich, Barbara, and Muhammad, Dedrick, "The Recession's Racial Divide," *The New York Times,* September 13, 2009.

Ehrlich, Howard J., *Hate Crimes and Ethnoviolence*. Boulder, Colorado: Westview Press, 2009.

Eltis, David and Richardson, David (eds.), *Extending the Frontiers: Essays on the New Transatlantic Slave Trade Database*, New Haven: Yale University Press, 2008.

Essed, Philomena, and Goldberg, David Theo (eds.), *Race Critical Theories: Text and Context,* Malden, Massachusetts: Blackwell Publishers, 2002.

Farkas, Steve; Johnson, Jean; and Duffett, Ann; "Stand By Me: What Teachers Really Think About Unions, Merit Pay and Other Professional Matters," N.Y.: Public Agenda, 2003.

Feagin, Joe R., *Racist America.* Second edition, N.Y.: Routledge, 2010.

Finkelman, Paul, *Defending Slavery: Proslavery Thought in the Old South, A Brief History with Documents*, Boston: Bedford/St. Martin's, 2003.

Frankenberg, Erica, "The Segregation of American Teachers." Cambridge, MA. Civil Rights Project of Harvard University, 2006.

Franklin, John Hope, *One America in the 21st Century: The Report of President Bill Clinton's Initiative on Race,* New Haven: Yale University Press, 2008.

Frazier, E. Franklin, *Black Bourgeoisie*, Glencoe, Ill.: Free Press, 1957.

Freire, Paolo, *Pedagogy of the Oppressed*, Myra Bergman Ramos, (trans.), N.Y.: Continuum, 2000.

Fromm, Erich, *Escape From Freedom,* N.Y.: Henry Holt and Company, 1941.

Fromm, Erich, *Man for Himself: An Enquiry into the Psychology of Ethics*, London: Routledge, 2002.

Fryer, Peter, *Staying Power: The History of Black People in Britain*, London: Pluto Press, 1984.

Fryer, Jr., Roland G., and Levitt, Steven D., "The Causes and Consequences of Distinctively Black Names," *The Quarterly Journal of Economics*, 119, no. 3, August 2004.

Gall, Franz Joseph and Spurzheim, Johan Gaspar, *Phrenology: And the Moral Influence of Phrenology*, Philadelphia: Carey, Lea, and Blanchard, 1835.

Gay, G., *Culturally Responsive Teaching: Theory, Research, and Practice*. N.Y.: Teachers College Press, 2000.

Geronimus, A.T. ; Bound, J.; Waidmann, T.A.; Colen, C.G.; and Steffick, D.; "Inequality in Life Expectancy, Functional Status, and Active Life Expectancy Across Selected Black and White Population in the United States," *Demography*, vol. 38, no. 2, 2001.

Giddings, Franklin H., *The Principles of Sociology: An Analysis of the Phenomena of Association and of Social Organization*, N.Y.: Macmillan and Company, 1896.

Ginsberg, Allen, "A Supermarket in California," *Collected Poems 1947–1980*, N.Y.: Harper Collins, 1984.

Ginsberg, M.B., and Wlodkowski, R. J., *Creating Highly Motivating Classrooms for All Students: A School Wide Approach to Powerful Teaching and Diverse Learners*. San Francisco: Jossey-Bass, 2000.

Giuliano, Laura; Levine, David I.; and Leonard, Jonathan; "Manager Race and the Race of New Hires," *Journal of Labor Economics*, 27, October 2009.

Glover, Karen S., *Racial Profiling: Research, Racism and Resistance*. Lanham, Md.: Rowman and Littlefield Publisher, Inc., 2009.

Goldstein, David, *Jacob's Legacy: A Genetic View of Jewish History*, New Haven: Yale University Press, 2008.

Gordon-Reed, Annette, *The Hemingses of Monticello*, N.Y.: W.W. Norton, 2008.

Gossett, Thomas F., *Race: The History of an Idea in America*, N.Y.: Oxford University Press, New Edition, 1997.

Gravlee, Clarence C., "How Race Becomes Biology: Embodiment of Social Inequality," *American Journal of Physical Anthropology*, vol. 139, 2009.

Green, Carmen R.; Ndao-Brumblay, S. Khady; West, Brady; and Washington, Tamika; "Differences in Prescription Opioid Analgesic Availability: Comparing Minority and White Pharmacies Across Michigan," *The Journal of Pain*, vol. 6, no. 10, October 2005.

Hacker, Andrew, *Two Nations*, N.Y.: Scribner, 2003, 1992.

Haley, Alex, *The Autobiography of Malcolm X*, N.Y.: Ballantine Books, 1964.

Hamilton, Kendra, "Embracing 'Black is Beautiful'—African-American Involvement in Fashion Industry, and Consumer Spending on Apparel and Beauty Care Products," *BNET Business Network*, January 4, 2001.

Hammer, Michael F, "Extended Y Chromosome Haplotypes Resolve Multiple and Unique Lineages of the Jewish Priesthood," *Human Genetics*, July 2009.

Handywerk, Brian,"Some Neandertals Were Pale Redheads, DNA Suggests," *National Geographic News*, October 25, 2007.

Hannaford, Ivan, *Race: The History of an Idea in the West*, Baltimore: The Johns Hopkins University Press, 1996.

Harlow, Caroline Wolf, "Hate Crime Reported by Victims and Police," Bureau of Justice Statistics, Special Report, U.S. Department of Justice, Office of Justice Program, November 2005, NCJ 209911.

Harry, B., and Klingner, J., *Why Are So Many Minority Students in Special Education?*, N.Y.: Teachers College Press, 2006.

Harvey, John, *Men in Black*, Chicago: The University of Chicago Press, 1995.

Herrnstein, Richard, *IQ in the Meritocracy*, Little, Brown and Company, Boston, 1973.

Hobbes, Thomas, *Leviathan*, Dover Philosophical Classics, 2006.

Hoberman, John, *Darwin's* Athletes, Boston: Houghton Mifflin, 1997.

Hoffman, Paul, "The Science of Race," *Discover*, November 1994.

Holzer, Harry J., and Neumark, David, "Assessing Affirmative Action," *Journal of Economic Literature*, 38, September 2000.

Holzer, Harry J., and Neumark, David, "What Does Affirmative Action Do?" *Industrial and Labor Relations Review*, 53, no. 2, 2000.

Holzer, Harry J., and Neumark, David (eds.), *The Economics of Affirmative Action*, London: Edward Elgar, 2004.

Hooks, Bell, *Teaching Community: A Pedagogy of Hope*, N.Y.: Routledge, 2003.

Ingersoll, Richard, "Revolving Doors and Leaky Buckets," in Carl Glickman, (ed.), *Letters to the Next President*, N.Y.: Teachers College, 2004.

Isaacs, Julia B., "Economic Mobility of Black and White Families," PEW Charitable Trusts, The Economic Mobility Project, November 13, 2007.

Jefferson, Thomas, *Notes on the State of Virginia*, Richmond: J.W. Randolph, 1853.

Jencks, Christopher and Phillips, Meredith (eds.), *The Black-White Test Score* Gap, Washington, D.C.: The Brookings Institution, 1998.

Johnson, Allan G., *Privilege, Power, and Difference*, Second edition, N.Y.: McGraw-Hill, 2006.

Jones, Jeffrey M., "Race, Ideology, and Support for Affirmative Action," in Alec Gallup and Frank Newport, (eds.), *The Gallup Poll 2005: Public Opinion*, Lanham, MD: Rowman and Littlefield, 2006.

Kahlenberg, Richard, *All Together Now*, Washington, D.C., Brookings Institution Press, 2001.

Kalev, Alexandra; Dobbin, Frank; and Kelly, Erin; "Best Practices or Best Guesses? Assessing the Efficacy of Corporate Affirmative Action and Diversity Policies," *American Sociological Review*, 71, August 2006.

Kaplan, H. Roy, *Failing Grades: The Quest for Equity in America's Schools*, Second edition, Lanham, MD: Rowman and Littlefield Education, 2007.

Kaplan, Jeffrey, (ed.), *Encyclopedia of White Power: A Sourcebook on the Radical Racist Right*, Lanham, MD: Rowman and Littlefield Publishers, 2000.

Katznelson, Ira, *When Affirmative Action Was White*, N.Y.: W.W. Norton Company, 2005.

Keane, Fergal, *Seasons of Blood: A Rwandan Journey*, London: Penguin Books, 1997.

Kilman, C., "Learning Lakota," *Teaching Tolerance*, 30, Fall 2006.

Kirp, D. L.; Dwyer, J. P.; and Rosenthal, L. A.; *Our Town: Race, Housing, and the Soul of Suburbia*, New Brunswick, N.J.: Rutgers University Press, 1995.

Kochar, Rakesh, "Growth in the Foreign-Born Workforce and Employment of the Native Born," PEW Hispanic Center, Washington, D.C. August 10, 2006.

Kochar, Rakesh,"Unemployment Rose Sharply Among Latino Immigrants in 2008," PEW Hispanic Center, Washington, D.C. February 12, 2009.

Kozol, Jonathan, *Savage Inequalities: Children in America's Schools,* N.Y.: Crown Publishers, Inc., 1991.

Kozol, Jonathan, *The Shame of the Nation: The Restoration of Apartheid Schooling in America,* N.Y.: Crown Publishers, Inc., 2005.

Kushner, David, *Levittown,* N.Y.: Walker and Co., 2009.

Ladson-Billings, G., *The Dreamkeepers: Successful Teachers of African-American Children,* San Francisco: Jossey-Bass, 1994.

Lavater, John Caspar, *Essays on Physiognomy,* Thomas Holcroft (trans.), London: Tegg and Co., 1878.

LaVeist, Thomas A.; Gaskin, Darrell J.; and Richard, Patrick; "The Economic Burden of Health Inequalities in the United States," Joint Center for Political and Economic Studies, Washington, D.C.: September 2009.

Lee, O., "Equity for Linguistically and Culturally Diverse Students in Science and Education: A Research Agenda," *Teachers College Record,* 105, 2003.

Levin, Jack, and Nolan, Jim, *The Violence of Hate,* Third edition, Boston: Allyn and Bacon, 2011.

Lieberman, Matthew D. "Social Cognitive Neuroscience: A Review of Core Processes," *Annual Review of Psychology,* 58, 2007.

Lindsay, Lisa A., *Captives as Commodities: The Transatlantic Slave Trade,* Upper Saddle River: Pearson Prentice Hall, 2008.

Liptak, Adam, "Justices, 5–4, Reject Corporate Spending Limit," *New York Times,* January 22, 2010.

Locke, John, *An Essay Concerning Human Understanding,* P. Nidditch (ed.), Oxford: Clarendon Press, 1975.

Logan, John, "Separate and Unequal: The Neighborhood Gap for Blacks and Hispanics in Metropolitan America," Lewis Mumford Center for Comparative Urban and Regional Research, 2002.

Lombroso, Cesare, *The Criminal Man,* Mary Gibson and Nicole Hahn Rafter (trans.), Durham: Duke University Press, 2006.

Losen, Daniel J., and Orfield, Gary, (eds.), *Racial Inequity in Special Education,* Cambridge: Harvard Education Press, 2002.

Lott, Tommy L, "Patriarchy and Slavery in Hobbes's Political Philosophy," *Philosopher's on Race: Critical Essays,* Oxford, England, 2002,

Lowenstein, Roger, "The Immigrant Equation," *The New York Times Magazine,* July 9, 2006.

Luo, Michael, "In Job Hunt, College Degree Can't Close Racial Gap," *New York Times,* December 1, 2009.

Luo, Michael, "'Whitening' the Resume," *New York Times,* December 6, 2009.

Madrick, Jeff, "Goodbye, Horatio Alger," *The Nation,* Feb. 5, 2007.

Malik, Kenan, *The Meaning of Race: Race, History and Culture in Western Society,* N.Y.: New York University Press, 1996.

Mann, Michael, *The Dark Side of Democracy: Explaining Ethnic Cleansing*, London: Cambridge University Press, 2004.

Marable, Manning, *The Great Wells of Democracy: The Meaning of Race in American Life*. Cambridge, Mass.: Basic Civitas Books, 2002.

Marcuse, Herbert, *One Dimensional Man*, London: Routledge and Kegan Paul, 1964.

Massey, Douglas and Denton, Nancy, *American Apartheid: Segregation and the Making of the Underclass*, Cambridge, Mass.: Harvard University Press, 1998.

Matthews, Donald R., *U.S. Senators and Their World*, Westport, CT.: Greenwood Press, 1980.

Mazumder, Bhashkar, "Sibling Similarities, Differences and Economic Inequality," Federal Reserve Board of Chicago, Working Paper, 2004.

McDonald, Steve; Lin, Nan; and Ao, Dan; "Networks of Opportunity: Gender, Race, and Job Leads," *Social Problems*, 56, August 2009.

McIntosh, Peggy, "White Privilege: Unpacking the Invisible Knapsack," *Independent School*, Winter, 1990.

McKinney, Karyn D., *Being White: Stories of Race and Racism*, N.Y.: Routledge, 2005.

McNamee, Stephen J., and Miller, Jr., Robert K., *The Meritocracy Myth*, Second edition, Lanham, MD.: Rowman and Littlefield Publishers, 2009.

Mellinger, Wayne Martin, "Postcards from the Edge of the Color Line: Images of African-Americans in Popular Culture, 1893–1917," *Symbolic Interaction*, 15, 1992.

Merton, Robert K., *Bureaucratic Structure and Personality*, The Free Press: Glencoe, Ill., 1957.

Mills, C.Wright, *The Power Elite*, N.Y.: Oxford University Press, 1956.

Mishel, Lawrence; Bernstein, Jared; and Shierholz, Heidi; *The State of Working America: 2008-2009*, Washington, D.C.: Economic Policy Institute, 2009.

Moore, Robert B., "Racist Stereotyping in the English Language," in Paula S. Rothenberg (ed.), *Racism and Sexism: An Integrated Study*, N.Y.: St. Martin's Press, 1988:

Morrison, Toni, *The Bluest* Eye, N.Y.: Holt, Rinehart and Winston, 1970.

Murray, Charles, *Losing Ground: American Social Policy, 1950–1980*, Basic Books, N.Y.: 1984.

Nalty, Bernard C., *Strength for the Fight: A History of Black Americans in the Military*, N.Y.: The Free Press, 1986.

Nieto, Sonia, and Bode, Patty, *Affirming Diversity: The Sociopolitical Context of Multicultural Education*, Fifth edition, N.Y.: Allyn and Bacon, 2007.

Obama, Barack, *The Audacity of Hope*, N.Y.: Barnes and Noble, 2006.

Olson, Steve, *Mapping Human History: Genes Race and Our Common Origin*, Boston: Mariner Books, 2002.

Orfield, Gary and Eaton, Susan, *Dismantling* Segregation, N.Y.: The New Press, 1997.

O'Reilly, Kenneth, *Nixon's Piano: Presidents and Racial Politics from Washington to Clinton*, N.Y.: The Free Press, 1995.

Paradies, Yin, "A Systematic Review of Empirical Research on Self-Reported Racism and Health," *International Journal of Epidemiology*, vol. 35, no.4, April 2006.

Pettigrew, Thomas F., and Tropp, Linda R.,"A Meta-Analytic Test of Intergroup Contact Theory," *Journal of Personality and Social Psychology*, vol. 90, no. 5, 2006.

Picca, Leslie Houts, and Feagin, Joe R., *Two-Faced Racism: Whites in the Backstage and Frontstage*. N.Y.: Taylor and Francis, 2007.

Popescu, Ioana, "Differences in Mortality and Use of Revascularization in Black and White Patients with Acute MI Admitted to Hospitals with and Without Revascularization Services," *Journal of the American Medical Association*, vol. 297, no. 22, June 13, 2007.

Powell, Michael, "Suit Accuses Wells Fargo of Steering Blacks to Subprime Mortgages in Baltimore," *New York Times*, June 7, 2009.

Powell, Michael, and Roberts, Janet, "Minorities Affected Most as New York Foreclosures Rise," *New York Times*, May 16, 2009.

Powell-Hopson, Darlene and Hopson, Derek, *Different and Wonderful: Raising Black Children in a Race-Conscious* Society, N.Y.: Prentice-Hall, 1990.

Rank, Mark R., and Hirschl, Thomas A., "Estimating the Risk of Food Stamp Use and Impoverishment During Childhood," *Archives of Pediatric and Adolescent Medicine*, vol. 163, 11, November 2009.

Relethford, John H., *Reflections of Our Past: How History is Revealed in Our Genes*, Cambridge, Mass: Westview Press, 2003.

Rhoden, William C., *Forty Million Dollar Slaves*, N.Y.: Crown Publishers, 2006.

Rhoden, William C., *Third and a Mile: The Trials and Triumphs of the Black Quarterback*, N.Y.: ESPN Books, 2007.

Rivera, Amaad, *The Silent Depression: State of the Dream*, United for a Fair Economy, Boston, 2009.

Robeson, Paul, *Here I Stand*, Boston: Beacon Press, 1958.

Roth, Philip, *The Human Stain*, N.Y.: Vintage, 2001.

Rothenberg, Paula, *Race,Class and Gender in the United States*, Eighth edition, N.Y.: Worth Publishers, 2009.

Rothenberg, Paula (ed.), *White Privilege: Essential Reading on the Other Side of Racism*, Second edition, N.Y.: Worth Publishers, 2005.

Rousseau, Jean Jacques, *The First and Second Discourses*, Roger D. Masters, (ed.), Judith R. Masters (trans.), N.Y.: Bedford/St. Martin's, 1969.

Rutstein, Nathan, *Racism: Unraveling the Fear*, Washington, D.C.: The Global Classroom, 1997.

Ryan, William, *Blaming the Victim*, N.Y.: Knoph Doubleday, 1976.

Satter, Beryl, *Family Properties: Race, Real Estate, and the Exploitation of Black Urban America*, N.Y.: Metropolitan, 2009.

Savage, Charlie, "A Judge's View of Judging Is on the Record," *New York Times*, May 14, 2009.

Scarville, Jacquelyn, "Armed Forces Equal Opportunity Survey," Defense Manpower Data Center, Survey and Program Evaluation Division, Department of Defense, Arlington, VA, 1999.

Sells, Michael, *The Bridge Betrayed: Religion and Ethnic Genocide in Bosnia,* Berkeley, Cal.: 1996.

Shapiro, Thomas M.; Meschede, Tatjana; and Sullivan, Laura; "The Racial Wealth Gap Increases Fourfold," Institute on Assets and Social Policy, Research and Policy Brief, The Heller School for Social Policy and Management, Brandeis University, May 2010.

Shreeve, James, "The Greatest Journey Ever Told: The Trail of Our DNA," *National Geographic,* Sunday, March 12, 2006.

Skorecki, Karl, "Chromosomes of Jewish Priests," *Nature,* 385, January 2, 1997.

Slater, Philip E., *The Pursuit of Loneliness,* Boston: Beacon Press, 1970.

Smith, David B., *Health Care Divided: Race and Healing a Nation,* Ann Arbor: University of Michigan Press, 1999.

Sniderman, Paul M., and Piazza, Thomas, *The Scar of Race,* Cambridge, Mass.: Harvard University Press, 1993.

Spencer, Herbert, *Social Statics,* London: John Chapman, 1851.

Steele, Claude, "Thin Ice: 'Stereotype Threat' and Black College Students," *The Atlantic Monthly,* August 1999.

Steele, Claude, and Aronson, Joshua, "Stereotype Threat and the Intellectual Test Performance of African-Americans," *Journal of Personality and Social Psychology,* 69 (5), November 1995.

Stern, Kenneth S., *A Force Upon the Plain: The American Militia Movement and the Politics of Hate,* N.Y.: Simon and Schuster, 1996.

Stouffer, Samuel, *The American Soldier,* 4 vols. Princeton, N.J.: Princeton University Press, 1949.

Sumner, William Graham, *What Social Classes Owe to Each Other,* N.Y.: Harper and Brothers, 1883.

Tatum, Beverly Daniel, *Why are All the Black Kids Sitting Together in the Cafeteria?,* N.Y.: Basic Books, 1997.

Thomas, Mark G., "Y Chromosomes Traveling South: The Cohen Haplotype and the Origins of the Lemba—the 'Black Jews of Southern Africa,'" *American Journal of Human* Genetics, 66 (2), February 2000.

Thompson, Diane E., "Why Servicers Foreclose When They Should Modify and Other Puzzles of Servicer Behavior," National Consumer Law Center, Inc., Boston, Mass., October 2009.

Thompson, Heather, *Whose Detroit: Politics, Labor and Race in a Modern City,* Ithaca: Cornell University Press, 2004.

Tropp, Linda R., "The Role of Trust in Intergroup Contact: Its Significance and Implications for Improving Relations Between Groups," in *Improving Intergroup Relations: Building on the Legacy of Thomas Pettigrew,* Malden, Mass. Blackwell, 2008.

Urquhart, Brian, *Ralph Bunche,* N.Y.: W.W. Norton and Company, 1998.

Van Ausdale, Debra, and Feagin, Joe, *The First R,* Lanham, MD.: Rowman and Littlefield Publishers, 2001.

Veblen, Thorstein, *The Theory of the Leisure Class,* N.Y.: Macmillan, 1912.

Vedantam, Shankar, *The Hidden Brain*, N.Y.: Spiegel and Grau, 2010.

Ward, Julie K., and Lott, Tommy L. (eds.), *Philosophers on Race: Critical Essays*, Oxford: Blackwell Publishers, Ltd., 2002.

Watkins, Steve, *The Black O: Racism and Redemption in an American Corporate Empire*, Athens, Georgia: The University of Georgia Press, 1997.

Weber, Max, *The Protestant Ethic and the Spirit of Capitalism*, (Talcott Parsons trans.), Mineola, N.Y.: Dover Publications, 2003.

West, Cornell, *Race Matters*, N.Y.: Vintage Books, 1993.

Wiggins, Jennifer B., "Damages in Tort Litigation: Thoughts on Race and Remedies, 1865-2007," *The Review of Litigation*, vol. 27, 2008.

Wilkinson, Richard, and Marmot, Michael (eds.), *Social Determinants of Health: The Solid Facts*, Second edition, Denmark: The World Health Organization, 2003.

Wilson, William, *More Than Just Race*. N.Y.: W.W. Norton, 2009.

Wilson, William Julius, *The Truly Disadvantaged: The Inner City, the Underclass, and Public Policy*, Chicago: University of Chicago Press, 1987.

Wingfield, Adia Harvey, *Doing Business with Beauty: Black Women, Hair Salons, and the Racial Enclave Economy*, Lanham, Md.: Rowman and Littlefield Publishers, Inc. 2008.

Wingfield, Adia Harvey and. Feagin, Joe R, *Yes We Can?* N.Y. Routledge, 2010.

Wise, Tim, *Between Barack and a Hard Place*, San Francisco: City Lights Publishers, 2009.

Wise, Tim, *Color-Blind*. San Francisco: City Lights Books, 2010.

Withrow, Brian, *Racial Profiling from Rhetoric to Reason*, Upper Saddle River, N.J.: Pearson Education, Inc., 2006.

Wong, Kate, "The Fate of the Neandertals," in John H. Relethford, *Reflections of Our Past: How History is Revealed in Our Genes*, Cambridge: Mass.: Westview Press, 2003.

Wong, Kate, "Twilight of the Neandertals," *Scientific American*, 301, (2), August 2009.

Woolf, Steven H., "The Health Impact of Resolving Racial Disparities: An Analysis of US Mortality Data," *American Journal of Public Health*, vol. 94, no.12, December 2004.

Wright, Michelle M., *Becoming Black: Creating Identity in the African Diaspora*, Durham, N.C.: Duke University Press, 2004.

Yancy, George, *Black Bodies, White Gazes*, Lanham, Md.: Rowman and Littlefield Publishers, Inc., 2008.

Zweigenhaft, Richard L., and Domhoff, G. William, *Diversity in the Power Elite*, New Haven: Yale University Press, 1999.

Index

ACORN. *See* Association of Community Organizations for Reform Now

affirmative action, 66, 68, 75, 86–87, 110, 130, 134–39, 145, 169, 206

Africa/Africans, xiii, 7–11, 17–22, 27–34, 38–39, 47, 52, 63, 89, 101, 131, 175

Allport, Gordon, 208–10

American Dream, xiv, 3, 136, 141, 179, 183, 189, 191, 194–95, 201, 205

American Indians. *See* Native Americans

Amnesty International, 163, 167, 216

Anglo-Saxons, 28, 48–54, 64, 67–68, 192, 220

Asians, xi–xv, 10, 14, 33, 35, 50, 52, 64–68, 76, 100, 108, 111, 120, 163, 167, 180, 184, 193

Association of Community Organizations for Reform Now (ACORN), 181–82

Baartman, Sarah, 22

bias, 53, 111, 121, 124, 132–34, 152, 154, 166–69, 189, 215

bigotry, 134, 156

Binet, Afred, 60–61

Blumenbach, Johann Friedrich, 18, 27–28, 33

Boas, Franz, 53–54

Bobo, Lawrence, 110

Bonilla-Silva, Eduardo, 110, 160

Brown v. Board of Education, 63, 69, 88, 117, 184, 197

Bush, George W., 85, 142, 152, 163, 190–91

capital punishment, 166–67

capitalism, xiii, 26, 31, 155

Carnegie, Andrew, 192

Carter, Jimmy, 112

Caucasian, xv, 27–28, 178, 183

Christianity, 18, 25–26, 30

Christians, 31–33

Civil Rights Movement, xi, 3, 135–36, 184, 208

Civil War, 35, 173–74

civilization, 19, 30–31, 36, 38, 41–42, 49, 52–55, 60, 131

Clark, Kenneth, 87–88

Clark, Mamie, 87–88

classrooms, xi, xiii, 42, 65, 91, 122, 170

Clinton, Bill, 6, 81, 112, 137, 162, 168, 176, 195, 200

Cohanim, 12

233

colonialism, xiii, 28
communication, 2, 76, 112, 122, 201–2, 215, 219
community, xiv–xv, 64, 86, 89, 132, 135, 161, 178, 197, 200–1, 204, 208;
    service, xiv, 102, 208–11
competition, xii–xv, 1–3, 5, 23, 31, 75–76, 79, 83, 85, 98, 109–11, 196, 209–11
Conley, Dalton, 179
consciousness of kind, 78
consumerism, 75, 98
corporate welfare, 190–91
Cose, Ellis, 82, 162
coworkers, 125, 129, 132
crime, x, 53, 61, 66, 82, 118, 160–70, 175, 189, 194
criminal justice, xiii, 14, 82, 90, 167, 211
culture, xi–xvi, 2–3, 5, 14, 18–19, 31, 36, 50, 53, 59, 65, 68–69, 76, 78–79, 82, 84–91, 93, 96–99, 101, 106–8, 112, 120, 123, 125, 130, 213, 218;
    of poverty, xvi, 123
Curry, George E., 137

dark-skinned, x–xiii, 14, 17–18, 32–33, 38, 41, 43, 47–48, 59–61, 63, 68–69, 76, 95, 97, 106, 110, 161, 164, 217, 219
Darwin, Charles, 10, 14, 17, 34–38
death penalty. *See* capital punishment
degradation, x–xii, 1, 52, 75, 85, 90
democratic, 50, 63, 175, 196, 204, 209
Department of Housing and Urban Development (HUD), 180, 184–85
Department of Labor, 137, 145
dialogue, xiv, 6, 102, 110–11, 133, 195, 197, 200–8, 215–16, 218–19;
    interfaith dialogue, 208
disabilities, 112, 120

discrimination, xiii–xv, 4–5, 14, 17, 43, 47, 59, 81, 87–88, 91, 93, 96–101, 107–8, 111, 120–21, 129, 132–34, 145, 151, 160, 163, 167–68, 173–76, 179–81, 184–85, 189, 192, 195–97, 199, 201, 205, 210, 216, 220
distrust, 98–99, 110, 134, 156, 191
diversity, ix, 2–3, 8, 81, 91, 112–13, 117, 119, 122, 137, 209;
    training, 117, 122–25, 133–35, 141, 202–4
DNA, xv, 8–15, 34–35, 67, 73, 167
Domhoff, G. William, 136–37, 144
domination, x–xiii, 6, 17–18, 25–26, 33–34, 55–56, 61, 87–88, 97, 107, 194

Economic Policy Institute, 142
education, x–xiii, 3, 5, 43, 60–70, 79, 88–90, 113, 118–23, 139, 146, 154–55, 196, 202
educators, x–xi, 43, 102, 112, 146, 170
equality, ix–xi, 1, 37, 48, 87, 102, 134, 145, 149, 162, 189, 197, 200–1
ethnic, 2–3, 43, 47–48, 54, 69, 90, 106, 117–18, 131, 133–34, 136–37, 145, 152, 169, 176, 178, 184, 191, 193, 195, 199, 211;
    ethnicity, xv, 14, 85, 97, 106–7, 111, 124, 130–31, 169;
    group, xi–xvi, 1–4, 12, 50–52, 60, 67–69, 77, 83, 88–90, 100, 111, 120, 130–31, 149, 161, 175, 180–81, 201, 208, 216, 219–20
ethnicity. *See* ethnic
eugenics, 51, 53–54, 60–61, 63, 65, 67
Eurocentric, xiii, 22, 33, 42, 79, 82–86, 88, 118, 120, 124, 219
everyday racism, 96–97, 215
evolution, 7–10, 14, 32–36, 60, 219
exploitation, xiii, 6, 17–23, 26, 28, 30–32, 34, 60, 95, 101, 194

exploration, xiii, 19–23, 26
expulsions, 112, 119, 122

FBI. *See* Federal Bureau of
   Investigation
Feagin, Joe R., 96, 99, 160
fear of strangers, xiii, 77
Federal Bureau of Investigation, x, 96,
   109, 207
Federal Equal Employment Opportunity
   Commission (EEOC), 132–34, 145
Federal Fair Housing Act, 184–85
Federal Housing Authority, 178
Franklin, John Hope, 162
Freire, Paolo, 123
Fromm, Erich, 78, 209

genetics, 41, 60
gifted, 120–21
A Girl Like Me, 88
Glover, Karen S., 164
Gossett, Thomas, 17, 33
government, 5, 51, 62, 66, 90, 99, 109,
   111–12, 132, 135, 145, 150, 155,
   164, 179, 184–85, 190–91, 195
graduation rates, 89, 120, 122, 193
Grant, Madison, 49–50, 56, 66

haplotype, 10–12
Harvard Civil Rights Project, 119
Harvard Educational Review, 65
hate, 54, 60, 73–79, 86, 99, 163, 211,
   213, 220;
   crimes, x, 2, 59, 96, 211
health care, ix, xv, 4, 43, 81, 84, 93, 97,
   109, 111, 143, 150–56, 189, 191,
   211
Herrnstein, Richard, 65
Hispanics, xiv, 135, 151, 183–84
Hobbes, Thomas, 17–18, 33, 62
Holocaust, xvi, 2, 52, 97, 209
home ownership, 178
hooks, bell, 124
Hooten, Ernest, 53

housing, xiii, 59, 93, 109, 173–74,
   177–79, 184, 189, 211;
   segregation, 173, 175, 179–81,
   184–85
HUD. *See* Department of Housing and
   Urban Development

ideology, 18, 26, 29, 48, 82, 86, 93,
   112, 191, 193–97
immigrants, xiii, 3, 48–53, 59–63, 66,
   68, 76, 79, 99, 101, 153, 156,
   175, 192, 211–13, 218
immigration laws, 51, 64, 213
income, xii–xiii, 14, 67, 69, 81–82, 85,
   101, 108, 136, 142–146, 151–52,
   180–82, 212
inclusivity, 117–25
indigenous people, xiii, 2, 9, 17–20,
   23–29, 31–33, 53, 63, 192
inequality. *See* social inequality
inner city, 5, 105, 117–21, 181
Institute on Assets and Social Policy, 144
integrated, 5, 65, 112, 121
intelligence, xv, 33–34, 43, 53, 60–69,
   190
IQ. *See* intelligence

Jefferson, Thomas, 8, 11, 38–42, 165,
   204
Jim Crow, 42, 87, 101, 107, 109, 160,
   174–75, 177
Judaism, 13

Kant, Immanuel, 17, 89
Kennedy, John F., 135
Kerner Commission, 4, 169

Las Casas, Bartolome de, 23–25, 29, 32
Latinos, xi–xv, 3–4, 9, 33, 51, 59–60,
   66–69, 76, 81, 99–102, 108, 110,
   112, 117, 120, 122, 131, 135,
   137–38, 143, 145–46, 150–52,
   159–60, 163, 167, 180–82, 184,
   193, 195, 218–19

light-skinned, xvi, 15, 37, 219
Lincoln, Abraham, 42, 173

Malik, Kenan, 62, 101
Mandela, Nelson, 22
Marx, Karl, 62, 111
materialism, xiii, 1, 3, 70, 75–76, 84,
    86, 93, 98, 156, 196, 203, 205,
    210
meritocracy, 70, 101, 109, 189–95, 203,
    205, 216
middle-class, 117, 119, 143, 177, 217
migrant, 212
migration, xv, 2, 8,–10, 61, 68, 77,
    174–75, 211–13
military, xiii, 18, 51, 61, 109, 173–185,
    194
minorities, xii–xvi, 2–4, 43, 47–48,
    63–69, 75–79, 87–90, 99, 108–10,
    117–18, 131, 134–39, 145, 150–
    52, 160, 163, 176–84, 191, 195,
    210–11, 218, 220
mortgages, 131, 144, 177–84, 190–91.
    See also subprime mortgages
Murray, Charles, 65
Muslims, 2, 59, 78, 163
mutations, 10
Myopia, 93–95
myths, x–xiv, 1, 6, 41, 68–70, 93,
    97–101, 130–31, 193–96, 213,
    216, 219

NAACP. *See* National Association for
    the Advancement of Colored
    People
National Association for the
    Advancement of Colored People
    (NAACP), 88, 109, 133, 182–83
National Commission on Fair Housing,
    178, 180, 185
National Urban League, 132, 145, 159
Native Americans, xi, xv, 19, 28–29, 33,
    48, 76, 163, 180, 184
natural selection, 10–11, 14, 34–37

Nazism, 33, 52, 56, 76, 78
Negro, ix, xiv, 35, 52, 166, 174, 218–19
New Deal, 87, 178
New World, xiii, 17–20, 23, 25, 28–32
No Child Left Behind, 68, 113, 118
non-whites, xiii, 5, 26, 110, 130–31,
    163, 181, 193–94, 196, 203, 220

Obama, Barack, ix, 6, 97, 110–11, 135,
    146, 153–56, 160, 162, 168, 179,
    191, 199–201
Olson, Steve, 11
origin of our species, x–xii, 7–10,
    34–36, 59, 89, 101, 220

parents, 9, 65–69, 98, 118, 131, 154–55,
    160, 196, 202–3
pedagogy, 118, 123
people of color, ix–xvi, 3–6, 17–18,
    26, 43, 47, 63, 70, 75–76, 81–87,
    90, 93–98, 101–2, 106–10, 124,
    129–38, 143–46, 150–52, 159–64,
    180–81, 184, 192–97, 200–6,
    208–13, 215–20
PEW Charitable Trusts, 143–44, 182,
    190
poverty level, 143–46, 180
power, x–xi, xvi, 4, 15, 18, 50–53,
    75–76, 82, 86–88, 91, 93, 106–9,
    135–39, 141, 156, 169, 194, 203,
    205, 210
prestige, 51, 210
primitive, ix, 14, 18–19, 26, 30, 32–33,
    59, 77
privilege, xi–xvi, 4, 18, 52, 75–76, 86,
    91, 124, 129–32, 141, 197, 205
public:
    housing, 178, 180
    policy, 66, 177–79

race relations, xv, 3, 43, 75, 84, 96,
    106, 110, 162, 173, 176, 195–97,
    200–8, 215

racial profiling, 101, 160–64, 215
racism, ix–xiv, 4–6, 7, 14, 17–22, 26,
    42, 47, 52, 59–64, 82, 86, 89–91,
    95–102, 105, 108–12, 122, 129–
    32, 151, 159–65, 169, 173, 176,
    178–82, 189, 192, 195–97, 199,
    201, 204–11, 215–20. *See also*
    everyday racism
redistribution of wealth, 142
Rousseau, Jean Jacques, 33, 62
Rushton, J. Philippe, 64

schools, 4, 66, 69, 79, 85–86, 93, 96,
    102, 112, 117–25, 132, 139,
    141, 146, 149, 161, 177, 184–85,
    201–2, 206, 209
scientific racism, 26–28, 33–34, 47, 52,
    54, 61, 64
segregation, 5, 53, 81, 88, 108–9, 121,
    173–74, 180, 184–85, 195
sentencing, 159, 166–67
separate but equal, 88
Skinner, B. F., 67
slave trade, xiii, 30, 63
slavery, 18, 24, 29–30, 34–38, 40, 42,
    48, 162, 164–65, 185, 193, 196,
    205, 207
slaves, 8, 18, 29–30, 38–40, 42, 164–65,
    173–74, 196, 207
social:
    change, xiii, 203, 208
    class, xvi, 4–5, 62, 82, 106, 136, 219
    inequality, xi, 33–34, 36, 42, 52, 64,
        69, 124, 141–46, 183–84, 195–96,
        205, 211
    injustice, 204–5
    scientists, xv, 4–5, 14, 110, 136, 144,
        168, 176
Social Darwinism, 37, 51, 62, 68, 101
society, ix–xvi, 3–6, 14, 37, 39, 47–51,
    53–56, 59–60, 62–64, 66–67, 69,
    75–76, 79, 81–82, 84–88, 90–91,
    93, 95, 97–98, 100–2, 105–9, 113,
    124–25, 131, 136, 138, 141–46,

    151, 155, 160–62, 164–65,
    168–69, 173, 177, 184, 189, 192,
    194–96, 199–205, 207–11, 213
Southern Poverty Law Center, 99–100,
    112
special education, 119–20, 131
species, 7–11, 17, 33, 35–37, 39, 41
standardized tests, 68, 90, 113, 118, 120
Startle Reaction, 77–78
Steele, Claude, 63
Steele, Shelby, 86–87
stereotypes, x–xiv, 4, 6, 9, 14, 28, 32,
    41–43, 63, 68–69, 75, 86–87,
    89–90, 93, 98, 101–2, 106–07,
    129–30, 134, 161, 195, 197, 199,
    209, 219
Stoddard, Lothrop, 47, 49, 54–56, 66
students, vii, xi, xiii, 4–5, 43, 53, 60,
    65, 68–69, 79, 81, 89–91, 94, 96,
    102, 112–13, 117–25, 131–32,
    138–39, 146, 149, 154–55, 161,
    170, 184–85, 193, 201–3, 206,
    209–10, 215
subprime mortgages, 181–83
suspensions, 89, 112, 124

tax:
    cuts, 142, 144
    taxes, 142, 146, 154–55, 203
Tea Party, 111, 154
teachers, 42, 68–69, 79, 89, 91, 112,
    117–25, 131, 155, 161, 185,
    196–97, 202–3, 206, 217–18
Thirteenth Amendment, 165, 174

U.S. Census, 120, 180
United for a Fair Economy, 146, 181
United Nations, 109, 145, 160, 180,
    185, 211–12
United Nations Committee on
    the Elimination of Racial
    Discrimination (CERD), 180, 185
United States Department of Justice,
    96, 167

upward mobility, xiii–xvi, 60, 98, 136,
176–77, 193

values, xii, xv–xvi, 1–2, 26, 49, 55, 74,
78–79, 107, 109–10, 120, 131,
134, 178–79, 195, 203–5, 209,
211
victims, x, xiii, 29, 43, 47, 59, 63, 86,
89–91, 96, 130, 163–64, 167, 189,
192, 195
violence, 2, 7, 15, 94–96, 118–19, 121,
189

war. *See* Civil War; World War I;
World War II
Washington, George, 42, 165, 204
wealth, xiii, 20, 26, 52, 62, 90, 132,
136, 141–42, 144–46, 179, 181,
190–92, 194, 211
West, Cornel, 168
white:
privilege, 88, 101, 121, 123–24,
130–32, 169, 195–96, 204, 209,
217

supremacy, 18, 50, 97, 101
whites, x–xvi, 3–6, 17–19, 26, 33,
35–36, 38–42, 47–48, 52–56,
59–65, 67–70, 76, 78, 82–86,
90–91, 93, 95–100, 102, 107–12,
120–21, 124, 129–31, 135,
143–46, 150–51, 153–54, 159–67,
176–82, 191–97, 199–201, 203–8,
213, 215, 217–20
Wilson, William Julius, 4–5
Wise, Tim, 154
women, xiii, 7, 22, 24, 30–31, 38, 42,
63, 82–84, 87, 90, 93–95, 102,
108–9, 117, 120, 133–39, 145,
151, 159, 165, 169, 176, 196,
210–12, 217
World Health Organization, 149
World War I, 55–56, 60–63, 174
World War II, 51, 56, 136, 175–77

Zweigenhaft, Richard, 136–37, 144

About the Author

H. Roy Kaplan received his PhD in sociology from the University of Massachusetts, Amherst. He teaches courses on racism in the Africana studies department at the University of South Florida, Tampa. Dr. Kaplan was the executive director of The National Conference of Christians and Jews for the Tampa Bay area. He served as an advisor to President Clinton's Task Force on Race Relations, and in 1998 was named a "Hero of Education" by the U.S. Department of Education for his multicultural work in Florida schools.

CPSIA information can be obtained at www.ICGtesting.com
Printed in the USA
LVOW121214221211

260676LV00002B/3/P